A FRONT SEAT AT THE OPERA

A FRONT SEAT AT THE OPERA

BY GEORGE R. MAREK

GREENWOOD PRESS, PUBLISHERS
WESTPORT, CONNECTICUT

TO HERBERT R. MAYES

TABLE OF CONTENTS

A FRONT SEAT AT THE OPERA

INTRODUCTION
Love and Hate

It was what they call a *gast-rolle* night at the Royal Grand Ducal Pumpernicklisch Hof—or Court theater; and Madame Schröder-Devrient, then in the bloom of her beauty and genius, performed the part of the heroine in the wonderful opera of *Fidelio*. From our places in the stalls we could see our four friends of the table d'hôte, in the loge which Schwendler of the Erbprinz kept for his best guests: and I could not help remarking the effect which the magnificent actress and music produced upon Mrs. Osborne, for so we had heard the stout gentleman in the mustachios call her. During the astonishing Chorus of the Prisoners over which the delightful voice of the actress rose and soared in the most ravishing harmony, her face wore such an expression of wonder and delight that it struck even little Fipps, the blasé attaché, who drawled out, as he fixed his glass upon her, "Gayd, it really does one good to see a woman caypable of that stayt of excaytement." And in the Prison Scene where Fidelio, rushing to her husband, cries "*Nichts, nichts mein Florestan*," she fairly lost herself and covered her face with her handkerchief. Every woman in the house was sniveling at the time.

WILLIAM THACKERAY: *Vanity Fair*

I have sat through an Italian opera till, for sheer pain and inexplicable anguish, I have rushed out into the noisiest places of the crowded streets, to solace myself with sounds which I was not obliged to follow, and get rid of the distracting torment of endless, fruitless, barren attention.

CHARLES LAMB: *A Chapter on Ears*

THACKERAY AND LAMB stand at opposite poles. Thackeray likes opera; Lamb hates it with equal eloquence. And each gives expression in uncommon words to what is a common feeling. For opera has to an egregious degree the power to make people jump to one or the other side of the fence. People, if they are at all responsive to music, either love opera or hate it. Few can take it or leave it alone.

This love and hatred are probably more apparent in regard to opera than to any other art. I know of no literate person who likes novels but totally dislikes plays. I know of no lover of painting who has only scorn for sculpture. But I know a good many musically educated people, indeed I know some professional musicians, who cannot or will not recognize the charms of opera. They may admit that opera contains some good (though hardly simon-pure) music. They admit that Wagner and Verdi were splendid composers. But this admission cannot lead them to an evening in the opera house..

Why is that? Why does this division exist? Why is it virtually impossible to induce some frequenters of Carnegie Hall to go to the Metropolitan? And why is so much errant nonsense said about opera's being "an artificial art"? (As if all art were not "artificial" in the true sense of the word.) I believe it is because the attitude toward opera which leads to enjoyment needs at the outset a certain amount of—not tolerance, for that is too condescending a word—but of loving imagination. For most of us all music comes to life only when it is interpreted. Those of us who are not scholars and who do not read a score and hear it in our own mind's ear as it should sound, hear music only as someone can make it sound. That someone is either a conductor or an executant musician. But in opera the someone becomes a plural of considerable number and complexity. The difficulties of interpretation multiply, the annoyances of bad interpretation become more frequent. Bruno Walter once said that he had never in all his life conducted an opera performance which thoroughly satisfied him. He is no doubt unusually exigent. But even with allowance for a tolerance born of lesser knowledge, the wholly satisfying performance of an opera is a rarer thing than a wholly satisfying violin recital. If, therefore, we go to an opera performance in a sharply critical mood and without a certain amount of predisposing imagination, there will be much to criticize even in a good performance. I do not mean to say that we must sit down in the opera house with the attitude that a mother brings to the annual Christmas school festival in which her eight-year-old daughter is playing the fourth angel. Opera needs to claim no greater immunity from criticism than any other form of artistic endeavor. But it does call not so much for an imaginative ear as for an imaginative eye, an eye which can see beyond little absurdities toward great truths. It cannot be denied that some opera singers are not the world's best actors, nor have they the most ingratiating face and form. If our eyes are unwilling to make allowances, the music cannot reach our ears. But there is more to it: operatic acting is, and must be by the very requirements of acting in time to music, a stylized and an "artificial" form of acting. We must meet it on its own terms just as we must get used to the "thou" and "thee," the "an if you list" and "am be-thought" of Shakespearian language. Opera demands, as does poetic tragedy, a co-operation of mood. Robust, powerful and sufficient though it is, opera needs a sympathetic audience.

All this is probably said in vain. For the people who do not like opera just do not like opera. They are not going to buy or read my book. I had better address myself immediately to the second group, those friendly, intelligent, warm and alto-gether virtuous people who do like opera. I am a member of this group in good standing — in fact, I am an old standing-room member. I have adored opera ever since the first time I heard *Die Walküre*, standing on the side of the family circle, seeing only that corner of the stage where glimmered a not too convincing fire which threw its light on the hilt of the embedded Nothung, and hearing music which made such an impression on me that I forgot my hat. To me opera sung by the human voice—certainly not excerpted and adapted for concert performance—is the most thrilling form of music and the entertainment most satisfactory in repetition.

I knew a claqueur once who spent his free evenings in a curious way. On those nights when he was not obliged to make professional applause and when he had done with his share of crying *"Bis! Bis!"* he bought himself a ticket, went to the opera and sat there all evening long in non-professional enjoyment. He took, so to speak, a bis-man's holiday. No doubt about it, we opera lovers are a peculiar lot: we can never get enough of it. When we are not hearing it, we are discussing it; when we are not discussing it, we read about it.

It is to opera lovers therefore that this book is dedicated. It is not a book of plot telling: such books are already available. It is not a history of opera nor an analysis of its music. It is a book which attempts to set before you unusual facts about operas and their composers, to recall the genesis and reception of famous operas, and to discuss certain performances in our country. My hope for it is that it will add to the enjoyment of people who enjoy opera already. If it will give them a little more food for conversation or a little broader reason for pleasure, then the book will have achieved its purpose.

Most of the material of the book is drawn from articles which have appeared in the programs of the Metropolitan Opera in the seasons of 1942-43 to 1947-48. My particular thanks go to *Opera Magazines, Inc.*, and to its editor, Mr. Ellis Meyers, for permission to use these articles.

But general thanks should go to the many writers who have written on the subject of opera, men like Ernest Newman, Brockway and Weinstock, Donald Francis Tovey, Dyneley Hussey, Edward J. Dent, Francis Toye, Lawrence Gilman, Alfred Einstein and Olin Downes. It is the breath of their scholarship which sets my light bark in sail.

PART I

A FEW GLANCES AT OPERA IN GENERAL

Contemporary blindness to the
light of genius is a rare disease.
However, not all good operas were
at once successful....

1. *Famous Failures*

CERTAIN MUSICAL HISTORIANS—those of the nobility-through-suffering school—keep telling us that the great masters lived in obscurity, that they died without the world's realizing their greatness, and that only post mortem did they receive their fame.

Unfortunately this fancy does not follow fact. "Some mute, inglorious Milton" is the exception in musical history, not the rule. Actually almost all great composers attained fame within their lifetime.

Bach, the oft-quoted example of supreme genius neglected, was respected and celebrated during his life. It was only after his death that his music fell into the "formless ruin of oblivion." And as against one Schubert of whose greatness the contemporary world had a shamefully small idea, there were Beethoven and Brahms and Debussy and Verdi and even Mozart; in all these men the people of their time recognized genius, though they did not fully understand or measure its extent. Beethoven was the most famous musician of his generation, and considered so important that he, fiery, dour, and of "somewhat lofty bearing," could allow himself flares of temper which his publishers and his aristocratic patrons (the "princely rabble") were willing to suffer.

We often hear that Wagner's music was reviled during Wagner's lifetime and that it took a long time before people began to understand it. This is only partially true. Wagner's idiom was (after *Rienzi*) so new and audacious that time had to elapse before his ideas could be assimilated. But while many people were shocked by this new music and disliked it, more were impressed by it. *Die Meistersinger* and *Tristan* had become long before Wagner's death immensely famous and popular operas. Wagner himself had become immensely famous. His works were so in demand that he could afford to be peremptory with publishers and opera directors. (He was.)

This is not to say that all those symphonies and operas which are today favorites were instantaneous successes. But the evidence shows that first-night failures were more often due to inadequate performances, stage accidents, or back-biting activities of an opposing cabal than to a lack of responsiveness from the people who bought their seats.

The first performance of *Tannhäuser* in Dresden in 1845 under Wagner's direction was a failure. One contributing cause was the extreme length of this first version. Equally important was the fact that the scenery for the second act, the Hall of the Wartburg, had not arrived in time, and that the audience was disappointed in having to look at a familiar setting, to which they were accustomed as representing the Grand Hall of the Emperor Charlemagne in Weber's *Oberon*. Another trouble was the Venus, the famous Schröder-Devrient, then somewhat past her prime, and "stouter than she used to be," to use William Schwenck Gilbert's words. Tannhäuser was sung by Tichatschek, who had already made a great success in *Rienzi* and who was the star tenor of the time. With all his good will toward Wagner, Tichatschek could not grasp the idea that opera should be drama, that the words should be understood and the action be acted. He knew that his popularity was due to his brilliant loud tones, and he meant to use them. The suffering and brooding of Tannhäuser he could not express. At the moment in the second act when minstrels, sings his hymn of the embrace of Venus, Tichat-Tannhäuser, sick of the pale praises of love sung by the other schek crossed the stage and directly addressed the frenzied words to the virginal Elizabeth!

Obesity was the cause of another famous failure. Of *La Traviata* Verdi wrote after the first performance, "*La Traviata* last night a fiasco. Is the fault mine or the singers'? Time will show."

The prima donna who portrayed Violetta, the camellia girl who was better than she ought to have been, was "a plump and pleasing person," to quote Gilbert once more. That a singer so obviously upholstered should waste away from consumption struck the audience as funny. They might have forgiven it had the action of the opera been laid in some mythical country far away, but *Traviata* was a modern-dress opera. It was a contemporary play given in contemporary costume. This alone was a daring innovation. And so the first-nighters hissed.

There are several examples of opera whose first nights were made hideous by the sabotage of rivals. *The Barber of Seville*, for instance. Rossini's impresario had suggested the famous Beaumarchais comedy as a subject for a libretto. But the barber Figaro had already served music twice before, once to a harmless composer named Mozart, and once to the revered (and now forgotten) composer, Paisiello. Rossini, who could be a diplomat, wrote to Paisiello and advised him of his intention. Paisiello could not have been pleased but preserved the amenities and replied, "Go ahead," in a polite letter. This letter Rossini made known in Rome. And as a further gesture, he titled his new work not *The Barber of Seville* but *Almaviva or The Vain Precaution*. Rossini's precaution proved to be the vain precaution. A number of Paisiello's friends and followers seized on mishaps at the première to provoke a storm. The accidental snapping of the string of a guitar, a cat that walked across the stage, Basilio's becoming entangled in his robe—all these were the signals for loud voices of disapproval.

Rossini conducted, and many years after he told Wagner what an ordeal he had gone through that night.

Even in the case of so bewildering a work as *Pelléas et Mélisande*—an opera so inward and hushed that only several hearings will disclose its beauties—it was not the public which reacted badly to it, but an intriguing, hostile faction. I am sure this must have surprised Debussy, who had had misgivings about the public's reaction to the work long before *Pelléas* was finished. He had revised his score several times, and it was seven years after he had completed the first version that the opera was finally produced. In the meantime, Maeterlinck had quarreled bitterly with Debussy. It seems that the part of Mélisande had been promised to the woman with whom Maeterlinck had been living and whom he had recently married, Georgette Leblanc. All of a sudden Maeterlinck learned that Carré, the manager of the Opéra-Comique, had decided to give the part to a young Scotch-American singer who two years before, on a Friday the thirteenth, had made a considerable success substituting in *Louise*. The young singer was Mary Garden.

Maeterlinck was furious. First he tried the law. When he learned that he had no legal right to choose the creator of the role, he jumped in a fit of anger through the window of his apartment (ground floor) and rushed away to try his cane on Debussy. Then he wrote a letter to *Le Figaro* in which he said, "They have managed to exclude me from my work, and from now on it is in the hands of the enemy. . . . The *Pelléas* in question is a work which is strange and almost hostile to me. . . . I can only wish for its immediate and decided failure."

When after 120 rehearsals the new work was finally given its public dress rehearsal on an April afternoon, a satiric pamphlet, a "Select Program," was sold at the doors of the Opéra-Comique. During the performance, Mary Garden's somewhat less than Sorbonne French accent provoked snickers, especially when she sang, "*Je ne suis pas heureuse.*" At the first regular performance there was still more laughter. But it calmed down (Carré had taken the precaution of hiring a claque) and the opera succeeded. The seventh performance of *Pelléas* was a sell-out. In spite of the lack of spectacular qualities in *Pelléas*, it has renewed its success on every occasion when a sensitive actress (such as Mary Garden or Marcelle Denya) has portrayed Mélisande.

The reception by the critics was a mixed one. Romain Rolland called *Pelléas* "one of the three or four outstanding achievements in French musical history." But one critic said that the score contained "not a trace of melody"—which statement is an exact translation of what Beckmesser says of Walther's song in *Die Meisersinger*. There will always be a Beckmesser.

2. *Once in a Lifetime*

WHY DO SOME artists create only once in their lives an enduring masterpiece? Having created it, why are they unable to
repeat? The *succès unique* is a frequent and fascinating occurrence in art, and one which has received insufficient attention
from the historians. Curiously, the one well-shaped work is
not usually the last by the artist; it is not the culmination of
trial and experience. It is neither the swan song nor the first
chirping of the bird. The great success often appears some-
where in the middle of the composer's career. The reason for
its time and place is difficult to discover. Is it because there
comes only once in certain artists' careers the happy conflux
of outer and inner circumstances which lifts their talent to
a summit? Or is it really possible to use up all one's resources
on a single work?

Whoever will look into this puzzle should turn his attention
to the author of *The Professor* and *Shirley*, who, at the age of
thirty-one, wrote the one and only novel on which her fame
rests. For it was then that Charlotte Bronte published *Jane
Eyre*. He might also examine the case of her sister, of whose
writings only *Wuthering Heights* endures. Swift and Cer-
vantes and Gautier would provide further material. He might
find out why a strait-laced professor of mathematics could—
only once—produce so free a fancy as *Alice*. Or, for that matter, how the American clergyman, Clement Clarke Moore,
after compiling the *Hebrew and Greek Lexicon* and other
worthy and dull stuff, could pen *'Twas The Night Before
Christmas*.

When it comes to one-hit opera composers, there is a possible but by no means complete explanation. That is, that the

composer was presented with a libretto which kindled his imagination to full flame. A good story inspired good music. And a good story helped to keep the opera alive in the theater. Surely that was the case with Rossini, a genius of highest facility and brightest sparkle, who wrote forty operas before he was thirty-seven years old, of which forty only *The Barber of Seville* possesses an adequate libretto and only *The Barber of Seville* remains altogether alive.

One-hit composers occurred most frequently in France, about the middle of the past century, that incredibly prodigal time in the history of music during which Meyerbeer, Brahms, Grieg, Saint-Saëns, Schumann, Bizet, Berlioz, Liszt, Wagner, Verdi, Gounod, César Franck, Smetana, Offenbach, Johann Strauss were all alive and furiously setting down black dots on ruled paper. Take the case, for example, of Jacques Halévy, who wrote more than thirty operas, only one of which has endured. Indirectly we owe *La Juive* to a tenor of brains and culture. Nourrit, the great French tenor, was tired of portraying nothing but handsome young men destined to love in vain and in vanity. He asked Halévy to make the part of Eleazar a tenor instead of the traditional bearded baritone father. Nourrit sang the first performance. *La Juive* has remained a favorite with tenors.

It was one of Caruso's great parts and was the last role that he sang, on Christmas Eve, 1920, eight months before his death.

What is considered by many as the perfect opera was written by Halévy's son-in-law, Bizet. *Carmen* is a work that seems to have sprung, complete and Minerva-like, from his brow. It is so much better than anything else Bizet wrote that it seems almost to have come from a different mind. *Les Pêcheurs de perles*, *La Jolie fille de Perth* and *Djamileh* all have their moments, but they are moments only. Only *Carmen* is packed to bursting with original inventions, with theatrical surety, with melodic richness.

Look up at the placques that frame the Metropolitan curtain. In the late nineteenth century, when they were put up, Gounod was considered sufficiently important to have his name engraved there along with those of Gluck, Mozart, Verdi and Wagner. At that time he was the paterfamilias of French music, resplendent in reputation and in beard, the musical glass of fashion and the mold of form, the authority of authorities. This prodigious fame is due solely to one opera. Gounod wrote a dozen: but only two of them, *Faust* and *Roméo et Juliette*, are still given outside of France, and of the two only *Faust* remains truly popular. *Faust* was his fourth opera, and in it he found the winning combination: sweet and pleasant melodies applied to a libretto which took Goethe's vast and philosophic poem and reduced it to a simple-minded story of boy loses girl with the help of a bogey man. Why Gounod didn't succeed equally well with the other world-renowned boy-loses-girl story—why, in other words, *Roméo et Juliette*, though at first almost as popular as *Faust*, has not remained in the repertoire is one of those mysteries. The fact remains that *Faust*, faulty, frivolous and pretty, turned out to be probably the most popular of all operas, and while at the Metropolitan Opera House its frequency has now been eclipsed by *Aïda*, it is still very much in the running there too.

Gounod's academic rival was the formidable Charles Louis Ambroise Thomas. Like Gounod, he wrote many, many operas. Like Gounod also, his two best are written respectively to a plot by Goethe and one by Shakespeare. But *Hamlet* is hardly known, while *Mignon* remains beloved, if for nothing else but "*Connais-tu le pays?*"

One can go on to the composers of other nations. Of Bellini, only *Norma* remains active; of Weber, only *Der Freischütz*; of Smetana, only *The Bartered Bride*, though *Dalibor* or *The Kiss*, both of which he wrote later, should be revived.

Then there is that hardy double-feature of the opera house

known in quiz programs as "Cav and Pag." Mascagni wrote *Cavalleria Rusticana* as a young man of twenty-seven. He entered the opera in a competition, won the first prize and such acclaim as to change him from actual starvation to world-wide renown. After that, he labored on works like *L'Amico Fritz*, *Iris*, *Lodoletta*, and as late as 1934 on a spectacular opera called *Nerone*, which possibly pleased Mussolini but definitely not the Italians.

The fate of Leoncavallo is even more puzzling because he wrote his own librettos and was therefore not dependent on anyone but himself. After *Pagliacci*, written when he was quite young, a string of operas came from his pen. One of them, *Zaza*, was popular for a time at the Metropolitan because of Geraldine Farrar, but all of them are now forgotten.

*The shuddering, the indignation,
and the publicity are gone. The
music remains. . . .*

3. *Immoral Operas*

NOTHING IN ART is so temporary as immorality. One generation's shocker is the next generation's schoolbook. The novel
which was discussed while the children were out of the room
becomes a few years later reading for high school girls. Nor,
of course, are the girls any the worse for it. There is no evidence
that "immoral" works of art have ever produced immorality.

Yet in the history of art the charge of immorality against
this work or that one has created enormous ructions, frightful
diatribes, nasty splits—and no little advertisement. Thus it was
with *Tom Jones* and with *Tristram Shandy*, with *Tess of the
D'Urbervilles*, with James Joyce's *Ulysses* and with Manet's
The Picnic. Thus it was also with many operas.

After more than a century and a half, we listen to *The Marriage of Figaro* with undiminished delight. We find it beautiful,
and so it is. We think it sparkling, and so it is. We consider the
plot innocuous—but so it most certainly was not. *The Marriage
of Figaro* was based on a comedy by Beaumarchais, a comedy
which was satiric, bitter and politically purposeful, and which
played a not unimportant part in the French Revolution. The
model for the *dédaigneux* count who insisted on his privilege
of spending the first night with every commoner's bride was
in 1786 not difficult to recognize. *Le Mariage de Figaro* was
not only immoral, it was dangerous.

Mozart suggested the subject to Joseph II's theater-poet,
Lorenzo da Ponte. Da Ponte, a Jack-of-all-adventures (his
Mémoirs read like a road-company Casanova) and a smooth
intriguer, submitted the libretto to Joseph II. According to

the *Mémoirs*, Joseph said: "But this *Mariage de Figaro*—I have just forbidden the German troupe to use it!"

" 'Yes, Sire,' I rejoined, 'but I was writing an opera, not a comedy. I had to omit many scenes and to cut others quite considerably. I have omitted or cut anything that might offend good taste or public decency at a performance over which the Sovereign Majesty might preside. The music, I may add, as far as I may judge of it, seems to me marvelously beautiful.'

" 'Good! If that be the case, I shall rely on your good taste as to the music and on your wisdom as to the morality. Send the score to the copyist.' "

Da Ponte was hardly telling the truth. We are grateful to him for that. *The Marriage of Figaro* was performed to the acclaim of the Viennese, aristocrats and commoners alike.

That the charge of immorality should have been leveled against the creator of *Tristan* is to be expected. Even *Tannhäuser*, besides being considered by some Parisian critics as "*la chose la plus idiote qu'on n'ait jamais entendue*," was considered indecent.

In the case of *Tristan* the charges of immorality were grave and vehement. For *Tristan* is indeed sensuous and revealing music, though it must require exceptional obtuseness to see in this, the most exalted music of love, nothing but a piece of erotica. Lawrence Gilman discusses this in his book, *Wagner's Operas*, and shows that serious minds held such a view by quoting George Moore, who wrote that the music of Wagner is "a Turk lying amid the houris"—music with "cruel claws and amorous tongue that feeds upon my flesh."

Here are some contemporary critical dicta about *Tristan*: "A wolf's den of love." "Nudity set to music." "A psychological torture chamber." "Higher cat music." "*Monstrum*." "Libidinous chaos of sound."

The best of these blossoms is an article by a French neurologist called Moreau, who claimed that "the music of Richard Wagner acts exactly like several other specific brain poisons—alcohol, morphine, absinthe, etc. Novices reject this poison vehemently, but nine-tenths come back to go through the experience once again until they succumb, and the now-desired poison destroys their bodies. Thus it is with the Richard Wagner poison. One hundred to two hundred bars are enough to tempt the organism to repetition. Then whole acts are devoured. Only the most powerful can withstand it." The doctor counsels in all scientific seriousness to interne the composer in a sanatarium for the insane, "and to watch him for a decade, to forbid all of Wagner's music, and above all to burn all the scores and piano arrangements of *Tristan and Isolde.*"

The conservative and certainly not erotic Verdi did not escape the charge of libidinousness when he decided to set to music Alexander Dumas' titillating drama, *La Dame aux camélias.* For here was a play which treated in realistic and sympathetic manner of an actual contemporary courtesan. (Her grave is in the Montmartre cemetery, decorated by a sculpture of camellias in a glass, though the camellias were Dumas' invention.)

As Francis Toye relates in his biography of Verdi, the play "was regarded by the old-fashioned as a deliberate attack on the institution of marriage, a defense of free love, a plea for easier divorce. . . ."

In England clergymen preached against *La Traviata,* and there were severe letters in the *Times,* thus proving George Bernard Shaw's contention that "an Englishman thinks he is moral when he is only uncomfortable."

But even the more tolerant French have their share of prissiness. Gounod's *Faust* was viewed with alarm by the censor. He raised particular objection to the Cathedral scene. The manager of the Théâtre Lyrique arranged to have a representative of the Church attend the rehearsals, and when the censor again protested, he was asked to lay his objection before Monseigneur de Ségur, the Apostolic Nuncio. This high dignitary could not understand what the fuss was about and approved of the Cathedral scene whole-heartedly. So the censor went away satisfied; he never did find out that Monseigneur de Ségur was blind.

Carmen, too, offended. I quote from that valuable guide, the *Metropolitan Book of the Opera* by Pitts Sanborn: "Leuven, conservative member of the management of the Opéra-Comique, balked at the idea of a *Carmen* opera peopled with thieves, gypsies, cigar girls. 'Isn't she assassinated by her lover? At the Opéra-Comique! A family theater! A theater for the promotion of marriages!' he demanded. 'We rent five or six boxes every night for these meetings of young couples. You are going to put our audience to flight. No, it's impossible!' And he begged Halévy (the librettist) not to let Carmen die. 'Death has never been seen on this stage, do you hear, never! Don't let her die! I beg of you, my dear child!' (Halévy was then a child of forty!)"

Puccini's *Tosca* was considered fare too strong for opera and too sordid, because, besides containing a torture scene, an assassination, an execution and a suicidal leap, all of which are standard operatic equipment, it also contains an attempt at rape. How some of the critics barked! Presently, however, these Sardou melodramatics were no longer taken seriously, but that was perhaps less the fault of the plot than the fault of some performances of *Tosca* wherein, as someone put it, an elderly Scarpia chases an elderly Tosca, trying to extract from her that price which it was as obviously impossible for her to give as for him to make use of.

The classic instance of a real operatic scandal at the Metropolitan is the case of Strauss's *Salome.* It raised eyebrows, veils, dust and indignation, and nearly resulted in impresario

Conried's resignation. Conried first offered the part to Farrar, who refused it. Fremstad was the first Metropolitan Salome and the opera was first heard at a dress rehearsal for an invited audience on a Sunday morning—when most of the people came to the opera house directly from church. But it was the first public performance which started the storm. The house was sold out at double prices. First there was an operatic concert; the opera itself started around ten o'clock. There was some commotion all through the performance; during the final scene many of the people in the first rows of the orchestra and in the boxes nearest the stage ostentatiously got up and left. The next morning the *Times*, in addition to a long and beautifully written review by Richard Aldrich, published a special news report under the heading, "How the Audience Took It."

"Ten extra policemen were required last night to handle the crowds.... Many of the women in the Metropolitan Opera House last night turned away from the dance. Very few men in the audience seemed comfortable . . . in the galleries men and women left their seats to stand so they might look down upon the prima donna as she kissed the dead lips of the head of John the Baptist. Then they sank back in their chairs and shuddered." Five days later it was announced that no further performances of *Salome* would be given.

Lest you feel such prudery to be an American trait, let me say that the play, *Salomé*, aroused moral indignation in its day and so did the first performances of the opera when given in Europe. When Oscar Wilde first read the play to Sarah Bernhardt at the house of their mutual friend, Henry Irving, she was captivated by it and decided immediately to act the part. She went so far as to put it in rehearsal at the Palace Theater in London. Then England's censor, the Lord Chamberlain, stepped in and forbade the presentation, evoking a law still in force in England which prohibits the performance of plays with Biblical characters, unless the characters sing. By this law the opera could have been produced had it existed at the time, though certainly Strauss's music heightens rather than lessens the "immoral" quality of the play. At any rate, Wilde was furious over the fact that "the greatest tragic actress of any stage" was forbidden to appear in his work and that he was therefore cheated of hearing "her flute-like voice." Frank Harris tells us that Wilde was so angry he declared he would "settle in France and take out letters of naturalization." He should have done so, as Paris certainly treated Wilde kindlier than London. Sarah Bernhardt offered consolation by promising to give the play at her own theatre in Paris, the Porte St. Martin, but she never got around to doing it. And Wilde never became a French citizen. By the time Strauss began writing the music, the author of the play—a condemned and unforgiven man—had drunk himself to death.

The production of the opera took place December 9, 1905, in Dresden. It was the musical sensation of Germany that year, as Strauss at that time had for the musical world all the fascination of Peck's Bad Boy. I quote from the report of the première published in *Musical America:* "According to mail-advices just at hand, Richard Strauss scored an overwhelming success with his music-drama, *Salome.* That the opera was produced at all is due to the tireless energy of Strauss himself, for it is now a matter of history that the only manager having the courage to produce it was Count Seebach, Intendant of the Royal Saxon Opera House. That the new opera is a stupendous work from a purely physical standpoint is evident from the fact that it required two stage-managers, Herr von Schuck, who supervised the musical portion, and Wilhelm Wirk, of the Munich Opera House, who acted as stage manager. One hundred and four musicians were necessary for the orchestral part of the performance.

"As soon as the roles were distributed, nearly every one of

the singers offered to strike. Frau Wittig handed the role of
Salome back to Count Seebach, stating that it was an impossibility. She desired to know, among other things, how she, a
solo singer, could dance for ten minutes and sing immediately
afterward for a full quarter of an hour. Burrian, the tenor,
declared that owing to the difficulties of his part, he had to
study it not act by act, but measure by measure. It required
several months for the soloists to learn their roles, after all
difficulties had been adjusted, and then followed two weeks
of daily rehearsals with the orchestra.

"About ten days before the première, Strauss came to Dresden and supervised the final rehearsals. The house was sold
out, and the critics were forced to attend the dress rehearsal
on the previous evening.

"According to the general consensus, the score is a remarkable one, Strauss outdoing himself in his musical daring."

All the Dresden critics said more or less the same thing,
that the music was extraordinary and overpowering, that the
public burst into enormous applause at the close and that
Strauss had to take twenty-five curtain calls.

But as Wagner had learned with *Tannhäuser*, a Dresden
success did not insure a general success in Germany. For that
the opera had to be produced in Berlin, the musical capital of
Germany. Here Strauss ran into difficulties with the Emperor,
just as Wagner had before him. It seems that Kaiser Wilhelm,
who was an ardent admirer of Leoncavallo, disliked *Salome*
sight unseen or sound unheard. He banned the opera. The
London *Daily Mail* reported at the time, "*Salome* has caused
serious unpleasantness between the Kaiser and Strauss. Strauss,
being a royal servant in his capacity as one of the conductors
of the Berlin Opera, was informed by the Kaiser that His
Majesty thought the writing of an opera on such a theme as
Salome was unworthy of him and not conducive to the ad-
vancement of pure art. To this Strauss replied that he was

not going to take lessons on the qualities of art from anyone, no matter how highly placed, unless his inherent knowledge on the subject was superior to his (Strauss's) own. A coolness ensued, and it is said that the contract with Strauss in regard to his position as director of the Berlin Orchestra will not be renewed."

On this cue, some of the German critics thought it the better part of valor to be shocked by the opera. Arno Kleffel, writing in the *Allgemeine Musik-Zeitung*, expressed his surprise at the enthusiastic reception which Dresden gave *Salome*, saying that it went to prove that "the time has come when the most perverse depravity, in general the basest and most repulsive that can be imagined by human brain, can nowadays be produced on the stage successfully."

Kaiser Wilhelm did not hold out too long against public curiosity. *Salome* was given at the Berlin Royal Opera a year after the Dresden première. The *Musical Courier* reported on this event as follows: "Emperor William did not attend the performance. As is well known, the monarch for a long time, on account of the 'perversity' of the text, opposed the production. For a man of his convictions, this was going a long way. After deciding in favor of the opera, His Majesty instructed General Intendant von Hülsen to make the performance in every way as true as possible to the intentions of the composer. One slight but striking innovation is said to have originated with the Emperor himself, and a very happy idea it was—namely, in the closing scene, after the soldiers had killed Salome, a bright star suddenly appeared in the blood-red heavens—a symbol of Christianity." This is the kind of corny stagecraft that the Kaiser could well have invented.

Now, to get back to our Metropolitan, it took twenty-seven years until *Salome* was again unveiled. The business of the final kiss was toned down and played in shadow, but probably even this precaution was unnecessary. Nobody seems to have shown any moral ill-effects from the performance, not even the members of the radio audience, to whom *Salome* was brought that season.

Thus the author of *Salome's* text was vindicated in his belief — written in the introduction to *Dorian Gray* — that "there is no such thing as a moral or immoral book. Books are well or badly written. That is all." Obviously this applies to operas as well.

Consider the librettist: he toils
and he spins, but nobody cares...

4. *The Forgotten Man of Opera*

CAN YOU TELL me offhand who wrote the libretto for *La Traviata* or *La Bohème* or *Rigoletto?*

Of all creative occupations, that of the libretto writer seems to be least grateful. Anyone who has ever tried to write words to be sung knows what a devilishly difficult job that is. What Mozart said still holds true—that is, that in opera the text has to be the obedient daughter of the music. But for all the obedience, ingenuity and work that have gone into opera librettos, most of the writers (there are exceptions) have not only earned no fame, but are solidly wrapped in such obscurity as used to be proverbial of the vice president of the United States. Most people who go to the opera do not even understand the words they wrote—let alone remember their names.

What kind of men were these who would undertake so subservient a task? Why did they do it?

It is difficult to unearth the answers. In the New York libraries, which are exceptionally well stocked in musical matters, there is surprisingly little material on this subject, possibly or probably because no one has bothered to undertake a thorough research of the librettist subject. There exist letters from Verdi to his four librettists, there exist letters from Puccini to his playwrights. But these present the composers' side; there is no vice versa. From Verdi's letters we get Verdi's specifications, and from Puccini's letters we get mostly grumblings. The lesser half of the team does not often speak. (I am excepting the Strauss-Hofmannsthal relationship. These fascinating letters, which let us into the workshop of two equal partners, do set forth both sides.)

We might suppose most of these librettists were simply hack

writers and that if they lived today they would be doing scripts for soap operas. But such is not the case. Some of the librettists were by no means nonentities, and had made names for themselves with successes of their own before they bowed to the tyranny of music.

But in the make-up of most of them there must have been a deal of gentleness and submissiveness, a second-fiddle trait which made it possible for them to work for an overlord. For, to be sure, the composer was, as he should have been, the boss of the collaboration. And practically every opera composer was an exacting boss, having his own ideas about the words and being extremely particular about what went into the libretto.

Such a gentle, yielding soul was Piave, the third of Verdi's librettists, who wrote the texts for *Ernani, Rigoletto, La Forza del Destino, La Traviata,* and others. He was the resident poet and stage manager of the Fenice Theater in Venice, and in all turned out about sixty librettos for various Italian composers. He was utterly devoted to Verdi. Verdi gave Piave explicit instructions on every aria and duet. Piave filled in the words and worked out the plot. Realizing that he was not a very good poet, he said: "What's the difference? The sublime notes which the Maestro has adapted to my verses will make them appear beautiful." His favorite slogan was, "The Master wishes it so, and that is enough." He not only tailor-made the librettos to order, but was helpful to Verdi by taking off the composer's shoulders the burden of many rehearsals. He aided with the copying of the parts. He helped solve, through great tact, the censorship trouble which had arisen over *Le Roi s'amuse.* Piave persuaded the officials that in the guise of *Rigoletto* the play was harmless. All this he did with good humor and placidly. No wonder Verdi was fond of Piave and treated him with characteristic Verdian kindness! Long after Piave had ceased to be useful to him, Verdi defrayed all expenses of Piave's long illness and settled ten thousand lire on his illegitimate daughter. He even persuaded six famous composers, among them Auber and Thomas, to contribute to an album of songs, the royalties of which provided the daughter with a small income.

Piave was drawn to Verdi in admiration of the composer. Boïto's collaboration was preceded by long-standing unfriendliness. Boïto's first job for Verdi was writing the words to the *Hymn of Nations*, which Verdi composed for a festival in London in 1862. But after that the two men became estranged. Boïto had written a public letter attacking Italian composers, and Verdi, as the most eminent Italian composer, felt himself personally wounded. It was not until seventeen years later that Boïto went to work with Verdi on the "chocolate venture," as Verdi called *Otello*. In the meantime, Boïto had written one or two librettos for others, had published some good poetry, had joined Garibaldi's expedition and fought for Italy's freedom, and had written the music for the opera *Mestifole*, which was a sensational failure at La Scala, but which happens to be an excellent opera, one that should be revived. Boïto at first disliked Verdi's music, being smitten by Wagnerian music drama. Only after Boïto had heard *Aïda* did he change his mind. He finally brought to Verdi an adaptation for *Otello* which was both operatically serviceable and truly poetic, in fact, a masterpiece of a libretto!

Boïto was a much greater personality and an infinitely abler writer than Piave. Yet he, too, was, I think, at least partly submissive. Certainly as a composer he stood in awe of Verdi and was willing to sacrifice his own musical career to be of help to the greater master.

Verdi was a reasonable man. But Puccini—! There is probably the most turbulent partnership in opera—the triple partnership of Puccini, Illica and Giacosa. Illica was a writer of Italian comedies and a successful librettist; he wrote, among others, *La Wally* for Catalani and *Andrea Chenier* for Giordano. Giacosa was one of the best-known Italian playwrights of his time. For thirty years he was acclaimed by the Italian theatrical public. Not only that, but he was a popular lecturer, wrote good short stories and was editor of a magazine. How could such a man accept the bludgeonings of Puccini?

The two dramatists started their collaboration with Puccini on *La Bohème* and continued with *Butterfly* and *Tosca*. Illica had a quick, agile mind, and was concerned only with what was immediately picturesque and effective behind the footlights. Giacosa was slow, cautious and elegant, a filer of phrases. Puccini was a nervous, irritable and unconscionably severe taskmaster who made the two librettists write and rewrite over and over again. This is shown by Puccini's letters to his publisher, Ricordi, whom he used as a sort of go-between to relay his instructions to the two men. Puccini minced no words when he was annoyed with their work, which was most of the time. During the writing of *La Bohème*, he said such things as, "Illica sent me a copy of the solo of Schaunard. ... A very poor thing ... a mere piece of pudding." "He chooses to give himself airs. Must I blindly accept the fiat of Illica?" Under these conditions, it took two years to produce the *La Bohème* libretto, while it took only eight months to compose the music. The text of the last act was rewritten five times. On many occasions Ricordi had to step in to keep the partnership from breaking up. Illica had a violent suppressed temper, and Giacosa would fall into moods of deep depression. It was only Ricordi's skill which kept the men together. Actually the two poets were most valuable to Puccini, as we realize when we look at the other librettos for Puccini operas. Yet there was no balm in Gilead, ever. There was, however, one librettist who never quarreled with his composer. In that particular case, the composer even held him in exaggerated esteem. That librettist's name was Richard Wagner.

5. *What Happens
Between the Acts?*

A TURTLE HAS NOTHING on a musical prejudice: they are both
hard-shelled and long-lived. People who do not like opera,
flexible though they may be in other respects, persistently
continue to assert, and with great positiveness, that all opera
librettos are nonsense. I even know some people who are fond
of opera but who nevertheless think that one should look down
one's nose at *all* librettos, that all are bad and none should be
seriously considered.

I can probably cite as many bad librettos as the next man,
but I am far from agreeing with this supercilious attitude
toward the dramatic part of opera. In fact, I have a great respect for many librettos. An unprejudiced and scientific survey
leads one to the profound conclusion that there are two kinds
of librettos: good ones and bad ones. But most of the operas
with which we now come in contact have good ones. If some
of them are not dramatic masterpieces, almost none of them is
altogether meretricious. It is virtually impossible for an opera
to live if it is chained to a dead-weight libretto. Donald J.
Grout, professor of music at Cornell University, concludes
his book, *A Short History of Opera*, by saying: "As we look
back over the past, there is borne in upon us with irresistible
force a certain feeling of futility. The thought of so much
buried beauty is saddening .…" While there may be several
reasons why a particular operatic beauty stays buried, a poor
libretto is certainly one of the chief reasons.

It seems to me that plays age quicker than other forms of
literature. All but the greatest date noticeably. Anyone who

has gone with high anticipation to the revival of a play he once found exciting, only to find it in resurrection tepid and dull, will know the truth of this. I have had that experience with *The Front Page, R.U.R., The First Mrs. Fraser* and others. Even the work of better playrights—Ibsen and Shaw—reveals its age. The fact that we can accept *La Tosca* at all, that in a good performance we still—after all this time—become worked up over Scarpia's villiany and Tosca's sufferings, is a testimonial to Sardou as well as to Puccini. We would not, of course, go to a performance of *Tosca* without the music, unless perhaps another Sarah Bernhardt were to play the role. Still, when we hear the opera, it is not only the music that we hear and respond to, but a combination of music and play. That combination owes something to the worth of the play. We are wrong if we discount the drama.

To name specific examples, I believe that *Carmen, Boris Godunov, Pelléas et Mélisande, Die Meistersinger, The Marriage of Figaro, Der Rosenkavalier, Gianni Schichi* and of course *Otello* are first-class operatic plays, and that *La Bohème, Louise, Tosca, Falstaff, La Traviata, Le Coq d'or* and *Die Walküre* are more than acceptable from the dramatic point of view.

It is of course the music that counts in all these operas, as well as in the borderline cases such as *Rigoletto, Madama Butterfly* and *Götterdämmerung*, where the drama is of doubtful value. Good plays or mediocre plays, music is the magician. A remarkable magician, too, who forces us to look where we are supposed to look and guides us so that we do not miss things that ought to be in the play. This is true of even the best librettos. Because we concentrate on the music, the operatic play has an easier time of it than the stage play and can get away with more inconsistencies. It is extraordinary what we don't notice because of the music.

I said just now that *Die Meistersinger* was a good libretto,

So it is. It has an amusing plot, it brings us a vivid picture of an interesting period, it has lots of charm, its people are believable characters and one of them is a great dramatic creation. But don't forget that the plot is supposed to revolve around a singing contest. The competition on St. John's Day is to be a public one, and anyone can enter provided he is a Meistersinger and a bachelor or, as Beckmesser says, a widower. But what kind of prize contest is this? What do we get in the last act? Where are the contestants? Did you ever hear of a contest where there are only two entrants, one of them being an illegitimate substitute? There is not the slightest suggestion that other singers are going to compete. If Hans Sachs's scheme did not work, and if Walther did not appear on cue and sing his previously rehearsed prize song or a reasonable facsimile thereof, would the prize go to Beckmesser by default just because he was the only contestant? In the first act, when Pogner announces the contest, Kothner says enthusiastically, "Come on, all bachelors!" Between the first and the last acts, what has happened to all the bachelors?

It is obvious that the magic music carries us over this dramatic hole so that practically no one notices the omission. I dare say that few people, even among those who know *Die Meistersinger* well, have ever thought to question the proceedings. There is a similar puzzle in another splendid libretto, *Der Rosenkavalier*. Will you tell me how it happens that the august and elegant Marschallin, Fürstin Werdenberg, comes to the shabby inn where the third act takes place? Her appearance there is even more inexplicable than the appearance of the strait-laced elder Germont at Flora's gambling party in *La Traviata* at which I always ask myself, "What is he doing here?" In *Der Rosenkavalier*, what happens between the end of the second act and the beginning of the third act? Who has talked? Who has told the Marschallin of Octavian's scheme to get rid of the Baron? Obviously not Octavian himself, because when she appears he is quite as astonished as the rest and says to her, "We had something different in mind, Marie-Therese." Neither Faninal nor Baron Ochs could possibly have informed her. But here she is, a charming and resplendent *dea ex machina*, in a bistro. And of course we are glad to see her, for she is shortly to take part in the trio, the most beautiful music of the opera. Ernest Newman in *More Stories of Famous Operas* points out this dramatic inconsistency and notes that it must also have occurred to Hofmannsthal and Strauss, for the score carries at this point an added stage direction which does not appear in the original text, calling for the servant to run out when the police commissioner enters. But even this afterthought does not explain the situation. Not nearly enough time elapses for the servant to have gone to the Marschallin's palace, to have summoned her and to have brought her to the suburban inn. Indeed, not enough time elapses for a woman like the Marschallin to have put on her hat!

What happens between acts two and three of *Tristan?* This has baffled me for years. There is no explaining the events subsequent to the fall of the curtain of the second act. Tristan draws his sword, shouts, "On guard, Melot," then lets his sword fall and sinks wounded into Kurvenal's arms. Isolde flings herself on him and the curtain falls. In the next act we learn that the faithful Kurvenal has carried Tristan away on his broad shoulders and that Tristan has lain like dead since that day. Now, since the wound will not heal, Kurvenal has sent for the only physician who can heal it, for Isolde. But why did all this happen? Did Isolde turn away from the wounded Tristan and pay no further attention to him? Impossible. Then why did she not take care of his wound immediately? And why did not Isolde flee with Tristan if Kurvenal insisted on bringing Tristan back to his native land? Did Mark hold her back? That is most unlikely. We can't believe it knowing King Mark as we do. Did Kurvenal spirit Tristan away in secrecy? Aside from the fact that such an action would have been almost impossible without Isolde's knowing about it, why did she not follow? She intimates (in one of the most beautiful passages at the close of the second act) that she wishes to follow Tristan wherever he leads, and she knows that he leads to death. Why does she not go with him at once? Later, when the second ship arrives, Brangäne tells us that she confessed, as soon as Isolde had disappeared, the secret of the potion to the king. Learning the secret, the king himself embarked in greatest haste in order to reach Tristan and to give Isolde to him. He comes too late, and it is of course proper to the tragedy that he come too late. But why did Brangäne wait all this time? And what made her confess finally? None of these questions is ever resolved. It does not matter—because of the music.

I cite these instances only to show that strong librettos can afford little weaknesses. But a strong libretto it must be if the entire opera is to remain alive and healthy.

*There are operas that have
remained only a gleam
in their creators' eyes....*

6. *Some Operas that
were Never Written*

IF YOU SHARE with me an admiration for Sherlock Holmes of
Baker Street, you will know that between moments of deduc-
ing why there was a fresh nick in the stone parapet and why
Watson was better shaved on one cheek than on the other, and
why the dead man did not have an Underground ticket in his
pocket, he was also working on a number of cases about which
we know nothing but the titles. Such cases as "The Adventure
of the Paradol Chamber" or "The Case of the Amateur Mendi-
cant Society," casually mentioned by Dr. W., remain unwritten. Because they remain unwritten, we Holmes idolators
think that they must have been particularly fascinating cases.

Similarly, there are a good many operas of which we know
little more than the titles or one or two musical fragments or
outlines of the libretto. Some of these projects, entertained
fleetingly or seriously by the composers, seem as tantalizing as
the unwritten Holmes stories.

There are, for example, many unwritten Faust operas. The
legend which inspired music in Wagner, Liszt and Berlioz, and
on which Boïto based his *Mefistofele* and Gounod his pretty
and famous gumdrop, also appealed to many another operatic
composer. Weber thought of doing a Faust opera. And so did
another composer who indeed could have done justice to
Goethe's vast conception—Beethoven.

In Beethoven's case, Faust was only one of a dozen ideas
with which he toyed. It is generally supposed that the failure

of *Fidelio* disgusted Beethoven with opera, and that he never again meant to write for the stage. This is not correct. Before and after *Fidelio*, Beethoven applied to well-known contemporary librettists for texts. Grillparzer, the famous Viennese dramatist, worked with Beethoven on two operas, and the composer nearly drove him mad with demands for revisions. Beethoven also wrote to the then most popular author of heroic bombast, Kotzebue, requesting a libretto for an opera of the poet's own choosing and of any nature—"romantic, serious, heroico-comic or sentimental, as you please"—which sounds reminiscent of Polonius. There is even evidence to show that he started to work on a text supplied him by the librettist of *The Magic Flute*, Schikaneder.

Beethoven also considered *Macbeth* (both the Shakespearean original and an adaptation by his friend Collin, for whose play he wrote the *Coriolanus* Overture); Schiller's *Fiesco, Romeo and Juliet, Orestes, Attila, Melusine, Antigone*, a tragedy by Voltaire, a text by the poet Schlegel, one of the translators of Shakespeare into German; the return of Ulysses, and several other subjects. But again and again he rejected the librettos, perhaps because subconsciously he felt no real affinity for the stage. In one of his letters Beethoven confesses, "It is so difficult to get a good poem." He then says strangely, "I could not compose operas like *Don Juan* and *Figaro*. They are repugnant to me. I could not have chosen such subjects; they are too frivolous for me."

Like Beethoven, Debussy remained a one-opera composer. He too worked on many plans. He too was attracted to Shakespeare, and considered *Comme il vous plaira* as a subject for music. Of this no sketches are extant though two fragments of a proposed *King Lear* have been published. And, paradoxically, Debussy, who hated Wagner, considered an opera on the Tristan legend. Can you imagine the difference between the Wagnerian *Tristan* and a Debussian Tristan? Or would they have shared some inner and fundamental similarities? This is speculation, just speculation. The Tristan opera never went beyond the idea stage; Debussy's most serious uncompleted project was an opera called *La Chute de la maison Usher*, in which title you will recognize the Edgar Allan Poe tale. Gatti-Casazza paid Debussy an advance of two thousand francs for the production rights of this opera, for Gatti knew the worth and the success of *Pelléas*. Debussy did not want to take the money, nor did he promise to deliver the opera, as he was "such a lazy composer." But Gatti insisted, and in the course of several visits assured the composer that the Metropolitan would do everything to give the new work a worthy production. Debussy had opportunity to convince himself of what the Metropolitan was capable, for in 1910, when the company made a guest appearance in Paris, Debussy attended a performance of *Aïda* in which Caruso sang and which Toscanini conducted.

Debussy worked hard and long on *The Fall of the House of Usher*. He steeped himself in the atmosphere of the Poe story, and we know that he invented for the music a strange orchestral effect involving the low tones of the oboe contrasted with violin chords. Nothing remains of this music. Like Brahms, Debussy was a critical destroyer of unfinished or unsatisfactory manuscripts.

It is curious to reflect that as we might have had another Tristan, so might we have had another Pelléas. Puccini read and liked the drama and wrote to Maeterlinck asking whether he could buy the story for an opera libretto. Maeterlinck had to tell him, "Alas! How willingly would I give my poem to the composer of *La Vie de Bohème*, if I had not already given it to Debussy!" Maeterlinck's disappointment is obvious; for Puccini was considerably more famous than Debussy. But what would have happened to the whispering love of Pelléas and Mélisande if it had been expressed in the sweep of Puccini melodramatics? Later Puccini himself admired the Debussy music. It had, he said, "extraordinary harmonic qualities and the most delicate instrumental effects. It is very interesting, in spite of its coloring, which is somber and unrelieved, like a Franciscan's habit."

Puccini's unwritten operas include a *Marie Antoinette*, a *Notre Dame*, and a *Tartarin*. This last project he discussed with the dying Daudet, who was thrilled at the prospect of having his unheroic hero set to music. These three unwritten operas are not nearly a complete catalogue of the subjects which Puccini considered seriously. Indeed, we might say with only a little exaggeration that it would be difficult to find a dramatic subject Puccini did not consider. Puccini was happy only when he was working, miserable as soon as he had written *fine* to an operatic manuscript, and bored with any opera which he had completed. He immediately began the search for a new one. He bombarded all his friends with pleas for suggestions. He searched through books, he ran to see the popular plays. He conferred with D'Annunzio and relinquished what started out as a promising collaboration only after D'Annunzio had failed twice to deliver a satisfactory libretto. The search took him to so unlikely a subject as *Lorna Doone*, to a play about the actor David Garrick, to a novel called *Two Little Wooden Shoes* by Ouïda, author of *Under Two Flags*, and to *The Florentine Tragedy* by Oscar Wilde.

Verdi weighed earnestly for a long period of time an opera on *King Lear*. This is not surprising in the composer of *Otello* and *Falstaff*, who "preferred Shakespeare to all other dramatists." At Verdi's direction, a friend of his, Somma, worked out a libretto. Verdi's letters show how carefully he went into the matter. In his *King Lear* he wished to give particular treatment to the part of the Fool, "so original, so deep." He also cautioned Somma "not to make Lear's part too exhausting." But *Re Lear* never was completed, perhaps because Verdi at the last was held back by his original hesitancy: "I am appalled by the need to span such a tremendous canvas in a narrow frame without detracting from the originality and grandeur of the characters."

One of the strangest of all unwritten operas is a huge project by Wagner. He worked on an opera to be called *The Victors* the year before he began *Tristan*. This was to be an opera on Buddhism, and Wagner studied the religion and the philosophy in preparation for the opera. The sketch for the drama has survived. It is a turgid and vague plot, but its central motive is Wagner's favorite theme, the redemption of the world through Woman. Some characteristics of the heroine, Ananda, were probably made part of Kundry, and one musical motive in the Wotan-Erda scene in the third act of *Siegfried* was originally intended for *The Victors*.

The unwritten opera which might have been most interesting to Americans is a work of Dvořák. When Dvořák was living in New York and teaching at the Conservatory, he became interested in American literature. In a Czech translation he made the acquaintance of a poem which spoke of Indian hunters and the American forest in a strange, beguiling meter. Dvořák was so captured by the *Song of Hiawatha* that he wanted to make Longfellow's legend the basis of an opera, just as he meant to write a symphony in B minor about Niagara Falls. He never did either.

Perhaps the most engrossing of all non-existent operatic projects is the one with which Rossini toyed after the completion of *William Tell*. He said he would like to write an opera called *Joan of Arc*. Would Joan have addressed the French soldiers in a coloratura aria?

Old abuses and an old
defense, both from London. . . .

7.'*Twas Ever Thus*

ANY LOVER of opera knows that opera has its problems. Any lover of opera knows that opera has its enemies.

In our time some problems have been solved, some detractors have been convinced. Others have not. Most certainly they have not! But, in case we become impatient, let us remember that opera remains as an art agreeable, succulent and lively in spite of its problems, in spite of its heretics.

Let us also remember that some of the problems are of ancient vintage and some of the scoffers almost as old as the art itself. I have no new solutions for old problems, nor any new arguments for those who don't want to listen to what is for me the most exciting form of music. I have, however, a bit of historical argument to set forth which shows that some of the things which bother us today bothered other people at other times. It is an old story but an interesting one.

Let's take the problem of the composer. I don't know whether we have so few good new operas because the composers are inadequately compensated for the complex labor of writing them, or whether the composers are inadequately compensated because so few know how to write an opera which pleases the public. At any rate, as Benjamin Britten, the composer of *Peter Grimes*, has said, the creation of an opera demands from the composer "a freedom from other work which is an economic impossibility for most young composers." Obviously this is a bad condition, not made better by the knowledge that it has, to a certain extent, always existed. It bothered a good composer two hundred years ago. . . .

[41]

When George Frederick Handel went to England toward the end of the year 1710, he met Aaron Hill, director of the King's Theater in the Haymarket. Hill asked Handel, who was already a renowned composer, to write an opera for his theater. The opera *Rinaldo* was the result. It was given in February of 1711, mounted sumptuously, performed splendidly with a cast of Italian singers, and it had an immediate and spectacular success. (One of its melodies, by the way, was later taken over into *The Beggar's Opera*.) Because of the opera's popularity, the "song hits" of *Rinaldo* were published by a London music publisher, John Walsh. The sheet music sold so well that Walsh made $7,500 from the publication, obviously an enormous sum for the time. Handel, however, received very little for his labors. It was only later, when he ran his own theater in London, that he was able to make money. Naturally this inequality rankled in the composer's mind, so much so that Handel is supposed to have addressed a letter to Walsh which read, "My Dear Sir: As it is only right that we should be on an equal footing, you will compose the next opera, and I shall sell it."

Rinaldo was only the first of a long series of operas which Handel was to produce in England. His kind of "Italian" opera quickly became London's favorite form of theatrical entertainment. But with the friends came the enemies, and there were many people in London who disliked opera—for musical, moral and dramatic reasons. Among these were two eminent journalists, one of them himself a playwright—Joseph Addison and Richard Steele. In the *Tatler* and the *Spectator*, they attacked opera with force and wit. The tried, by every literary means they could devise, to check London's fondness for this entertainment. They were unable to do so.

But as much as a century later the point of their argument had not entirely dulled. I have come across a book by a certain A. Burgh, A.M., called *Anecdotes of Music, Historical and*

Biographical: in a Series of Letters from a Gentleman to His Daughter, which shows that the questions whether or not opera was a sensible entertainment, whether it took employment away from English actors, and also whether, if given at all, it ought to be given in English, were current problems in 1814, when the book was published. Mr. Burgh belatedly answered Addison and Steele, but his remarks were still of timely interest. I quote some of his ingenious, if sometime specious, arguments:

"Mr. Addison had, in a former number of this excellent periodical work, leveled his chief artillery of ridicule at the absurdity of going to an opera without understanding the language in which it is performed: 'an absurdity,' says he, 'which shows itself at first sight. It does not want any great measure of sense to see the ridicule of this monstrous practice.' But he never told the public that it was absurd to go to concerts of good music: on the contrary, he even recommends those of Clayton to public encouragement. Now, it may be asked, what entertainment there is for the mind in a concerto, sonata or solo? They are merely objects of gratification to the ear; and opera, at the worst, merely for the ear, is still better than a concert, or a pantomime entertainment for the eye. And, supposing the articulation to be wholly unintelligible, we have still an excellent union of harmony and melody for the ear: and, according even to Sir Richard Steele's account of Nicolini's [a famous singer in Handel's time] action, 'it was so significant that a deaf man might go along with him in the sense of the part he acted.'

"No one will dispute that understanding Italian would render our entertainment of an opera more rational and more complete; but without that advantage, be it remembered by the lovers of music that an opera is the *completest* concert to which they can go; with this advantage over those in still life, that to the most perfect singing, and effects of a powerful and well-disciplined band, are frequently added excellent acting, splendid scenes and decorations, with such dancing as a playhouse is seldom able to furnish.

"The ridicule and reasoning of Mr. Addison, from his high reputation as a writer, have been long and implicitly admitted, and imagined sincere; but besides his want of knowledge as well as love for music, when it is considered that his friend, Sir Richard Steele, was a patentee of the playhouse, and interested at any rate to depreciate the opera and exalt the English drama; and that Addison himself was not only exasperated at the untimely death of Rosamond, but at the opera's being crowded while his friend Mr. Smith's tragedy of Phaedra and Hippolytus was neglected; which, by the way, always has been neglected even when no opera was performed against it; for as Dr. Johnson says, it 'pleased the critics, and the critics only.'

"If we put these circumstances together, we shall ascribe some part of the *Spectator*'s severity to want of skill in the art of music, some to peevishness, and the rest to national prejudice, and the spirit of party in favor of our English theaters.

"London has now a sufficient number of inhabitants to supply a musical theater with an audience without injuring our own drama. People will be pleased in their own way: wherever there is the attraction of extraordinary talent, the public favor follows of course, either in regard to the playhouse or the opera; nor can it be justly said that native excellence has usually been robbed of its share of patronage by an unmerited partiality to foreigners. And this we may venture to assert, even though Mr. Addison has said, 'we know not what we like in music: only, in general, we are transported with anything that is not English: so it be of foreign growth, let it be Italian, French or High Dutch, it is the same thing.' But was this the case in his own time with respect to singing? Were not Mrs. Tofts and Mrs. Anastasia Robinson in very high favor, though English women? This he could not be unacquainted with, and therefore has wilfully misstated the case....

"As to the *understanding* having no share in the pleasure we receive at an opera, it may at least be allowed the negative praise, which was admitted by the gloomy fanatic, Cromwell, that 'being an unknown tongue, it cannot corrupt the morals of the people:' which is more than can be said of our own *Beggar's Opera* or the comedies of Congreve and Vanbrugh, which, however excellent in other respects, have certainly a most immoral tendency and are on that account highly reprehensible. We admit that the understanding may be gratified for the moment by the brilliancy even of licentious genius; but if this brilliancy be found to corrupt the hearts of the young and inexperienced, who are the chief support of public places, the opera must be acknowledged a more innocent, if not a more rational amusement."

A nice point: it is better to give opera in a foreign language because people then don't understand the immoral words it may contain! We can laugh at this; yet we are still not agreed on the question whether opera should or should not be sung in our language. And there are still people around who believe that we show "an unmerited popularity to foreigners."

PART II
OPERAS IN PARTICULAR

1. *Journey to Egypt*

ITALY'S MOST IMPORTANT operatic première occurred far from Italy. The first *"Celeste Aïda"* was sung in an Italian opera house in an Egyptian city under European influence, the opera having been originally planned as part of a celebration of French ingenuity.

Though both the Suez Canal and the Cairo opera house were already doing good business in the winter of 1871, this première was still musically and politically a most important affair. It was important enough for the Egyptian government officially to invite one of Italy's eminent critics to attend the evening, and important enough for that critic to heed the invitation, though for a Milanese to leave the domain of La Scala and *risotto alla Milanese* and to journey south, far south into a land of lamb and Sphinxes, was in those days no light undertaking. Filippo Filippi, critic of *Perseveranza,* did not flinch from his duty. He went.

This Filippi seems indeed to have been a courageous man. He began his career with an enthusiastic praise of *Rigoletto* and later championed some modernistic music in a pamphlet called *Riccardo Wagner.* In his memoirs (which unfortunately have never been translated into English) he has left us an account of his voyage and his first impression of *Aïda.*

Before we retell this travelogue we might quickly review the well-known but still memorable circumstances responsible for *Aïda*'s creation.

Ismael Pasha, Khedive of Egypt, a despotic, extravagant but also progressive young monarch who was in love with Europe and occidental ways, wanted something special to celebrate the opening of a new opera house he was building in Cairo.

This opening was to coincide with the grand opening of the Suez Canal. Through an agent he approached Verdi with a commission for an opera. Verdi refused. The Khedive then sent him an outline of a plot, which he had supposedly written himself. Verdi did not quite believe this. However, probably remembering Bülow's admonition that one should not criticize the compositions of royalty as one never knows who wrote them, he did not voice his doubts. He began to study the outline and found that he liked it. In fact, he suddenly decided that he liked it so much that he wanted to set it to music. He then asked his pupil and friend, Muzio, what should be the price for an opera commissioned by royalty for a royal occasion. Muzio advised him to ask the sum of four thousand pounds sterling for the rights of performance in Egypt alone. It appeared that the Khedive was willing to pay this exceptional price, and Verdi accepted the commission. Soon afterward Verdi learned that his skepticism as to the origin of the plot had been founded, that the story had actually been written by Mariette Bey, a friend of the Khedive and a well-known French Egyptologist, the discoverer of the Temple of Serapis and then director of the great Egyptian museum of Bulec.

Verdi went to work with his usual conscientiousness. He inquired into a number of historical facts such as the role of Ethiopia in ancient times, the meaning of the cult of Isis, etc. Then he worked on the plot itself, to which he contributed several important ideas. A prose version of the full libretto was prepared, and he then found an Italian poet, Ghislanzoni, to set the lines to verse. Even there, Verdi gave precise suggestions, often line for line.

All this took longer than expected. The première was now postponed to January, 1871. In the meantime, both events which were to have been celebrated by *Aïda* had already taken place. The Suez Canal had opened with the Empress Eugénie in attendance. Instead of *Aïda*, an Offenbach cycle was given in a series of performances in a wooden auditorium which, at the command of the Khedive, had been built in a few days. Included were *La Belle Hélène*, which was the Khedive's favorite opera, *La Grande Duchesse de Gerolstein*, *Orpheus* and *Barbe-Bleu*.

The Cairo opera house had also opened. At that opening the evening began with a cantata composed in honor of the Khedive. In the middle of the stage, around a bust of the Khedive, stood eight singers representing Justice, Mercy, Fame, History, Agriculture, Industry, Commerce, and (strangely enough) Music. This was followed by a performance of *Rigoletto*.

Mariette Bey went to see Verdi for a consultation. Mariette spent almost two years planning details of the costumes and the scenery, all of which were to be ordered in Paris. Verdi finished the opera in time for a possible performance in 1871, but the.outbreak of the Franco-Prussian War upset all the plans because not only ,the costumes and the scenery but Mariette Bey himself were shut up in Paris.

Verdi had a perfect right under the circumstances to produce *Aïda* at La Scala. Thus read his contract. But Verdi was a man of scrupulous honesty. He held up the Scala production because he felt that Egypt had first right to the opera. Paris surrendered in January 1871, but by this time it was too late to get the costumes to Egypt for a performance that season, so the opera was postponed until the next season. The interim was used by the director of the Cairo Opera House for a journey to Verdi at Sant' Agata to discuss the final details of production and to go over once again the choices of singers and conductor.

When Filippi decided to travel to Egypt, he knew that Verdi would not attend the première (Verdi had a dread of sea trips and also feared that in Egypt "they might make a mummy of him") and wrote to the composer offering his services in any way that would be useful. Verdi, who by this time was quite nervous about all the publicity that the new opera was bringing forth, and who never did like non-musical fanfares, replied with a rather short-tempered letter:

"What I am going to say to you will seem strange, very strange; but you must forgive me if I feel I must unburden myself of what is on my mind.

"You at Cairo? Why, nothing could be more important for *Aïda* in the way of publicity. To me it seems that art practiced in this manner is no longer art but a trade, a diversion, a sport, something to be run after, to be made, if not successful, at least notorious at any cost! The feelings roused in me are those of disgust and humiliation. I always remember with joy the early days in which, almost without friends, without any personal mention, without preparations, without any kind of influence, I came before the public with my operas ready to be shot at, only too glad if I were able to make some kind of favorable impression. And now what a pother about an opera! Journalists, singers, players, choristers and directors, etc., etc., all have to contribute their stone to the edifice of publicity, to make in this way a cornice of nonsensical trifles that add nothing to the merit of an opera and may quite possibly detract from its real value. It is deplorable, absolutely deplorable. . . ."

So Filippi started off without Verdi's blessing. He took a train on what was called the India Trunk Line, a train which went through Bologna en route to catch the P. and O. boats to the Orient. At Foggia an agent of the Italian Line boarded the train and tried to argue the critic into taking the Italian boat intsead of the English vessel on which he was booked. When Filippi refused, the agent snapped, "All right, go with the English; but remember, you leave later, arrive later, and you will be very badly served." This worried Filippi and he decided to talk it over with a man who was in the same compartment on the train, an Englishman in a long grey silk gown, looking somewhat like a rajah. The Englishman told him that there was no comparison between the two boats, that the English boat, the *Nyasa*, was a "colossus" of two thousand tons and that the Italian boat was only four hundred tons and "does a *danse macabre* on the sea. The strongest stomach cannot stand it." Filippi finally concluded that the Englishman owned stock in the P. and O. Company and that nowhere could unprejudiced advice be obtained. However, he took the English giant, and it was a full three days before he arrived in Alexandria. He found the food on the boat "fair" (I suspect he was being polite), and tasted curry, chutney and chili. He wondered at the English custom of serving sandwiches with sherry or brandy at 10:00 P.M. The other passengers were "stand-offish," read the *Times* until they knew it by heart and played whist. There was a piano on board, but the Prince Consort had just died and the captain decreed that all music was prohibited.

At the docks in Alexandria the beggars surrounded Filippi, but he was soon met by a government official and whisked away. He did a bit of sightseeing around Alexandria and dutifully visited Pompey's Column and Cleopatra's Obelisk. He went to the inevitable Offenbach operettas at the theater and listened to the discussions about the *Aïda* première. The whole town was talking of nothing else. Many people were planning excursions to Cairo for the occasion. The newspapers wrote daily articles about the opera, and there were many tall reports about the fantastic sum spent on the costumes and scenery, reputedly 700,000 francs.

From Alexandria Filippi went to Cairo and was much impressed by that city, though he found there "an air of vice." The Khedive was trying to make it into a modern French city. In fact, Cairo was by this time so French that *Paris Comique*, the French comic paper, published cartoons showing that the pyramids were advertising French products, "*Occa-*

sions exceptionnelles," while the Sphinx gazed down at the bewildered tourist who was muttering *"Ça manque de couleur locale."*

From his hotel Filippi looked out into the streets filled with camels and donkeys and Arabs, and proceeded to ride a donkey himself. He went to the park where the Khedive showed himself, seated in his beautiful European carriage, the veiled ladies of the harem following. The ladies were escorted by the eunuchs and were trailed on foot by a band of cocottes.

Filippi greatly admired the new opera house with its enormous colonnaded arcade. Opera was the Khedive's pet luxury. Every year his opera director traveled to Europe to engage singers who vied for engagements because of the high fees that were paid. The tenor Mongini, who was to sing Radames, got 125,000 francs for the season! Filippi attended the rehearsals and found the theater well equipped, orderly and disciplined, but with a tendency, as was also true of the Italian theaters, to work little. However, they were trying their best to do a good job with *Aïda*. Rehearsals lasted eight hours at a time. Both the stage manager and the conductor had had no rest for fifteen days. Musically and dramatically the opera was ready, but the mechanics still did not work, and the great movable scaffold for the Temple scene in the last act was not yet finished.

The Khedive, however, decided that he wanted to take a trip to the Upper Nile by Tuesday, the twenty-sixth, and therefore, come what may, ordered the dress rehearsal for Saturday, the twenty-third, and the première for Sunday, Deecmber 24, 1871.

On Saturday night the dress rehearsal was attended by all the subscribers (according to French custom, this *répétition générale* was in fact a performance), by the Khedive and his suite, and by the ladies of the harem. It lasted from 7:00 P.M. to 3:00 A.M., what with the delays and intermissions. The machinery worked badly and the ballet (which comprised forty young girls all brought from Paris, all accompanied by their mothers) did not come on in time. Things would have to go better the next night.

Tickets for the opening night had been sold out many weeks in advance. Speculators asked fantastic prices, of course. The house was filled on Sunday night long before curtain time. No one was fashionably late. "Much beauty and elegance, especially among the Greeks and the foreigners of high lineage," many Copts and Jews with their strange berettas and their violently colored costumes, were in the audience, but few Arabs. The ladies of the harem sat in three boxes at the right of the stage, protected from view by a white muslin curtain. The spectators promenaded between the acts and looked at themselves in the foyer mirrors which reached from floor to ceiling. Officials wearing the traditional red silk turbans of the Moslems stood in front of signs which read "No Smoking" and smoked.

The Khedive made a dramatic entrance after the prelude. The audience rose and cheered. From then on enthusiasm mounted. The first aria which stopped the show was of course the "*Celeste Aïda.*" After that every number was applauded and cheered, so much so that the conductor Bottesini turned around at one point, glared at the audience and shouted with a strong Milanese accent, "That isn't done!"

Filippi was enraptured by the scenery and costumes. The backdrops were authentic copies from Egyptian buildings. Amneris' diadem of pure gold was ornamented by symbols found on the monuments at Nubia. Radames' helmet and shield were of solid silver. The materials covering the throne in the third act were copies of pieces in the Louvre. The King's costume was blue with a white velvet tunic covered with gold and jeweled design.

The staging was excellent; as a matter of fact, it was so good that few changes have been made since then in *Aïda* staging, a tradition not entirely beneficial to the opera. There were native Arab trumpeters, a military band from Cairo and three hundred people for the triumphal march—which rather over-crowded the stage. Of course, a few things went wrong. The machinery still didn't work in the last act, the cellar was pitch dark, the Temple above too brightly lighted. Verdi had worried about the reception of this final duet because of its "vaporous style"; he need not have feared, for it too was cheered.

Filippi was so carried away by the performance and the glamor of the evening that he forgot to say much about the music. He ended his visit by meeting the Khedive and his chief eunuch. He then returned to Milan, where two months later *Aïda* had its European première.

Verdi took the greatest pains with this Milan performance, attending all the rehearsals and becoming more and more impatient with the tenor, who could not understand that Verdi wanted him to sing the words as well as the music correctly. This performance, too, was a triumph, though a few critics now began to accuse Verdi of Wagnerism. This for a time quite spoiled his pleasure in the opera.

Aïda became popular everywhere. Everyone loved it except a certain young man who addressed to Verdi a curious letter:

"On the second of this month, attracted by the sensation which your opera, *Aïda*, was making, I went to Parma. Half an hour before the performance began I was already in my seat, No. 120. I admired the scenery, listened with great pleasure to the excellent singers and took pains to let nothing escape me. After the performance was over, I asked myself whether I was satisfied. The answer was in the negative. I returned to Reggio, and on the way back in the railroad carriage, I listened to the verdicts of my fellow travelers. Nearly all of them agreed that *Aïda* was a work of the highest rank.

"Thereupon I conceived a desire to hear it again, so on the

fourth I returned to Parma. I made the most desperate efforts to obtain a reserved seat, but there was such a crowd that I had to spend five lire to see the performance in comfort.

"I came to the following conclusion: the opera contains absolutely nothing thrilling or electrifying, and if it were not for the magnificent scenery, the audience would not sit through it to the end. It will fill the theater a few more times and then gather dust in the archives. Now, my dear Signor Verdi, you can imagine my regret at having spent thirty-two lire for these two performances. Add to this the aggravating circumstance that I am dependent on my family, and you will understand that this money preys on my mind like a terrible specter. Therefore I address myself frankly and openly to you, so that you may send me this sum. Here is the account:

"Railroad: one way	2.60 lire
Railroad: return trip	3.30 lire
Theater	8.00 lire
Disgustingly bad dinner at the station	2.00 lire
	15.90 lire
Multiplied by 2	×2
	31.80 lire

"In the hope that you will extricate me from this dilemma, I am yours sincerely,

BERTANI"

In reply Verdi wrote to his publisher that "in order to save this scion of his family from the specters that pursue him," he would be glad to pay the little bill. But he deducted four lire for the two dinners: "He could perfectly well have eaten at home." He also asked for a receipt and a promise that this young man would never again hear any of his new operas, "so that he won't expose himself again to the danger of being pursued by specters, and that he may spare me further travel expenses!"

This is the only recorded example of money back if not satisfied in opera. . . .

The opinion of Signor Bertani was, as I say, the exception. Almost everyone now calls *Aïda* "the world's most popular opera." It is certainly that at the Metropolitan Opera House, where it has been performed more often than any other opera. It is that in Italy and in England. And if it is not quite the most popular opera in Germany, it is nearly so.

For *Aïda* is both the most Italian of operas and the most international. Though Verdi wished to incorporate into the score the "smell of Egypt," what he did was to transplant Egypt to Italy. Rather, he gave us an Italian Egypt, complete with Italian excellence in melody and Italian excesses in theatricality.

Verdi studied Egyptian mythology and inquired into Egyptian cults before he composed the music. Fortunately that did him no harm, and no trace of it can be heard in the music. He was too great an artist to put any obvious "local color" effects into the score. He would not have used any quotations even if someone could have told him the kind of music that had existed in ancient Egypt. *Aïda* does not smell of the lamp of archeological research. It contains no foreign phrases as does *Madama Butterfly*, where *The Star Spangled Banner* is as out of place as a hot dog stand would be in the Forum of Rome. But though *Aïda* is all Italian, it presents no difficulties, no obstacles, no strangeness to the operagoers of any nation.

Music is supposed to be international—though that is true only to a degree. But in opera music is married to a libretto, and it is sometimes the libretto that determines the degree of acceptance of the opera in various countries. Perhaps one reason for *Aïda's* ubiquitous popularity is the fact that the action of the opera is laid so far in the past that all nationalities can accept it as part of a common past. Distance here lends enchantment. But more probably it is due to the fact that the libretto is a simple one, containing a little bit of everything that's good in the theater — love, jealousy, patriotism, royal splendor, and the pomp and circumstance of war, all worked out in such a way that the most elementary theatergoer is able to find out what is going on, even if he does not understand a word of Italian. Whatever *Aïda* is, it is not subtle.

The music is not only consistently interesting, but it too runs the gamut. There is so much in *Aïda:* a show-off aria, wonderful heroic declamations, marches and stirring big choral effects, a quiet and melodious soliloquy, the magic softness and deep blueness of a southern night, music of rage and remorse, and finally the incomparable farewell duet.

Aïda is not only loved by the broad mass of people but also by the musically literate. Even the snobs who would have no truck with *Il Trovatore* have little to say against *Aïda*. Those who best understand the beauty and greatness of Italian opera admire *Aïda* the most.

Francis Toye, the English biographer of Verdi, speaks of its "wealth of melodic invention, its vivid contrasts, its luscious harmonic and orchestral coloring." Dyneley Hussey, who wrote the most interesting short book on Verdi I know, says that *Aïda* exhibits "more than any other, Verdi's inexhaustible melodic inspiration, which was capable of pouring out one great tune after another, without ever repeating ideas already used elsewhere, whatever family likeness there may be between them." Ernest Newman regards it as "the culminating point of the older Italian opera," lifting all its ingredients to the "highest possible point of expression."

These are all non-Italian writers. For that matter, perhaps the best comment on *Aïda* was written by a German who is musical but not a musician. You will find it in the chapter called "Full of Harmony" in Thomas Mann's *The Magic Mountain,* where Hans Castorp listens to the phonograph records and is particularly moved by the final scene of the opera.

The music which Hans Castorp so admired is not only judiciously distributed among the four acts — each act contains particular beauties and nobilities — but it is also impartially apportioned among the various characters. Perhaps that is one further reason why *Aïda* is so popular. It is a very practical opera. Some operas need exceptionally good interpretations in order to make their effects. *La Traviata* without a good Violetta is an impossibility, and it is more than a little difficult to sit through a *Tristan und Isolde* if either the Tristan or the Isolde is below par. But in *Aïda* one or another weakness in the cast does not necessarily eliminate enjoyment. *Aïda* is a stellar opera, but it contains a whole constellation. One dull star will not much mar its effect.

Aïda has outlived many poor performances. I have intimated that it suffers somewhat from the fact that its first production was so well staged that few managers have seriously bothered to restage it, at least in our country. (It fills the house even with poor staging.) In the course of years the Egyptian gestures which were first put into the opera have been repeated by rote and have sometimes become meaningless and even ridiculous (Alfred Frankenstein, the music critic of the San Francisco *Chronicle*, describes one of these gestures as "the double-breasted heart attack"). Since *Aïda* is a must for any impresario who puts on opera, no matter under what conditions, some of the popular-priced companies have tried to make up in pageantry—a huge crowd of people on the stage not knowing what to do, and sometimes horses, elephants and camels certainly not knowing what to do—what they lack in orchestras and singers.

This was already true in the late nineteenth century. Colonel Mapleson, in his memoirs, speaks of the *Aïda* which he presented in 1886 in Chicago. In addition to Patti and other stars, he had there "five hundred supernumeraries with blackened faces, in Oriental garb, chasing around to try to find their places. . . . The march was really most impressive. There were six hundred State Militia on the stage, each company marching past in twelves, the rear rank beautifully dressed, the wheels perfect. The finale of the act, with the military band and the 350 extra chorus members, together with the gorgeous scenery and dresses, was something long to be remembered!" We can imagine!

This took place the same year that *Aïda* was introduced at the Metropolitan. By that time, the opera was already well known to the New York public because it had first been performed here in 1873 (at the Academy of Music), two years after the Cairo première and before either Paris or London had heard the opera.

Surprisingly enough, at that first New York performance the critics of both the New York *Times* and the New York *Herald* took a cautious view of the opera. Though it had been enthusiastically received not only in Cairo but also in Milan, and though its fame must have been known here, the critics went into no raptures about it. The *Times* thought it was "clearly the offspring of an almost Wagnerian system." The *Times* man also said, "Loud applause was elicited last night by many portions of *Aïda*. To excite continuous admiration, however, the subject needs a closer acquaintance than one sitting can beget." He seems to have got his greatest pleasure from the scenery, which was brought from Italy, the models being the same as those of the Cairo production. "Artistically nothing finer could be wished than the reproductions on canvas of the gorgeous temples of Egypt. . . . An augmented orchestra, a complete brass band, a small corps de ballet — including a rather undisciplined force of Ethiopian juveniles . . . and brand-new dresses of every one of the two hundred human beings who, in the second act, are gathered at once upon the stage, were beheld during last night's entertainment."

The New York *Herald* also thought that much of the success of the performance "was due to the scenery, and we think this ought to be a lesson to managers when they produce such great works as *Le Prophète*, *L'Africaine*, *L'Etoile du nord*, etc., to put them upon the stage with an effective *mise en scène*."

The first performance of *Aïda* at the Metropolitan was—strangely—given in German. It was an all-German opera company which inhabited the Metropolitan the season of 1886. Anton Seidl conducted, Marianne Brandt sang Amneris, and the Aïda was "Frau Herbert-Förster," the wife of Victor Herbert. The New York *Herald* describes the event as follows: "It augurs well for the enterprise and the liberality of the Metropolitan Opera management that at the very outset of the season, and in spite of an extensive and most attractive repertoire, it offers to the public a work which, from not a few points of view, is a comparative novelty. Before last night Verdi's *Aïda* had never been heard in the German tongue. It has never been seen with all the pomp and circumstance of the Metropolitan Opera House resources. A great spectacle was expected by a great audience, and the public was not disappointed. Everything that the art of the costumes, a seething mass of supernumeraries, an excellent orchestra and conscientious artists could do to brighten the effect of the opera was certainly done." Nevertheless the critic had some reservations about the staging. "Singers and the orchestra," however, "surpassed expectation."

Since then, *Aïda* has been given more than three hundred times at the Metropolitan. Many of these presentations have been gala performances, with great singers, but the most thrilling must have been the one which opened the season of 1908, the first season under the directorate of Gatti and Dippel. In that performance Emmy Destinn made her debut as Aïda; Homer sang Amneris; Caruso, Radames; Scotti, Amonasro;

Didur, Ramfis. It was, in fact, a performance of debuts, not only for Emmy Destinn, but also for Angèlo Bada as the Messenger, for Giulio Rossi as the King, for a new chorus and new scenery. In addition, it was the debut of a new conductor, Arturo Toscanini.

2. *Troublesome Libretto*

WHY WOULD an opera composer choose as a libretto a totally unsuccessful play, a play which twenty years before had been given precisely once and had then created an unpleasant theatrical scandal? Wouldn't the composer, if he had any common sense, assume that having failed once, the play was likely to fail again? Why wouldn't he choose either an original or a reasonably safe plot for his opera?

It is hard to imagine what made Verdi — who had much common sense — turn to a play called *Le roi s'amuse* in order to extract from it a libretto called *La Maledizione*, which eventually became the opera we know as *Rigoletto*. The Verdi biographies say little and his letters say nothing about the reasons for his choice. One reason no doubt was that the same author had already furnished Verdi with one plot he liked. But *Ernani* had been only a moderate success. Nor can the whole explanation be that *Le roi s'amuse* furnished the composer those violent and dark dramatic situations which attracted him so strongly. If there's one thing that abounded in those days of 1849 it was bloody melodrama. The dagger was as over-used a stage property of the middle nineteenth-century drama as the telephone is of ours. And the innocent girl abducted was as frequent a stage occurrence then as is today the teen-age daughter getting into mischief.

Verdi undoubtedly did not foresee the troubles this choice of plot was to give him; but how much did he actually know about the difficulties of the original play?

Those problems were the usual ones met by "daring" or politically suspect subjects on the French stage, particularly if the subjects were used by new, not officially sanctioned authors. In reviewing what happened to *Le roi s'amuse*, we must of course think of Victor Hugo not as the marble-busted classic of French literature, but as a young (he was thirty when the play was produced) newcomer who had already caused much trouble with *Hernani*, and who was now concerned with a new romanticism, a cutting through the hallowed Alexandrines of the French classics. This appealed to the young men of France, to Nanteuil, Gautier, Balzac, Berlioz, etc. But it did not appeal to the academicians or the government.

Now Victor Hugo proposed to write a drama — about a king, to boot! — with this idea: "Take the most hideous physical deformity — the most repulsive, the most complete; place it where it best belongs, in the most infamous, the lowest, the most despised story of the social edifice; illumine this wretched creature on all sides by the sinister light of contrasts, and then endow him with a soul; put into this soul the purest sentiment that can be given to man—the paternal sentiment. What will happen? This divine sentiment, warmed in accordance with certain conditions, will transform this degraded creature under your very eyes. This little being will become great; this deformed being will become beautiful. This, in substance, is *Le roi s'amuse.*"

Just before the first performance one of the ministers, M. d'Argout, sent for the manuscript. Censorship in France was supposed to have been abolished two years before, so Hugo refused to comply with the demand. However, he called upon the minister, who said he had been informed that *Le roi s'amuse* contained unflattering allusions to Louis Philippe. The author denied this and insisted that he had simply shown Francis I in his true colors.

Opening night, the young leaders of French thought and all those who "like an interment" were at their posts in the theater. By that time the whole affair had taken on a political tinge. When the leaders of society and the fashionable people entered their boxes, they were not greeted, as had been the custom, by rounds of polite applause, but by the strains of the *Marseillaise*. Then, just before the curtain rose, a wild rumor went through the house that the king had been shot. This naturally so distracted the audience that they paid little attention to the first act. There was much talking during the first scenes. The play was not well acted, so what the audience did hear left them unmoved. The performance was also disturbed by various stage accidents. Blanche (Gilda) was carried off the stage heels over head, no doubt an effect not beneficial to the new romanticism. And in the third act the audience was shocked out of what wits they had left by seeing a king in a dressing gown.

The net result of all this was that the play was a complete failure and was hissed as only the French can hiss something they do not like. Members of the Academy and various other busybodies went the next morning to the minister and complained that the play was not only "a simple outrage on good taste" but downright indecent. Moreover, it did contain disrespectful allusions to Louis Philippe, "and all this at the very time when assassins were making a target of his sacred head." Further performances of the play were forbidden. Hugo felt that this was not only an encroachment on his but on general liberty. He meant to fight, and he instituted a suit to compel the Théâtre Français to perform his play. The trial took two weeks. Hugo lost the case.

This, then, was the doubtful property which Verdi turned over to Piave to be shaped into an opera. This opera he was writing for the Fenice Theater, which accepted the subject with some hesitation. Piave, who knew his way about in and out of government offices, told Verdi that everything was going to be all right; there wasn't going to be any trouble with the censor. Then, when the libretto was completed, trouble did strike. The censor forbade the performance, and rebuked "the poet, Piave, and the famous maestro, Verdi, for not having chosen a more worthy field in which to display their talents than that of a plot so revoltingly immoral and so obscenely trivial."

Piave was in despair, Verdi was furious. After considerable back and forth—Verdi forthrightly refusing to make changes which would make the whole play meaningless—a compromise was finally reached. The plot was left essentially unaltered, the "hunchback who sings" was permitted. But the names of all the characters were changed, the locale became a "minor absolutist Italian state" instead of France, and Francis, the king, became the Duke of Mantua. There's nothing like a little demotion for pacifying a government censor.

One of the main points of contention had been the sack in which Gilda's body was placed. This Verdi was allowed to keep, and in return he agreed to give up the business of the latchkey. This was the key with which Francis I could let himself into the room of the abducted girl. A key, a visible symbol of possession—that was too much!

All these changes were drawn up in a solemn contract which Verdi and Piave signed.

But though the opera, when it was given after some postponements, was a huge success, Verdi's troubles were not quite over. Now Victor Hugo did not like the plot. Hugo had previously objected to *Ernani*, which he regarded as a poor thing and not his own. *Rigoletto* did not please him either; he considered it "a counterfeit." To prevent its performance at the Théâtre des Italiens, he entered an action against the director of that theater. (Hugo seemed to have had a fondness for the law courts.) Again Hugo lost his case; not only that, he had to pay the costs of the suit.

Hugo later changed his opinion. He became an admirer of *Rigoletto*, and thought that two places in the opera (the duet in the second scene between Sparafucile and Rigoletto, and the quartet) were actually improvements over the play.

Victor Hugo, by the way, has left us one of the best definitions of music. "Music," he wrote, "expresses that which cannot be said and on which it is impossible to be silent."

3. *The Première of the Chocolate Venture*

Dear Boïto: It is finished.
   Here's a health to us... (and also to *him*...)
   Goodbye.

                                             G. VERDI.

THUS DID VERDI announce the completion of *Otello* to his friend and collaborator. This was in November 1886, and production of the eagerly awaited opera, Verdi's first in fourteen years, was announced for the following February. All details were kept secret, and the singers who were engaged promised not to reveal any of its music—as other singers had promised thirty-five years ago when Verdi was rehearsing *Rigoletto* and wanted to keep *"La Donna è mobile"* away from the stealers of melodies. Now, with *Otello*, secrecy was enforced not because of a catchy tune; Verdi wondered how the opera would sound in rehearsal, and how successful he had been with this music, so new in feeling and treatment. Up to the last Verdi insisted on his right to withdraw the opera if he chose.

   The première was one of the most important operatic events of the decade, rivaling in international attention the first performance of *Parsifal*, which had taken place almost five years before. Monaldi, a contemporary writer and a friend of Verdi's, has left us in his memoirs a vivid description of the event. For weeks preceding the performance, he writes, all Milan was in great agitation, the pulse of its life definitely accelerated. The hotels were crowded with famous guests from France, England, Germany and America. The prices for tickets were fabulous: a single orchestra seat cost forty dollars. On the day of the performance, the crowd began to gather, trying to get into the unreserved seats, and when the doors of the great gallery were opened, the spectacle was truly terrifying. "The enormous mass of humanity rushed into the corridors, pitilessly brushing aside the weaker ones."

Monaldi describes the unbelievably nervous, hushed silence that fell on the hall when Maestro Faccio, "a little pale but sure of himself," mounted the podium. The first applause, and it was thunderous, came at Otello's entrance — which is indeed as thrilling an entrance as any operatic hero could enjoy. After this initial demonstration, there were many moments during the act when the audience would shout for Verdi to appear, which of course he did not do until the end of the act. Then the powerful figure of the seventy-four-year-old man appeared on the stage surrounded by his singers, "and the outcry that came from the mouth of each of the spectators shook the hall. . . . Verdi slightly bends his head and smiles, the frantic enthusiasm of the huge assembly bringing tears to his eyes. He seems to feel the necessity to retire, which the public, with a tardy respect for his age, finally permits him to do."

As the opera progressed, the enthusiasm of the audience increased, reaching its climax in the fourth act, the most moving and the most lyrical act. After it was all over, when Verdi left the theater, a crowd of admirers lined the street and another crowd drew his carriage to the Hotel di Milano. Verdi was melancholy in spite of this great success. While ladies were still waving their handkerchiefs to him and the Amateur Mandolin Society was still serenading him from the street, he said to his friends: "I fired off my last cartridge; I have nothing left." But then the old man smiled and said, "My friends, if I were thirty years younger, I should like to begin a new opera tomorrow, on the condition that Boïto provide the libretto."

Monaldi also gives us an account of how Verdi taught the role of Otello to Tamagno, the famous tenor "who had been known up to that time only as a singer with a golden voice. In this performance, he became equally distinguished as an actor, a development first noticed in the scene where Otello kills himself. . . . In all the rehearsals Verdi had done his best to improve the acting of Tamagno. The great tenor gradually approached more and more Verdi's ideals, but in the suicide scene he seemed unable to please the composer. Countless suggestions had failed to move the singer. One day Verdi lost his patience completely and took it upon himself to act the scene. Those who were present were amazed to see the white-haired Verdi going through the leading role of his greatest opera. Standing at the bed of Desdemona, he suddenly fell and rolled backward down three steps. The spectators were so surprised they thought he was having a heart attack from over-excitement, but Verdi was only acting."

The première aroused particular and immediate notice in England, not so much because Shakespeare was involved but because Verdi was by that time almost as popular at Covent Garden as he was at La Scala. The London *Times*, two days after the première, carried a long review of *Otello* and a full description of the enthusiasm: "In other countries such enthusiasm would have been scarcely possible without the excitement of politics or of alcohol." The correspondent gave the opera its due but had reservations about the singers and the performance, complaining (sensibly) about the many encores: "The encore nuisance is even more rampant in Italy than among us, and sometimes leads to curious results. When, for example, Otello was compelled to leave his wife's chamber so that the famous recitative in unison for double basses preceding the entry might be repeated a second time, the border-line between the sublime and the ridiculous was distinctly passed, the more so as that the recitative was played indifferently the first, and very badly the second time."

An English lady by the name of Blanche Tucker Roosevelt (no relation to our Roosevelts so far as I know) was moved to write an entire book about the première. The book is called *Verdi, Milan and Othello,* and is written in the form of letters addressed to Wilkie Collins. Why the writer of *The Moonstone* should have been the recipient of these reports, and whether the author of *The Woman in White* was really interested in the opera about the black man is one of those unimportant but tantalizing puzzles I have been unable to solve.

The book makes good reading even today, in spite of the fact that Miss Roosevelt, being a feminine writer of the Victorian era, is excessively effusive. As a sample of her reporting and, more importantly, as a picture of what went on at that happy occasion in a happier Italy, I submit the following excerpt from the book:

"At last, at last the great day has come and gone, and Verdi has added the crown jewel to his diadem of triumphs. I cannot tell you the anxiety felt in the city before nightfall. As early as 5:00 A.M. everyone was astir, and when Gianetta brought my tea she informed me that she had already been to La Scala; the posters were unchanged, the opera would surely come off, unless—you may imagine I sent her about her business with her 'unlesses'—unless the tenor or the soprano, or the wig-maker, or some particular hinge of the cast, she explained, 'did not "run ill" before 7:00 P.M.' Speaking of wig-makers, she also reminded me that any number of ladies in the hotel were having their hair dressed even at that unearthly hour—not me —eight 'an may it please you,' making preparations exactly as if the occasion were a state ball or a royal wedding. These ladies will sit all day with bejeweled and elaborately dressed pates and not dare to lie down or sit back or lean over for fear of ruining their puffs, etc.

"You may imagine the excitement was not lost on me. I hastily dressed and before noon was in the streets. Streets? There were no streets—at least, no crossings—visible, and had the blocks of houses not divided the town architecturally, everything would have been run together, like honey, with human beings, human beings, human beings! I never knew how the day passed. Vergil ran up against the La Scala doctor and actually turned pale as the M.D. went to speak to him. 'Don't tell me!' Vergil cried. 'All right,' laughed Dr. L.; 'he is not quite well but will sing, of course.' The 'he' meant, naturally, the tenor. . . . An hour passed; men, women, children, beggars, hand-organs pealing forth Verdi tunes, Ernani's 'Fly with me,' and Manrico's 'Do not leave me'; pardon the vernacular. Leonardo da Vinci's statue gleamed out of the sea of faces like a white eaglet's plume drifting toward a storm-swept sea. The windows of the tall houses looking out on the quadrangle were a mass of shifting heads; balconies were freighted with excited humanity, and the Italian terraced roofs, where people were eating and drinking and shouting, were literally black with moving forms. But the exteriors of these old stone palaces were the most curious sight. The panels were a perfect kaleidoscope of light and color. You know the Italian women are fond of bright raiment. When they have not covered their heads with their pretty black veils, they wear veils in cream-color studded with artificial flowers; they wear hats which would shame a hothouse for brilliancy.

"The Piazza della Scala was a sight to see, and the cries of 'Viva Verdi! Viva Verdi!' were so deafening that I longed for cotton in my ears. Poor Verdi! Had he been there, he would certainly have been torn to pieces, as a crowd in its enthusiasm rarely distinguishes between glory and assassination. You will ask what I was doing in the streets at such a time, and I will answer: I don't know; I merely obeyed the common impulse—went where the others did; the truth is,

I also wanted to watch the Scala billboard, to see that no change would be made in the announcements. We all stood staring at the old theater, just as those idiots on the Paris boulevards on a summer night watch the magic-lantern, to read the different advertisements for enterprising firms; and this, you say, in dead of winter? Oh, an Italian does not feel the cold on an occasion like this. But to return. In case there had been any change of program, I need not say there would not have been found a person in all Milan courageous enough to have put up the notice. There was death in the eyes of some of those men, waiting like hungry wolves since the night before to be first to crowd into the pit and galleries. Well, at last, after dinner—I didn't dine, I swallowed food—we started to the theater. The carriage had to be sent off long before we reached the door, the horses could not make their way through the crowd. At best, human beings one by one between a line of police could struggle toward the entrance. I expected my dress would be in rags; however, I managed to get in whole, and once there the sight was indescribable. La Scala has never before held such an audience, and although it was fully an hour before the time to commence, every seat was occupied."

And after the performance: "The ovations to Verdi and Boïto reached the climax of enthusiasm. Verdi was presented with a silver album filled with the autographs and cards of every citizen in Milan. He was called out twenty times, and at the last recalls hats and handkerchiefs were waved, and the house rose in a body. The emotion was something indescribable, and many wept. Verdi's carriage was dragged by citizens to the hotel. He was toasted and serenaded; and at five in the morning I had not closed my eyes in sleep for the crowds were still sinking and shrieking, 'Viva Verdi! Viva Verdi!' Who shall say that this cry will not re-echo all over the world?"

4. *The Maurel Monopoly*

GOOD SIR JOHN, honest Sir John, sweet Sir John nearly drowned in the Thames. *Falstaff* nearly burned in the fire.

It was about a year before the première of *Falstaff* that the baritone, Victor Maurel, approached Verdi with a singular request. Maurel knew about the progress of the opera and hazarded the safe guess that it would make a world-wide sensation. He proposed to Verdi that the composer give him the exclusive rights to *Falstaff*. Letting the cat of selfishness out of the bag of secrecy, as Thackeray said, he put forward in all seriousness the demand that no one but he was to play old potbelly. Verdi's face when he heard this must have been something to see. He had dealt with egocentric requests before and had been angered before. This time he became really enraged —so furious indeed that he threatened to destroy the score. He wrote to his publisher, Ricordi, "If I had to choose between accepting those conditions and burning the score, I would light the fire immediately and put Falstaff on the funeral pyre myself, together with his great belly."

What made Maurel think he could get away with this strange attempt at cornering the market? Well, first was he not a personal friend of Verdi's, and second, had he not done a brilliant job as Iago at the world première of Otello? Even further, he, Maurel, had been instrumental in guiding Verdi's thoughts toward this Shakespearean comedy. Or so he says in his memoirs.

About two years before Verdi started work on Falstaff, Maurel had sent him the manuscript of a version of *The Merry Wives of Windsor* which was used by the great French actor, Coquelin. Verdi, who was at that time convinced that he had done with composing, refused the manuscript. But two years later he wrote to Maurel: "There's a play on in Paris, Shake-speare's. Is it the same we talked over two years ago?" At this hint, Maurel journeyed to see Verdi and had dinner with him in Genoa. At the dinner Verdi told him: "You got me all upset two years ago. I could not get your idea out of my head. I am working on it now. Boïto has prepared a libretto."

That may all be true. Yet it is possible that Maurel's sug-gestion was only the result of putting two and two together, and that Falstaff would have been created without this sug-gestion. Maurel knew that Verdi's great love was Shakespeare. Verdi went to Shakespeare not only when he needed an opera libretto, not only when he was composing *Macbeth* or *Otello* or a *King Lear* (which never went beyond preliminary drafts) —but also for reading enjoyment. Many times in his letters Verdi refers to Shakespeare and quotes him, many times Verdi makes clear that he considered him, as Coleridge did, "the greatest genius that perhaps human nature has yet produced." Therefore, after the success of *Otello*, wouldn't the old man turn again to his favorite poet, if he were to write another opera?

Maurel also knew that Verdi had for a long time wanted to write a comic opera. He had written a comedy only once be-fore, in his youth: *Il Finto Stanislao* had been a complete fail-ure. Though there are comic scenes and characters in Verdi's operas, comedy was really a strange realm to him. And one of the miracles of *Falstaff* is that with this one work he made him-self master of the field. That phenomenon is like Beethoven, who made only one attempt at a violin concerto—and turned out the supreme example in that medium. Maurel was further-more aware that Verdi had refused a French Shakespeare lib-retto called *La Mégère apprivoisée*, better known as *The Taming of the Shrew*. Verdi thought that it needed a Doni-zetti or a Rossini to set that comedy to music. Knowing all this, it needed no super-subtle deduction on Maurel's part to come forward and suggest the famous *Falstaff*. It was obvious, by the way, that *Falstaff* in opera would *have* to be a baritone or bass part.

It is more probable that the actual setting in motion of the *Falstaff* opera came from Boïto, Verdi's collaborator on *Otello*. This is only conjecture. We know, however, that Verdi wrote to Boïto: "Do you realize, when you are drawing your portrait of Falstaff, the enormous number of my years? I know that in reply you will exaggerate the state of my health, saying it is robust and of the best. . . . That may be; none the less you will agree with me that it may be thought very rash of me to undertake such a task. Suppose I find the strain too great and cannot finish the music? Then your time and labor would have been wasted to no purpose. For all the wealth in the world I would not have that happen."

But once he started *Falstaff*, Verdi loved the undertaking. He still insisted that he began it as a "mere pastime, without any preconceived idea, without any plans—I repeat, to pass the time." But the peasants around Sant' Agata knew from his continually smiling face that he was writing a comedy with which he was pleased. He was enormously proud of the libretto, as indeed he had every right to be. Boïto's contribution, good as it is in *Otello*, is even better in *Falstaff*. Here he had to deal here with one of Shakespeare's careless plays: a sequel which shows the characteristic of so many sequels—lagging inspiration. Boïto managed to put back some of the charm, the lustiness, the good coarse nature which the Falstaff of *Henry IV* possesses. In part, Boïto made a successful merger of elements in three plays, retaining good features of all three.

Verdi took great pains with the production of the opera. He chose the cast for the La Scala première and decided exactly how the sets were to look. La Scala in turn did the handsome thing and sent Hohenstein, their scenic designer, to Windsor to study the old English houses.

The ensemble rehearsals were to begin on January 6, 1893, but the cast asked for a postponement of one day, for January 6 was a Friday! The eighty-year-old Verdi directed all the exhausting rehearsals himself, spurring on the artists and bringing out subtelties of diction and delicacies of singing which they themselves did not know they could achieve. What a première it must have been! Again people came from all over Europe to do homage to Verdi. Again the crowds lined the streets to watch him pass.

That Verdi forgave Maurel's earlier arrogation is proved by the fact that it was Maurel who created the title part. Verdi was exactly right when he prophesied that if Maurel were to excel in the part, it would become his own quite naturally. What Maurel had wanted he got without a written contract. For *Falstaff* became his, and he sang it all over the world, at the premières in Paris, in London, and at the Metropolitan in New York on February 5, 1895. He was so taken up with the part that he began to make a detailed study of the Falstaff character—even after the première. He became a minor Falstaff authority. He discovered, for example, that a Sir John Falstaff had really lived in England 150 years before the time of the play. Maurel went into the subject so thoroughly that Verdi warned him against too much study, too much cerebration. He wrote him two letters which are so remarkable, so unexpected, so different from a composer's usual adjuration to a singer, that they deserve to be quoted. As far as I know, these letters have not previously been reprinted. (Maurel published them originally in *La Revue de Paris*.) Here they are:

I admire your research on *Falstaff*. But be careful. In the predominance of a reflective tendency is a sign of decadence. That means that when art becomes a science, something baroque results that is neither art nor science. To do well, yes! To do too well, no! Don't try too hard to adjust your voice. With your great talents as a singing actor, with your accent and pronunciation, the role of Falstaff, once learned, will emerge already created, without your searching your brain and without your studying to obtain different vocal effects, studies which might even be injurious to you. Study little, *au revoir, à bientôt.*

VERDI.

And again:

You already have the *Falstaff* libretto. As soon as it is printed, you will have the partitura. Study, examine as much as you like the verses and words of the libretto, but don't bother too much with the music. Don't think it strange that I tell you that. If the music is sufficiently characteristic, if the character of the person is well understood, if the emphasis of the dialogue is correct, the music flows by itself and resolves itself.

When Maurel was sixty-one years and his singing days were over, he settled in New York. Here this versatile baritone became not only a singing teacher but a stage designer. He fashioned the settings for the first production of Gounod's *Mireille* at the Metropolitan Opera. He also wrote several books on the art of singing and an autobiography called *Ten Years of a Career*, which was translated into German by a woman not usually associated with literary efforts, Lilli Lehmann. It is from these reminiscences that some of the facts of this article are taken.

5. *The Lady of the Fictive Camellias*

EVERY TIME a good Violetta and a believable Alfredo step onto the stage, *La Traviata* glows in all its lambent colors and charms an audience which understands none of the words of the love story but can quite believe the drama itself.

La Traviata is assuredly one of those operas that I would take with me to a desert island. I hold it in special affection, with a more personal feeling than I have toward the other two members of the famous triumvirate, *Rigoletto* and *Il Trovatore*. Perhaps the story has something to do with this. Old-fashioned as it may be, it is still more modern than the wildly improbable brother conflicts of *Il Trovatore* and far more neighborly and close to our lives than the curse of Monterone.

The story must be good—consider how often it has been told and in how many ways! First, it was a real life story, then it was a novel, then a play, then an opera, then several motion pictures. And once it was even a minstrel show!

Alexander Dumas based his novel on the life of a well-known courtesan whom he knew personally. So, it seems, did most of the writers of that romantic Parisian period, the only difference being that Dumas saw her fictional possibilities. Her real name was Alphonsine Plessis, which she changed to the more euphonious Marie Duplessis. According to Dumas, she was elegant, witty, soft-spoken and, of course, beautiful; "she looked like a piece of Dresden China" and "she lacked neither intelligence nor disinterestedness." She died of consumption at the age of twenty-three. Another contemporary writer, Jules Janin, describes her thus: "As she swept grandly by, one involuntarily exclaimed: 'There goes a courtesan or a duchess!' " The first time Janin met her, he was sitting with Liszt. She approached them and spoke to Liszt, although she had never met him. She told him that his playing had made her dream. Liszt was puzzled as to who she could be, this strange woman who addressed him without knowing him and yet treated him with condescension as though she were a queen. . . .

How much of all this is recollective idealization is impossible to say. A good deal, no doubt. Janin wrote an exuberant foreword to a special de luxe edition of the novel in which he gave a description of the life and character of Duplessis and ascribed to her the combined graces of Queen Victoria and Ethel Merman. Surely it is a case of literature clothing the naked truth. Even the camellias are literature: Dumas invented them.

Dumas, the son of one of the world's greatest story tellers, was motivated to write by the simple fact that his father, who had made and lost several fortunes, was at the moment out of funds. In Paris they still tell the story that the young man, meeting a friend of the boulevard, suggested that they should dine together. Dumas said, "I have just fifteen francs in my pocket, and I dare say we can manage on that, although not too well." Young Dumas was delighted when on the way to the restaurant he saw his father on the other side of the street. "Wait a minute," he said, "I will run across and get some money from my father and then we can dine well." The friend watched him converse with Dumas *père* for three minutes. Then Dumas the younger returned looking rather crestfallen.

"Well, has he paid up?"

"No, and what's more, he has gone and borrowed my fifteen francs."

Since it was necessary that the young Dumas support himself, as his father's son he naturally turned to writing. After the publication of a volume of verse (the customary debut of a French author) he quickly published several novels. *La Dame aux camélias* had a moderate success but far from a sensational one.

I have reread the novel recently. It is a masterpiece. It is by no means a bittersweet old confection. Its people and their lives are not merely seen through a stereopticon but they are portrayed in the fullness of life, and what they do and feel is completely believeable. This is all the more remarkable because the social problem of the novel is dated. Armand's sister probably could get married today without his having to give up Marguerite. In fact, Francis Toye observes that "doubtless a certain section of society nowadays would rather welcome her as a rather interesting addition to the family." And if worse came to the worst, Armand might even break loose from his father and go to work. But in spite of these commonsense objections, Dumas' art is sharp and powerful enough so that at no time does the book seem like mere camellias and old lace. The atmosphere of passion sweeps one along; one cannot smile at it. Everything about this love is real: the jealousy, the ecstasy, the happiness of their life in the country, the cynical friends, the remorse and the final simple and heartbreaking letters of Marguerite.

The novel is told in the first person. The author, who represents himself as a friend of Armand's, tells the latter's story because, he says, not being experienced enough to invent people, he must draw from reality. At the beginning of the novel the author goes to an auction to purchase a copy of *Manon Lescaut*. There he sees a distraught and febrile young man who bids unsuccessfully against him and who calls on him later to ask for the book. It is a book the stranger had once given to one whom he loved dearly. Gradually, Armand unfolds the story of this love. Later, the two go to Marguerite's grave because Armand is obsessed with the longing to see her face once more. The scene in which both of them exhume the body is so powerfully written that Dostoievsky might have done it. On the other hand, the scenes in the country are brushed with the gentlest poetry. It is almost unbelievable that this could be the work of a twenty-year old writer.

Certainly we must not think of it as an old-fashioned romance by an immature novelist. A romance it is, but a fresh and perennially appealing one written with youthful zest but sure ability.

The opera, however, is not based on the novel but on the play which Dumas fashioned from his novel. We do not know how Verdi became acquainted with the play, but it is perfectly plausible that he saw it, for he was in Paris at the time it was being performed.

Actually, the play, good as it is, is inferior to the novel. It has less imagination, less poetry, less power, though it does retain some of the novel's emotional impact. Dumas wrote a "practical" play.

The success of the stage production—far greater than that of the novel—was due originally to the provocative quality of the theme and later to the fact that it gave opportunity to a good actress. It is effective, of course. But only at one point does it seem to rise to the poetic worth of the novel. That is in the third act, when Marguerite, living in the country and happy with Armand, speaks of her love to her friends:

MARGUERITE: I can speak frankly to you, to you two who believe me, because you listen to me with your heart: for moments I forget what I was, and the I of other days separates itself so completely from the I of today that two different women emerge, the second one hardly remembering the first. When, wearing a white dress, covered with a big straw hat and carrying on my arm the cloak to protect me from the coolness of the evening, I step with Armand into the little boat which we let drift and which comes to rest under the willows of the next island, nothing and nobody suspects, not even I, that this white shadow is Marguerite Gautier. . . . I have made men spend more money on bouquets than would be needed to nourish an honest family for a year; well, one flower like this one which Armand gave me this morning is enough now to perfume my day. You know well what it is to love: how the hours shorten themselves, how they carry us to the end of weeks and months without a jolt and without fatigue. Yes, I *am* very happy! But I want to be happier still; you do not know all. . . .

NICHETTE: What?

MARGUERITE: You told me not long ago that I did not live as you did; you will not be able to tell me that for long.

NICHETTE: What do you mean?

MARGUERITE: Without Armand's suspecting anything, I am going to sell all the furnishings of my Paris apartment, which I never even want to see again. I shall pay all my debts; I shall rent a little place near yours; I shall furnish it quite simply, and we shall live like that, forgetting and forgotten. In the summer we'll come back to the country, but in a house more modest than this one. Where are those who ask what happiness is? You have taught it to me, and now I shall be able to teach it to them if they wish.

NANINE: Madame, there is a gentleman here who asks to speak to you. . . .

(The gentleman is, of course, father with the bad news.)

Dumas wrote the play in eight days. He scribbled it on various pieces of paper that were lying on his table. The second act, he says, was written in five hours, and in the whole play there are not twenty-five corrections. He showed the completed play to his father, who said, "It is original, it is touching, it is audacious, it is new. It will have an immense success if the censor will let it be played. But the censor will never let it be played."

He knew what he was talking about. The play was a stepchild for three years. It was refused by several theaters, and held up by the censors until one of Napoleon's powerful ministers interfered. The censor said to one of Dumas' friends: "My dear sir, authorization would do no good. The public would never permit the piece to reach the second act. We must prevent the son of the great Dumas from sustaining such a humiliation." A. M. de Beaufort, *juge de la censure*, was sure that the public would throw the seats on the stage before the end of the second act. Incidentally, in later years this man became director of the Vaudeville (where the play had its première), and during a financial crisis of the theater he quickly ordered a revival of *La Dame aux camélias* to bail him out.

When the play was being cast, one famous actress turned it down because she too was sure that it was an impossible subject. She said to Dumas, "Your play deals with a world of which I know nothing."

"At your age?" replied Dumas. "Then you will never know it."

But the success of the piece was, as Dumas *père* had predicted, immense. The play was acclaimed by the first-night audience "with a deluge of tears and a tempest of applause." Not that there were no voices raised in protest. Many people saw in it an attack on marriage and family. (When the play was first given on the American stage, "the heroine was represented as a virtuous young lady whose only fault was that she was a coquette.") Dumas tells of one lady who came to all the initial performances and planted herself in one of the boxes, carrying a large bouquet of flowers in the center of which she had hidden a whistle. Thus she was able to whistle at the play while pretending to savor the perfume of the flowers!

What was new and shocking about the play was not the sympathetic treatment of a courtesan on the stage. That was an old theme and had in fact been recently done by Victor Hugo in *Marion Delorme*. But *Marion Delorme* was set in the removed period of Louis XIII. Dumas put on the stage not an historic courtesan but a woman in modern dress surrounded by people of the same society as the spectators in the theater. This contemporary quality of the play was also one of the reasons the opera was a failure at its first performance.* An opera in modern dress and dealing with plain people seemed

*See the chapter entitled *Famous Failures*.

to the Venetians of 1853 short-change, cheating them of the historic and heroic trappings that they were accustomed to expect from opera. When *La Traviata* was given again the following year, the opera was costumed in the period of Louis XIII. It was then a success.

The libretto follows the play fairly exactly. It compresses the action and eliminates several scenes and minor characters. For some unfathomable reason, Verdi eliminated the poetic last line of the play, "Sleep in peace, Marguerite! Much shall be forgiven you, because you have loved so much."

La Traviata is, then, a faithful musical version of the play. But it is the music, of course, which makes it live and gives it enchantment beyond anything that Dumas set down. What Henry James said of the play is much more pertinent to the opera: "*Camille* remains in its combination of freshness and form and the feeling of the springtime of life, a singular, an astonishing piece of work. . . . Some tender young man and some coughing young woman have only to speak the lines to give it a great place among the love stories of the world."

6. *The Lady with the Knife*

EVEN THOSE who did not hear Jeritza the first time she appeared
as Tosca at the Metropolitan in 1921 can remember the tremendous excitement she generated by singing *"Vissi d'arte"*
lying on the floor. The prone position gave so sensational a
fillip to the performance that a few weeks afterward a story
appeared in the *American Weekly* complete with sexy pictures, a signal distinction in those days when opera stars were
not generally worthy of Sunday-supplement attention.

Exploration in older newspapers, magazines and books has
yielded some more generally forgotten sidelights on the early
history of *La Tosca*, which, though they are hardly original
discoveries of mine, are so seldom told that they may bear
repeating:

Tosca started out as a phenomenally successful play written
by that sure theatrical craftsman of the nineteenth century,
Victorien Sardou. Sardou was one of Sarah Bernhardt's favorite playwrights, as she was of course his favorite actress: he
wrote not only *Tosca* but *Fédora, Cléopatra* and other plays
for her. Puccini had seen Sarah Bernhardt as Tosca when she
appeared in the part in Milan. This was long before he started
to work on the opera, even before he had finished *Manon
Lescaut* and composed *La Bohème*. The play made a strong
impression on him; he saw its possibilities for an opera because,
though he understood little French, he was able to follow the
action. To Puccini, who kept his eye on the foreign market
as well as the Italian opera house, this was one of the tests of a
good libretto. He applied that same test later when he saw
Madame Butterfly in English, and again when he attended a
performance of *The Girl of the Golden West* in New York.

A few years after seeing Bernhardt, Puccini heard that the

aging Verdi had remarked that if he were not so old he would like to use *Tosca* for an opera text. After Puccini had finished *La Bohème* and was looking around for a new subject, he thought again of Sardou's play, only to find that another composer (a pupil of Puccini's father) was just about to begin such an opera, and had in fact asked Illica, Puccini's librettist, to work with him.

Then developed a plot almost as shady as that in the opera itself. Puccini, Illica and his publisher Ricordi (who was also the publisher of Franchetti, the other composer) met and agreed to dissuade Franchetti from using the play. They did this by pointing out to him that the subject was too strong and the situation too unsuited for setting to music, that the audience would be repelled by torture on the stage; that, in short, everything was wrong with *Tosca* and he had better give it up. He was finally persuaded to do so, whereupon Puccini set to work immediately on the same story. Something similarly disagreeable though not so flagrant had occurred with Leoncavallo over *La Bohème*. It seemed to be a particular weakness in the character of Puccini, who was in other respects most generous but who on two occasions deemed literary property most desirable when it belonged to somebody else.

While Puccini was in Paris for the production of *La Bohème*, he called on Sardou to discuss the projected *Tosca*. Sardou was then an old man, with all the crochety sureness that a successful career can give, a formidable autocrat, an expert on everything. Even Sarah Bernhardt, says Verneuil in his biography, was deferential to him and never addressed him except as *maître chéri*. Sardou invited Puccini to dinner, and after the coffee and liqueurs asked him to play a little of the music for the forthcoming opera. The fact was that Puccini had as yet composed not a note for *Tosca*. But he calmly sat down at the piano and played for a long time, stringing together a medley of arias from his previous operas, all of which Sardou liked. The old man declared himself satisfied to leave his play in the hands of the Italian.

As always happened when Puccini was working on an opera, the fashioning of a libretto was the time of *Sturm und Drang,* while the music flowed comparatively easily from his pen. Again, as in the case of *La Bohème,* Puccini drove his librettists frantic with his insistence upon careful work, upon condensation, sharpening of the dramatic effects, changes and more changes. That there was undoubtedly much to correct can be indicated by one example of many: in the original version of the libretto a regulation tenor aria was provided for Cavarodossi *while* he was being tortured.

The opera had its world première in Rome on January 14, 1900. The performance took place in an atmosphere of general nervousness because the rumor had been spread that enemies of Puccini's (remember that he was by this time a highly successful Italian opera composer) were going to throw a bomb in the theater. Mugnone, the conductor, was ready to strike up the Italian national anthem at the first sign of disturbance. But nothing happened except that latecomers caused so much confusion the curtain had to be lowered and the opera started again ten minutes later. It achieved only a mild success that night, which hardly presaged the opera's later international popularity.

About three and a half years afterward, Puccini went to Paris to supervise the production of *La Tosca* at the Opéra-Comique. Sardou was also there and promptly took over. Even before the Paris première Sardou had conferred with Puccini frequently in tones of uncontradictable authority. Puccini wrote to Ricordi from Paris in 1899: "This morning I spent an hour with Sardou, who told me of various things in the finale that he does not like. . . . In the revival of the play, which Sarah will give on the twentieth, Sardou has introduced an enormous flag of the Castel Sant'Angelo; he is keener about that than about the opera at the moment." Sardou even sketched the scenery for Puccini, who kept the drawing as a memento. Sardou insisted that Tosca should end her life by leaping from the castle into the Tiber. Puccini pointed out to him that this might be acceptable except for the fact that the Tiber didn't happen to flow past the side of the castle but was nearly fifty feet away. "He, calm as a fish, answered, 'Oh, that's nothing.'" Puccini concludes his letter by saying, "On Tuesday morning I must go to see Sardou again—so the Magician has decreed. Perhaps he will insist on killing Spoletta too. We shall see."

When it was time for the Paris production, the seventy-five-year-old "magician" took over the reigns again and behaved as if he were not only the author but the stage manager and the composer of the music. Puccini expected him any day to push the conductor out of his place and wave the baton himself. However, Sardou finally acknowledged that the libretto was not only good but actually superior to his play; by that time, no doubt, he felt that all of the opera was his own.

The Paris performance was an enormous success with the public, though most of the critics condemned the opera. André Messager, the composer (who had conducted the première of *Pelléas et Mélisande* the year before), particularly disliked the work; he found the subject "unmusical." Sardou is said to have replied to these criticisms, "A play which has been given three thousand times is always right!"

One other little known *Tosca* anecdote belongs here. It comes from an old magazine where it appeared in the form of an interview with Puccini by an anonymous writer. Puccini tells of a performance in Milan, when he sat in the audience next to a pretty girl. By this time *Tosca* was a complete success. The audience was enthusiastic, the applause frantic. The young lady became extremely annoyed because Puccini did not clap or shout.

"Why don't you applaud this masterpiece?" she said.

"Masterpiece?" replied Puccini, and laughed sarcastically.

"Don't you like this music?" she asked in amazement.

"No," said he, "it is the work of an amateur."

"You know nothing of music, or you wouldn't talk like that."

"Yes, I do know music," said Puccini, and proceeded to prove to her according to the laws of harmony and counterpoint how poor a work *Tosca* really was. He told her this aria suggested Verdi and that chorus was stolen from Bizet. When he had finished, the young lady said, "Is that your real opinion? your sincere conviction?"

"Absolutely," he replied.

"Very well," she said with a little laugh, and left him. At breakfast the next morning, when Puccini picked up the newspaper, he saw a headline, "Puccini on *Tosca*." There he read word for word his remarks of the night before. The pretty young lady had been a music critic, had known all along with whom she was sitting in the theater, and all the while Puccini had thought he was duping her, she had been fooling him.

Tosca had its American première on February 4, 1901, at the Metropolitan, more than two years before the Parisian opening. Scotti, whose impersonation many of us remember, was the first Scarpia at the Metropolitan. Tosca was sung by Milka Ternina, who looks quite stunning in her photograph with the now traditional walking stick and the bouquet, and who must have been very good indeed. Odell, the recorder of the doings of the New York stage, wrote: "No one who saw Bernhardt's performance can ever forget the great scene in Scarpia's apartment. . . . I have seen and heard many famous singers as Tosca, and none but Milka Ternina ever approached Mme. Bernhardt in that 'big' episode."

Incidentally, Sarah Bernhardt was in New York at the time of the première. As a matter of fact, she had played Tosca here about two and a half months before the opera was performed at the Metropolitan. One might suppose that the popularity of the opera would have lessened the public's interest in the play. On the contrary, Bernhardt played Tosca in Paris until 1909 and appeared in New York as late as 1913 in the part, always with enormous success.

Reynaldo Hahn has given us a description of her performance. He relates that, with the greatest flippancy, she would leave her dressing room before the stabbing scene exclaiming lightheartedly, "*Allons, tuer Coq.*" (Coquelin, the famous Cyrano, was then playing Scarpia.) But once on the stage: "What a feeling for effect and what technique in the way in which, after the murder of Scarpia, she wets the napkin to wash away the blood she has on her hands, in which she examines her dress to make sure that she has not stained it, with which she looks out of the window by raising herself lightly on tiptoe! . . . The exit is a miracle of execution. Sarah half opens the door, puts her head out to peer into the corridor, then her shoulders, then her whole body, with the undulating movement of a reptile; the door closes softly, very softly, while the train of her dress disappears. . . . And while the curtains are lowered, we imagine that Tosca, furtive, palpitating, slinks off against the walls, silent as a shadow."

Maria Jeritza was one of Puccini's favorite Toscas. Her picture, in that role, occupied a place of honor among the innumerable photographs which cluttered his desk. Incidentally, most of those pictures have remained there just as he left them despite exposure to war and occupation.

* * *

I had occasion to see this for myself when I was traveling in Italy as a correspondent in 1946. I had flown to Rome and was trying to reach Milan. Since at that time the normally eight-hour journey took thirty-six hours—assuming it would be completed at all, which was always doubtful—I persuaded an army public relations officer to permit me to use the official courier plane then making daily trips between Rome and Milan. I was one of only two civilians aboard and as such, was handed a sheet of rules which included the following remarkable sentence under Rule No. 9:

LAVATORY AND AIRSICKNESS: There are lavatory facilities on board; also facilities for airsickness which is accompanied by nausea which will be shown to the passengers by a crew member.

Halfway in our journey, at Livorno, the plane came down and we were informed that the airfield at Milan had been flooded by heavy rainfall and no further air transportation was available until the field became dry, which would be no one knew when. After many negotiations I managed to hire a car and a driver. We started traveling north in a pouring rainstorm.

It was cold, dismal and—as I realized when we were crossing the Appenines in a fog—dangerous. At one point, we passed through a village called Torre del Lago. Suddenly I recalled that this was Puccini's beloved home, and I asked the driver to take me to the composer's house. It stands at the end of a little street, right next to the lake. No one was around, nor was there even a marker. Yes, one: a metal sign in English designating the house "off limits," as incongruous a sign as the one that had been placed in the center of the Grand Canal of Venice reading, "Speed Limit on the Grand Canal, 10 Miles P. H."

The house was shabby and silent, the garden completely overgrown. I finally roused an old man who had the key, and he let me in. All the rooms were in disorder, but Puccini's furniture, his scores, books and letters were still there. The Germans, said the old caretaker, had visited the place, but strangely enough had not robbed it. Only in two spots did they leave characteristic evidence of their visit. In the center of the house Puccini had built himself a small private chapel; he and his wife are buried there, and his grave is decorated by a marble sculpture on which the names of his operas are engraved. The chapel had small stained-glass windows; these the Germans had smashed. In addition, they had broken through a glass case and had made off with Puccini's death mask.

7. *The Original Bohemians*

THE LITERARY BIOGRAPHER of the beret set started his writing career by contributing articles to a trade paper of the hat business.

Henri Murger was the son of a tailor, and though, after a scanty education, he was apprenticed to a lawyer, his one certain ambition was to become a poet and a writer. He began earning his few francs by contributions to the small literary journals which perennially vegetate in Paris, and to trade periodicals.

Like the chronicle of those other but very different Bohemians, the members of the Pickwick Club, *Les Scènes de la vie de Bohème* appeared first serially in a magazine called *Le Corsair*. But unlike the *Pickwick Papers*, the first success of *Bohème* was confined to literary circles. Murger still found life impecunious, until one day a young playwright named Barrière, who had read the serial, proposed to him that they should turn the book into a play. At this time Murger was living in the sort of attic in the Latin Quarter that is the scene of the first act of *La Bohème*, and on the afternoon when the playwright presented himself, he found the novelist in bed. Murger readily fell in with the playwright's suggestion, and the dramatist proposed that they should settle details over an *apéritif* at a café. "I'm sorry to say that I cannot come," replied Murger with some embarassment. "Why not? Surely you are not ill," urged Barrière. "No," responded the novelist, "but the fact is I haven't a pair of trousers to put on." One of his Bohemian friends had borrowed Murger's only pair of trousers that morning.

About a year later, the play was produced at the *Variété*. It met with phenomenal success. From his poor unknown state, Murger was catapulted into the position of one of the leading contemporary writers. He bought himself, presumably, a second pair of trousers and left the Latin Quarter. As is often the way of French writers, he turned from a Bohemian into a conservative and well-dressed gentleman and became the owner of a villa at Marlotte in the Forest of Fontainbleu. Like the other stately writers of France, his ambition was to be elected to the Academy and to wear the ribbon in his buttonhole. He continued to write, of course. He still drew the models for his characters from the association of his youth in the Latin Quarter. But neither the sequel to *Bohème—Scènes de la vie de jeunesse*—nor any other of his subsequent writing could compare in freshness, humor, spontaneity and reality to the biographical first work in which he invented nothing but wrote of his own life, setting down each evening what he had experienced the preceding day. . . .

Bohème is one of those literary properties the fame of which extends far beyond those who have actually read the novel. Many people who have never even heard of the book know what a Bohemian is. In that sense the book is enduring; it describes a set of people and a state of mind which I trust will exist as long as young writers and artists set out in search of the indefinite. "Bohemian," then, is one of those adjectives which have become generic, like "Rabelaisian" or "mid-Victorian." The term, incidentally, has nothing to do with Shakespeare's Bohemia on the sea coast, though it also is a geographical mistake. The French used to call vagabond gypsies *"Bohèmes"* because they were thought to come from Bohemia. Use of the word to describe young artists leading an irregular life was introduced into English by Thackeray.

I have already said that the novel was a biographical work. Each of the characters is modeled on an actual person. Rudolph is Murger himself, presented of course with the poetic license regularly issued to writers who describe themselves. In real life Murger did not treat his writings as cavalierly as Rodolfo does in the opera. Writing was a difficult task for Murger. To the end it frightened him because he was always conscious of his lack of education. He used to work at night, surrounded by a number of lighted candles, stimulating his mind by incessant cups of coffee. He would put ten sheets of paper before him and write the same idea down in ten different fashions, then choose the one which pleased him best. His own uncertainty was perhaps the cause of Murger's extreme restlessness; he couldn't remain in the same place for more than an hour or so. He was nicknamed by his friends "the wandering Christian."

Schaunard is Alexandre Schanne, a likable and humorous fellow who was one of Murger's closest friends in 1841, and who much later published a book of memoirs called *Souvenirs de Schaunard*. It is through this book that we know a good deal of the background of Murger's characters. Schanne was generally referred to among his Bohemian friends as Schannard. (That was probably a play on the word *canard*.) Murger gave this name to one of his characters. The printer, however, reversed the first N and made a U of it. The error was not corrected, and so it is as Schaunard that he still leads his life in the novel and in the opera. Schanne wanted to be both a painter and a musician and never could make up his mind whether "to quit the easel for the piano." He climbed the tower of Notre Dame and perched there to observe the blue of the sky in order to paint a "proper blue." He then wrote the symphony celebrated in the novel: "*Symphony on the Influence of Blue in Art*." Schanne used to play it frequently to his friends though it was never published. At his father's death, Schanne gave up both his artistic careers, took over his father's business and became a successful manufacturer of children's toys.

As to Marcel, he is a composite of two artists, both "Bohemians," both close friends of Murger: Lazare and Tabar. Lazare was the most prosperous of that set of Bohemians, and Tabar the most talented. You remember from the opera the various stages that Marcel's picture, *The Passage of the Red Sea*, undergoes. Tabar actually did begin such a picture, but the cost of the models and costumes proved beyond his means. He therefore changed the composition; it became—don't ask me how—*Niobe and Her Children Slain by the Arrows of Apollo and Diana*. For this subject it was possible to use nudes. The painting was a heap of fourteen corpses, all modeled by the devoted Bohemians, who in modest undress posed in turn, and finally had the satisfaction of viewing their bodies exhibited on canvas in the Salon exhibition of 1842.

Colline is modeled on two friends, both philosophers and writers who took life tragically but not seriously: Jean Wallon and Trapadoux. Wallon wore an ecclesiastically cut coat which was stuffed with books, each of the pockets bearing the name of a public library. Trapadoux was a tall, spare, gloomy man with a thick beard; he wore a tall hat and a long green coat, whence he derived his nickname of "the green giant."

Benoit, the landlord, was actually a well-known landlord in the Rue des Cannettes.

All these friends used to meet in the Café Momus. The most celebrated café in opera was a real place. Schanne writes of it as follows:

"The Café Momus was located at Number 15 of the silent and gloomy Rue des Prêtres Saint-Germain-l'Auxerrois. . . . Murger and his friends preferred the upstairs room where smoking was allowed. There they were to some extent private and free from intrusion, the master of the establishment seeing to this. But if he overwhelmed us with attention, it was on account of the ambition to write which he himself harbored. He even showed himself especially friendly toward Trapadoux and other 'literati' whose advice he would ask. At closing time this refreshment housekeeper and courtier of the Muses would stand beside the counter smiling or not at the customer, according to whether the latter was a wielder of the pen or the brush."

It is less certain who the real-life Mimi was. In the novel she was probably a composite drawn from a number of the girls whom Murger and the Bohemians knew. The chief model for the character of Mimi was a girl named Lucile, a poor, sickly plant grown up in the shade of Paris. Murger romanticized her, for she was, according to Schanne, actually a predatory female, and though her face at times wore an angelic expression, she was devoid of all moral sense. She died of consumption—not in the garret but in a hospital, for Benoit would not allow a death in his house. Murger was not informed of her death in time to claim her body, which according to law was sent to a school of medicine for dissection. The business of the muff in the final scene of the opera is based on an actual incident: Lucile very much wanted a new dress before she died.

Musetta is at least partially drawn from a girl called Mariette, a model highly esteemed by both painters and sculptors, fully conscious of her plastic value and ready to reveal it at a slight provocation. Schanne tells that "one evening at Lazare's, a dozen of us were met, amongst whom was the austere Jean Journet, who had constituted himself in the name of 'Phalanstère,' the lay apostle of virtue. The idea struck our host to offer the spectacle of the Temptation of Saint Anthony. . . . After he had whispered to Mariette, she suddenly threw to the ground everything that covered her, and went and sat down on Jean Journet's knees. . . . The apostle remained for a moment confused and undecided. But he suddenly rose, which caused the temptress to slip to the floor. Then he rushed out like a madman, and the staircase echoed with his maledictions."

Mariette later left the Latin Quarter and led an irregular life in regular fashion, thereby amassing a considerable sum of money. With this she resolved to go to Algiers, where her sister was living. She embarked at Marseille on board the *Atlas*. The ship sank to the bottom of the Mediterranean.

These then are the characters from which Murger drew the novel that made the beret famous. Puccini was enchanted with the book and immediately urged his two librettists, Illica and Giacosa, to turn it into a libretto. But there were so many incidents in the novel, and the story was so rich in detail, that Illica's first extraction from the novel contained from fifteen to twenty acts. The shaping of the four acts of the opera then became a more than usually bitter struggle between the short-tempered Illica and the shorter-tempered Puccini, with their friend and publisher, Giulio Ricordi, acting as moderator.

While Puccini was working on the music, his friends and he formed a *La Bohème* club for their private amusement. The club was an Italian forerunner of the Algonquin Round Table, or something like it. It even had statutes such as:

> Article 1. The Members of the *La Bohème* Club, true knights of the spirit, for whose benefit the club has been founded, take an oath to cultivate well-being, and still better eating....
> Article 4. The treasurer is empowered to abscond with the funds....
> Article 6. It is strictly forbidden to play fair.
> Article 7. Silence is prohibited.

This kind of fooling seems a little childish today, even as Bohemianism itself does in our superadult world. But romantic and lovely music never becomes childish. Its beauty and melodiousness are uninfluenced by changes which take place in the harsher realm of reason. And *La Bohème* is music of the most beautiful and melodious species. It is, in my opinion, Puccini's masterpiece, perhaps surpassed in dramatic incisiveness by certain parts of *Tosca* and of *Turandot*, surpassed in humor by *Gianni Schicchi*, but never surpassed in its total impression and all-round charm. Here is an opera with not a dull moment in it. Here is an opera the music of which can still catch us, enchant us and move us after we know every twist and turn of it. Even peacock tenors and hen sopranos cannot kill our affection for Mimi and Rodolfo. When once in a lifetime, under the guidance of Toscanini, we get a *La Bohème* that is the real *Bohème* and we hear the music as it must have sounded to Puccini, then we realize that the cheapness which we sometimes ascribe to certain parts of Puccini's music is far more due to the exaggerations of everyday performances than to the score itself. Let's make no mistake about this: *La Bohème* is the work of a genius. It is both Puccini's finest work and his most appealing.

8. *Dangerous Role*

ASK ANY REASONABLY young opera singer to what role she aspires, and chances are that she will answer Carmen. It is (or ought to be) a fascinating part, the perfect operatic opportunity for acting and singing. All singers love it, and those who have been successful in it prefer it to all other roles.

Yet more singers have come to grief in *Carmen* than in any other opera. The bullfighter's girl makes the critics see red. You may remember how the scribes brought down their hatchets on Jeritza and Ponselle. Indeed, it is said that Ponselle withdrew from singing because the adverse criticism she received as Carmen had so unnerved her. Nor was this the first time that popular and well-established artists, singers who were by no means a flash in the pan, had been panned in a flash for interpretations of Carmen which seemed more a betrayal than a portrayal of the role. The loyal Huneker, who adored Mary Garden, had some unkind things to say about her Carmen.

Carmen is not a taxing role musically. But it is difficult to act, because seduction is almost as hard to manage on the stage as intoxication. To carry off serious seduction convincingly, the singer must be a really good actress and sedulously avoid conjuring up any May Westian images. In *Carmen*, the line that divides the fascinating from the ridiculous is indeed very thin.

What made the famous Carmens famous? What arts and artifices did they use in the part? What were the features of their interpretations? We do not know exactly. We must attempt to reconstruct their performances from contemporary accounts.

It seems to me, as I read these accounts, that the famous early Carmens, however much they might differ in details of technique, had one thing in common, namely, that they charged the part with venom and viciousness; that, in other words, they modeled the role more on the bold original character study of Mérimée than on the Bowdlerized version which the librettists extracted from the novel.

This seems already to have been true of the original Carmen, Celestine Galli-Marie. "The gypsy girl . . . is an odious creature at best; and Mme. Galli-Marie accentuates the least attractive side of her character. The actress's gestures are a very incarnation of vice, and there is something licentious even in the tones of her voice. . . . She was fascinating by reason of her animal beauty and in the exposure of her animal instincts. There was the swaying of restless hips, the curving of amorous arms, the languishing eye that encouraged, promised, pursued." Sounds good.

Minnie Hauk was the first Carmen who became famous in the part outside of France. She created the role both in England and in the United States. Herman Klein, in *The Golden Age of Opera*, described her thus: "The gypsy appeared strutting forward with hand on hip and flower in mouth. . . . The voice itself was not remarkable for sweetness or sympathetic charm, though strong and full enough in the middle register; but, somehow, its rather thin, penetrating timbre sounded just right in a character whose music called for the expression of heartless sensuality, caprice, cruelty and fatalistic defiance. We felt all this and more as the opera proceeded and the gypsy's ardent and impulsive (yet repulsive) nature continued to unfold itself. . . . In the scene with Don José, Mme. Hauk struck her first harsh note, that strange mocking note, strident and vicious, that distinguished her angry Carmen from all others save Calvé's." That there was no daintiness in her interpretation one can guess from her own *Memories of a Singer*. She writes: "Carmen, as I play the character, with her hands tied behind her back swings to and fro on a three-legged stool while she fascinates Don José. I swung too realistically, until I toppled over." Mme. Hauk then details how she rose to her feet and with hands still tied behind her, kicked the stool straight again and once more seated herself, singing all the while.

Galli-Marie was French; Minnie Hauk was an American, Pauline Lucca was an Austrian. From all nationalities have come interpreters of the Spanish girl who is really French. Of Lucca's performance Joseph Bennett wrote: "In working out her conception of the part, Mme. Lucca does not shrink from realism for the purpose of making things pleasant. Taking the broadest view of Mérimée's conception, she makes Carmen a very tigress, with cruel claws ready to dart forth and rend and tear on the smallest provocation. The slightest brush the wrong way turns our fascinating gypsy into a fiend. Mme. Lucca takes care that this shall be seen, almost as soon as she comes upon the stage, in the furtive, vindictive glance, and in the hard, set expression that falls like a cloud of night upon the whilom smiling face. . . . The same couchant fierceness runs through the entire course of the character, and, more than the sensuousness which passes with Carmen for love, puts upon it a distinguished stamp. . . . Her byplay (in the final scene) while Don José pours forth his complaints and entreaties, was a study, and showed better than words could do the varying emotions felt; now rage distorted the gypsy's face, succeeded by an expression of unutterable boredom at having to witness agony to her incomprehensible. Then came scorn, defiance, pride, as the plaudits of the bullring bespoke the triumphs of Escamillo; and lastly, despair on seeing that the time of reckoning had come."

Emma Calvé is generally considered to have been the finest interpreter of the part. Certainly in America she was the most popular, the model to which all others were compared. Herman Klein extolled her portrayal in *The Golden Age of Opera*.

"It had the calm, easy assurance, the calculated, dominating power of Galli-Marie's; it had the strong sensual suggestion and defiant resolution of Minnie Hauk's; it had the panther-like quality, the grace, the fatalism, the dangerous, impudent coquetry of Pauline Lucca's; it had the sparkle and vim, the Spanish insouciance and piquancy of Zelie de Lussans. That is to say, it combined them each and all in some degree; and the wonder of the melange added to exquisite singing, made Calvé's assumption from first to last superlative."

To Krehbiel she was "a woman thoroughly wanton and diabolically equipped with the wicked witcheries which explained, if they did not palliate, the conduct of Don José. Here we had a woman without conscience, but also without the capacity for even a wicked affection; a woman who might have been the thief whom the novelist describes, who surely carried a dagger in her corsage, and who in some respects left absolutely nothing to the imagination, to which a drama like *Carmen* makes appeal. She came upon the stage as Mérimée's heroine stepped into his pages: 'poising herself on her hips, like a filly from the Cordovan stud,' and with a fine simulation of unconsciousness she seemed every moment about to break into one of those dances which the satirist castigated in the days of the Roman Empire."

And Wagnalls, in *Stars of the Opera*, writes this about her: "This Carmen wore high-heeled slippers, 'tis true, but somewhat worn down and scuffed, as they must be if she was in the habit of running over cobblestones of Seville as she ran to the footlights on her first entrance. And her skirts, far from being well-setting and so short as to reveal shapely ankles and a suspicion of lace petticoats, were of that slippy, half-short length. . . . But this Carmen had an eye to color—she could hardly otherwise be a coquette—and in her hair at the nape of her neck was deftly tucked a large crimson flower. Her hair, however, was carelessly pinned and even tumbled down later on—a stroke of realism which was added to by the way she coiled it up and jabbed it into place again. . . . This performance was a revelation, a character study of a creature who recklessly holds that it is right to get all the pleasure you can and wrong not to have what you want."

It is rumored that to develop her interpretation Calvé actually lived with gypsies. The story goes that she traveled to Spain and, putting her maid up in the hotel, headed unattended to the gypsy quarter. There she remained for four weeks. In *My Life* Calvé writes: "How do you expect me to imitate Galli-Marié? She was small, dainty, of an entirely different build. I am big. I have long arms. It is absurd for me to imitate anyone but the gypsies themselves." The story also goes that Calvé invited a number of her gypsy friends some months later to a performance of *Carmen* at the Opéra-Comique in Paris; her strange guests were overjoyed because her interpretation was so authentic.

Incidentally, a curious Carmen must have been that of Lilli Lehmann, who made her debut at the Metropolitan in that part. Not being by nature endowed as a seductress, she emphasized the sinister side of the character. Krehbiel thought that it was "a conception which will not come easy to the admirers of the late Brünnhilde and Isolde; and indeed she was a puzzling phenomenon to the experienced observers."

Nearer to our own day, one of the most famous Carmens was Geraldine Farrar, also one of the most unbridled. According to one critic: "In the first act Carmen is supposed to have a little tussle with one of the chorus girls; Farrar ends up by mopping the floor with the chorus girl, for 'realism.' " But certainly it was not realism alone which made her fascinating in the part. Here is another contemporary description: "Miss Farrar's Carmen is brown of skin, raven-black of hair, lithe but not restless of motion and relatively simply clad. The piercing eyes, fixed or roving, turned inward or outward, individualize its aspect, with a vivid flowered shawl and curiously single-colored and straight-lined costumes for superficial aid."

Carl Van Vechten wrote in *Music and Bad Manners* that she enlivened the first act "with sundry blows and kicks. More serious still were her alleged assaults on the tenor (Caruso) in the third act which, it is said, resulted in his clutching her like a struggling eel, to prevent her interference with his next note."

I have mentioned that Huneker did not care much for Mary Garden's Carmen. Yet she was one of the most noted and popular of Carmens for many years. Here are some accounts of her interpretation:

"A new and astonishing wig became scenically and symbolically important in the first act, a shiny affair banged low over the eyes and with locks trailing in front of the ears. In Spain they say the wearer of such a hair cut is what Pooh-Bah calls not a young lady but a young person. Miss Garden's Carmen was just that."

"I shall never forget the effect of her turning the deathspade toward the audience with a gesture which seemed to mean that she was merely bent on turning it from herself. . . . She was wanton, rutilant, fescennine* in her beguilement: an emulsion, no doubt, of all the carnal temptings."

"In the famous wooing scene in the tavern she 'la-las' the captivating Spanish dance music while tripping a few simple steps before the fascinated Don José."

"Approaching José in the opening scene, for the first attack she circled menacingly around him; in answer to his indifference she did not toss the rose to him but crushed it against his lips; at the gypsy camp, she returned his ardent love-making with the insolence of striking a match on the sole of her shoe

---

*These mean glittering and scurrilous. I had to look them up.

to light her cigarette; at another time she mused quietly over the cards but snapped them angrily to show her displeasure; before the gates of the arena she snapped her fan in similar fashion and at last threw it to the ground. . . . Expressive, too, was her way of sliding into speech whenever the whim caught her; and the hard tones of her lower voice were mocking cruelty."

Could it be that our Carmens have become too ladylike?

9. *Was it a Failure?*

ERNEST NEWMAN, whose *Stories of the Great Operas* is indispensable to those who love opera and even to those who write about it, says that it will be a long time before the legend dies that *Carmen* was a failure and that this failure caused Bizet's death.

Who started this legend? We don't know. We do know that no less a celebrity than Tchaikovsky has contributed to it. Tchaikovsky felt a passionate admiration for the opera. And in one letter to Nadejda von Meck he says: "I am convinced that in about ten years *Carmen* will have become the most popular opera in the world. But no man is a prophet in his own country; in Paris, *Carmen* did not win real success. Soon after its first performance Bizet died, though in the bloom of youth and health. Who knows, perhaps the failure of his opera killed him?"

I have been curious to find out for myself exactly what was *Carmen's* reception. How the public liked it we can know only through the reports of the journalists who were there. But those reports do show us something. Here, then, is a summary of what the leading critics of Paris wrote immediately or shortly after the first performance.

First of all, there is no doubt that *Carmen* had some handicaps to overcome. It was given in a theater in which, from stalls to gallery, the respectable bourgeois element held sway. And there is nothing more respectable than a Parisian middleclass audience. Everything connected with this family opera house was as proper as a Schrafft's restaurant. It was the place where marriageable *jeunes filles* with a *dot* could be best observed. Not quite the right audience for an opera based on a novel which had been a *succès de scandale*. Moreover, the scandalous aspect of the opera was emphasized. No doubt the manager of the opera house, DuLocle, knew what he was doing when he publicly warned his friends not to bring their families to *Carmen* until they had seen it themselves, but such pre-advertisement seems hardly to have created a mood for calm appraisal of the music.

With the critics, also, *Carmen* had a handicap to overcome. And what a strange handicap! The belief was current that Bizet was an admirer of Wagner's theories. Four years after the Franco-Prussian War, Wagner was hardly a popular figure in Paris. And Bizet's music, because it was new and unusual, was accused of being influenced by Wagner: reason enough to approach it with reservations. Léon Escudier, a well-known critic of the time, shows this in an article in *L'Art musicale*.

"The music of the future has been a standing joke for some years, and it is high time that we heard the last of it. The leader of the school, since it must be so called, Richard Wagner, has been banished from our theaters and concert rooms. Had it not been for the war, which gave this gentleman an opportunity of making his opinion of us public [he refers to Wagner's silly pamphlet, *Eine Kapitulation*], we might even now be at the mercy of his braying German trumpets, to the destruction of all real music. . . . But Mr. Wagner has sowed such baneful seed which should be stopped from reaching maturity. . . . These remarks apply particularly to M. Bizet. Let us discuss his *Carmen*. This work is by no means without merit. The hand of a musician who knows his business thoroughly is plainly seen in it. But it is all head and no heart. . . ."

Another well-known critic, Arthur Pougin, wrote in *La Chronique musicale* a mixed review which starts by calling *Carmen* an "abnormal work" and ends by acclaiming it "an opera of brilliant promise."

Paul Bernard, the critic of the *Revue et gazette musicale de*

Paris, also liked some of the music and thought that "the stars helped to make *Carmen* a success." He particularly mentioned the lavish costumes and the colorful décor. "But the decoration M. Bizet certainly prefers is the one which he now has in his buttonhole. His nomination to the rank of Knight of the Legion of Honor reached him the very morning of *Carmen's* première. One must acknowledge that it was one of the most privileged days in his life." All of this certainly does not sound like a failure.

But we get the clearest picture of *Carmen's* première from the best critic in Paris at the time, Ernest Reyer, himself an opera composer and a perspicacious champion of new music. He was the critic who succeeded Berlioz on the *Journal des débats*. M. Reyer wrote a detailed and thoughtful account of *Carmen*:

"The *Carmen* of the Opéra-Comique is a very much sweetened, very purified edition of the novel which everyone has read, except perhaps young girls. . . . They have not succeeded in disguising their heroine to a point beyond recognition, and if they had not stopped before the slightly brutal death of Carmen, it would have been very necessary to punish vice, not being able to reward virtue. In summary, such was the show at the Favart Theater, the gypsy has not entirely lost that tart relief that she has in the novel, and that sufficiently explains to the intelligent reader the passion of Don José. . . . The reputation that has been established here at the Favart Theater as a safe refuge for the more puritan families will be found somewhat impaired. Nevertheless, if one looks carefully, it will not be difficult to discover in the repertoire of the Opéra-Comique some presentations which have not been precisely for the young women of Saint-Cyr." Of the music he has this to say: "In *Carmen*, the composer could hardly dispense with looking for the Spanish atmosphere. His memories have helped him there. This does not mean to imply reproach of memory or plagiarism, for it would be absolutely out of place so to point to a composer with as much talent and imagination as M. Bizet. . . . The song of the first act, with its very original chromatic phrase, comes straight from South America; they sing it a great deal in Havana; they will sing it a great deal in Paris. . . . It is really charming, above all, the section which starts with the ingenious melody accompanied by the orchestra. M. Bizet is a past master in the art of instrumentation and none other has found the secret of fine harmonies and pleasing accomplishments of sounds. I have said this about *Djamileh*, about *L'Arlésienne*, which is a jewel; I can well repeat it in regard to *Carmen*."

He then comes to what seems to me the most important evidence on the question of *Carmen's* success or failure. "I want to cite the parts that the public received particularly well and which must be for that reason the most successful. They cheered the '*Habanera*' of the first act; the cigarette girls' chorus is delightful, and there are excellent passages in the duet between Carmen and Don José!" And he goes on citing number after number, aria after aria, deserving of praise.

From all this I think it is fair to conclude that *Carmen*, despite the boldness of its subject, despite even the fact that the chorus girls smoked cigarettes and that this made everyone nervous, had the same first-night fate of many another good opera. Which is that the public liked it and quickly recognized it as exciting music, and that some of the critics had their cautious reservations, as critics are wont to have. But it is clearly evident that *Carmen* was not a failure!

10. *Genius and the Public*

"WHEN A TRUE genius appears in the world, you may know him by this sign, that the dunces are all in confederacy against him." This was the opinion of the author of *Gulliver's Travels*.

Oscar Wilde was of the same opinion. "The public is wonderfully tolerant," he wrote. "It forgives everything except genius."

Such illustrious but somewhat prejudiced authorities lend weight to the popular belief that a genius is not understood by his contemporaries. In the chapter "Famous Failures," I have already discussed the fact that certain romantic biographies have made us familiar with the picture of the starving genius in his garret, a man to whom the world pays no attention, who dies embittered and fameless and who then is discovered by a posterity incredulous of such ill treatment and remorseful of its neglect.

All this is quite affecting. Add a girl to it and you have an opera libretto. Add two girls and make the garret large and you have a scenario. But the fact is that one has to look long and far in the history of art to find the genius who was entirely unappreciated by his contemporaries and who was entirely ignored or misunderstood. In most cases, when a great talent appeared in their midst, people sat up and took notice. The attention may not have been as pronounced nor as lucrative as we of a later day believe it should have been. But it was there all the same; audiences and readers alike have almost always known when they were face to face with an opera or a book of import. And most new works of art have become popular with the public—who usually know what is what long before the critics do—in a relatively short time. That popularity is not always so sensational as that which greeted *The*

Pickwick Papers, when people used to stick their heads out of the window to look for the postman who was coming down the street with the latest installment. The fame of Beethoven's Fifth Symphony, of *Carmen,* of *Wuthering Heights* grew more slowly. But the general rule might be formulated that within ten years of a great work's appearance, it has its solid audience.

Fame, however, differs from finance. And it is true that, because of thieving or merely inadequate systems, many writers and composers were compensated poorly for their work. But the fact remains that they did not pass unnoticed. Even Poe, that tragic example of a writer who almost did starve to death, had fame, and quite a lot of it.

Boris Godunov is often cited as the example of the masterpiece which had no success whatever during the composer's lifetime. And Mussorgsky himself is cited as an example of a neglected genius. Is that true?

Not exactly. It is true that Mussorgsky, belonging to a special group who called themselves the Comrade Composers (we know them as the "Russian Five") and who had as their motto the search for "the unusual, the original, the unheard of and the unseen," did have to fight a gross amount of enmity, stupidity and misunderstanding. Perhaps one reason for this was the very fact that he belonged to a clique, that he shared their excesses as well as their virtues, and that therefore he was attacked by the traditional and conservative elements in Russian musical life. (One of his attackers was Tchaikovsky, who guessed wrong quite regularly: he liked neither Brahms nor Wagner.) It is also true that the opera was beset by difficulties because it was so "unusual," so "original" and so "unheard-of." But for all that, when the work was thrown into the musical pond of Russia, it made a big splash.

Boris Godunov in its first version was turned down flatly by the committee which decided the acceptance of new works

for the Imperial Theater. The opera was deemed unsuitable
because the most important part was given to the chorus—
which in the committee's opinion made the work too dull for
stage presentation—and also because there was no leading
feminine role. Mussorgsky then altered and expanded the
opera. He added the "Polish act," introduced a love scene
between the False Dmitri and Marina, and made various other
improvements. In this revised version the opera was privately
performed several times. Three scenes of the opera were also
given at the Marie Theater in St. Petersburg. This public but
incomplete performance was a great popular success. Mussorgsky, much elated, went to Rimsky-Korsakov's house for supper and everyone drank champagne to the success of a
complete performance. However, the conservatives in the
theater were still afraid of the work.

But now Mussorgsky's cause received aid from a woman
who was both determined and in a position to make her deter-
mination felt. The committee's hands were forced by a
Madame Platonova, one of Petersburg's most popular operatic
stars, who liked Mussorgsky and his new music, and who decided that *Boris* must be given a hearing. Never under estimate
the power of a woman! When it was time for her to renew
her contract, she stipulated as the prime condition that *Boris
Godunov* be given as a benefit performance for her. It seems
extremely unlikely, no matter how idealistic the lady was or
what her motives may have been, that an opera star would
have made such a stipulation if she had felt that *Boris* would
play to an empty house. Is it not more reasonable to assume that
she knew that the opera would be a success with the public
and that it had value, at least the value of being new and controversial? Benefit performances in Russia were important to
actors and actresses; on those occasions not only did the pro-
ceeds of the evening go to them, but it was also their special
evening, their fête, and they would receive flowers and gifts

from all their friends and from those members of the imperial family who liked the star and had a more or less valuable jewel to spare. It is inconceivable that the lady would have chosen for such an event an opera foredoomed to failure.

At any rate, Madame Platonova described in a letter addressed to Stassov, an intimate friend of Mussorgsky's, how she went to Gedeonov, the director of the Imperial Theater, and forced him to go over the heads of the committee and produce the opera against their wishes. Gedeonov sent for the chairman of the committee. "When he arrived, Gedeonov, pale with anger, met him in the antechamber.

" 'Why have you turned this opera down?'

" 'By your leave, Excellency, the opera is no good!'

" 'Why not? I have heard excellent accounts of it!'

" 'By your leave, Excellency, another reason: the composer's friend, Cui, is always abusing us in the Petersburg *News*; only the day before yesterday . . .' and he drew a crumpled copy from his pocket.

" 'Well, your committee can go to blazes, do you hear? I shall produce this opera without their permission!' shrieked Gedeonov, beside himself with rage.

"The next day his Omnipotence sends for me again. 'Now, my good madame, just see what you've brought me to! I'm likely to lose my place all on account of this *Boris* of yours! I can't for the life of me see what you find in it—and let me tell you I have no sympathy whatever with these newfangled fellows, for whom I shall probably have to suffer!'

" 'All the more honor to your Excellency,' I replied, 'for interesting yourself so energetically on behalf of these young Russian composers, with whom you are quite unable to sympathize'. . . . So, finally, the production of *Boris* for my benefit took place. The success was tremendous." This, even discounting a lady's enthusiasm, does not sound like failure. But as to that first performance we have not only her testimony, but also Rimsky-Korsakov's word. He says: "On January 27, 1874, *Boris Godunov* was produced with great success in the Marinsky Theater. We were all triumphant."

Even a severe critic of the new school, B. Baskin, wrote in a periodical called *Russian Thought*, ten years after the opening: "Let's state the fact that the opera had success and a pretty solid one; the composer and the performers were called forth after the tableaux, as well as after each act."

Why then, in the face of this, was the opera so rarely performed after its première that we have come to think of *Boris* as a contemporary failure? Because *Boris* was, as I have mentioned, considered a controversial opera, and though it was received with rapture by the younger element, its somber, strange music offended the right-wingers. And these included a number of powerful writers and critics (Cui, the composer, and a close personal friend of Mussorgsky among them) who exclaimed against the opera and for a time got the upper hand, the more easily so because both the imperial family and the management of the opera house were frightened by the "democratic elements" of the opera, by the sympathetic treatment of the plain people. They heaved a sigh of relief when this "shame covering the surface of all Russia," as the director of the theater expressed it, was taken off the stage. There were also those who felt that Pushkin's drama, which in its turn had come in for some sharp critical comment when new, was now something holy, a national shrine not to be tampered with. Mussorgsky had adapted Pushkin's work to the needs of an opera libretto and naturally had taken liberties with it. One historian wrote three letters to a publication called *The Citizen*, protesting against the outrage Mussorgsky had committed; the editor who gave space to these letters was Fjodor Dostoievsky.

But there were also voices raised in praise. A few critics and writers like Stassov were convinced that as time went on "one of the greatest pearls of the Russian folk art" would come into its own.

I have taken this example of a famous failure to show my belief that even in the case of an opera which was kept off the stage by a dogged clique of censors, theater officials and critics—that even in the case of a composer whose music had nothing in it of the easy and pretty appeal, there were people who realized what he had to offer and who gave him understanding and acclaim.

11. *Those Unappreciative Audiences*

AND STILL a few more words on my favorite topic: the defense of the public, past and present, but particularly past.

It is easy to make fun of the past. To look back into time and feel superior is a game that anyone can play. It is a pleasant game, too. It feels good to come across absurd notions which are no longer held; it makes us feel wise to meet problems which bothered our grandparents but which have now been solved.

That is why there will always be a market for entertainments of the retrospective, oh-so-quaint school. Plays like *Berkeley Square*, movies like *Meet Me in St. Louis* were successes. So was the revival of *Man and Superman* in 1948, and not because it is a good play (I think it is a terrible play) but because we like to laugh over the fuss raised by questions which we think have since been answered.

We are also very sorry for our forebears who failed to appreciate a great work of art immediately. Hindsight is particularly easy in art. We believe we would have been more perspicacious. But, honestly, we haven't as much right to feel superior as we think we have.

Let us consider the case of one of the greatest of all operas, *Don Giovanni*. Is it possible for us today to imagine what a task it must have been for operagoers of the last decade of the eighteenth century to assimilate an opera so unlike anything they had been used to? The impact of the work must have been tremendous, but could they make head or tail of it? If we did not know that *Don Giovanni* was a success from the first, would we not guess that so novel and difficult an opera would have been doomed to initial failure and that it could only gradually have made its way?

We do know that the people in Prague were enraptured with *The Marriage of Figaro*. Did the director of the opera there, when he commissioned Mozart to write another work especially for the Prague opera house, expect to receive a second *Marriage of Figaro*, a charming, ebullient, fast-paced, intriguing, happy and elegant comedy, sure of success? One knew where one stood with *The Marriage of Figaro*. It was a comedy, and with the exception of one plaintive aria, its mood was that of clear-cut joy. Its characters were eighteenth-century aristocrats and servants, clearly drawn, the kind of people audiences knew well. But along came *Don Giovanni*, which was neither a comedy nor a tragedy but both, with a most equivocal hero. What was he supposed to be? It was hard to tell whether to be sympathetic with him or to despise him. One knew only that he was *il dissoluto punito*, that he was a libertine and that—as in every previous form of the story—the libertine had to be punished. But though in the libretto Don Giovanni commits quite an impressive number of plainly dirty tricks, Mozart gave him in the music so many attractive traits that one could hardly help feeling friendly toward him. Was he then a hero or a villain? Was he supposed to be liked or disliked? And what of the play itself, this play called a "*dramma giocoso*"? Was it a drama or was it a joke? Comedy and drama pass heel to toe in *Don Giovanni*. In fact, they merge into each other. They merge even in two of the principal characters. The comic and tragic are blended in Don Giovanni and Donna Elvira in such a way that we cannot be certain how to take them. This is a long distance from *The Marriage of Figaro* or any other preceding opera which presented either comic figures or tragic figures but not people who were alternately or at the same time both. This blend of *Don Giovanni* is, of course, high art, but it could not have been easy for its first audiences.

The very fact that the characters cannot easily be defined,

that they are not in any sense, either musically or dramatically stock characters, gives *Don Giovanni* much of its fascination. Mozart's imagination reached so deep that, though the characters are complete and full, he nevertheless gives our own imagination the chance to fill in the last outline. When we do this, some of us see different things from others. It is a characteristic of certain works of art that they can be interpreted in several different ways, each valid. *Hamlet* is a prime example. How many different interpretations are there, have there been, and will there continue to be, of *Hamlet!*

If Don Giovanni himself is mysterious, Donna Anna is equally and perhaps more so. The conception of Donna Anna as the woman who is really in love with Don Giovanni is actually a superimposed conception. It springs from the romantic German nineteenth-century interpretation of Donna Anna and can be traced, partly at least, to a story written by the romantic E. T. A. Hoffman, the German Edgar Allan Poe. In this story, called *Don Juan: An Imagined Meeting*, he interprets the opera. He believes that Donna Anna was the woman in whom Don Giovanni might have found the fulfillment of all his desires. But he met her too late, and all he did was to violate her. She too feels that Don Giovanni, not the colorless Don Ottavio, is the man destined for her love. Though she works for his destruction, she is consumed by passion for him. Fanciful as all this may be, the curious aspect is that the interpretation should have taken hold. The reason must be sought in the music. This music is so charged with the highest beauty, it is so full of mystery, that the explanation given by the libretto—that Donna Anna is simply seeking revenge—does not seem to be adequate. Because of her glorious music, we are not satisfied with the conventional though perfectly proper plot-motive; thus we have dreamed traits and mysteries into Donna Anna which she may not possess.

I have wandered rather afield from the première of *Don*

Giovanni and from my point that the opera must have been a difficult one for its first audiences. Added to the unusualness of the characters was the unprecedented orchestration, heavier, more forceful, more dramatic than any heard before in the opera house. This orchestra, "blasting" forth with trombones (I am trying to speak from the contemporary point of view) was a frightening instrument. Mozart's scoring for *Don Giovanni* stands in about the same relation to the orchestration of that time as *Götterdämmerung* does to *Der Freischütz*. Yet *Don Giovanni* was, as we all know, an immediate success in Prague. Nor was Prague unique. Though the opera did not please the Viennese, it was a success in Berlin (four years after Prague) and within a generation it had made its way to the major opera houses of the continent. The number of articles, essays and appreciations published within thirty years or so (unfortunately too late to do Mozart any good) proves that *Don Giovanni* was judged an important work and that people grappled with it.

The best minds of the time were enchanted by the opera. In this connection it is interesting to find that Goethe wished that the music which (he guessed) would some day be written about *Faust* could have been written by Mozart "in the character of Don Giovanni." (What he would have said of Gounod's *Faust* is anyone's guess. Gounod, by the way, had himself painted holding the score of *Don Giovanni* in his hand.) To Schiller, who voiced the hope that a new, loftier and more noble form of tragedy might grow out of the form of opera, just as originally tragedy itself had grown from the choruses of the Bacchus feast, Goethe replied, "If you could have been at the recent performance of *Don Giovanni*, you would have seen that all your hopes about opera have been realized." He added, however: "This work is unique, and Mozart's death has destroyed the hope of ever receiving something like it again. . . ."

New York heard it in 1826, thirty-nine years after the world première in Prague. During these thirty-nine years *Don Giovanni* had become so renowned that its fame preceded it to America.

How did it fare in America?

The story of Don Giovanni's journey here is an interesting one. Lorenzo da Ponte, the opera's librettist, was then living in New York, an old man, a fugitive from his own intrigues and debts. He had come here after an eight-year sojourn in London, had tried unsuccessfully to become a tobacco and liquor dealer, and was now making a modest living as a teacher of Italian. He taught at Columbia College; he owed this job to his friend, the Reverend Clement Moore, author of *'Twas the Night before Christmas*.

While Italian opera, especially *The Barber of Seville*, was not unknown in New York, the first real gala season of Italian opera there was given in 1825 at the Park Theater. Da Ponte, who says in his memoirs that to establish Italian opera in New York was the object of his aspirations, seems not to have been directly concerned with the importation of the illustrious Manuel Garcia for this season.

Garcia, the extraordinary jack-of-all-trades of opera, was impresario, conductor, stage manager and composer for his own troupe, besides singing both tenor and baritone roles. In 1825, he was appearing in London with great success. Two men, Price, the manager of New York's Park Theater, and a certain Dominick Lynch, a rich wine dealer fond of music, went there to engage Garcia. His company consisted of himself, then fifty years old; his wife, Joaquina; his son, Manuel Garcia Jr., twenty years old; and Maria Felicita Garcia, seventeen years old and later known as the famous Maria Malibran. There were three other members of the company, but by and large it was a family affair.

They came over and opened the season with *The Barber of*

Seville to a fashionable audience which was, according to the New York *Evening Post,* "surprised, delighted, enchanted." One distinguished member of that audience was James Fenimore Cooper, who had just realized a formidable success with the first of his *Leatherstocking* series.

Garcia was no longer at the top of his form. According to an English magazine, *Harmonicon,* he was "half worn out." The same magazine expressed surprise that this meager troupe should cross the Atlantic to produce opera, and added, with the arrogance of those who have already heard a great many operas, that "our trans-Atlantic brethren have no experience in this kind of musical representation and therefore will not perhaps be very nice. . . ."

Da Ponte immediately went to see Garcia and proposed to him that "my *Don Giovanni*" be given by his company. Garcia agreed, provided that he could get a sufficient cast together. No one in his company was capable of singing Don Ottavio. An adequate tenor was found, but as Garcia did not wish to incur additional expense, Da Ponte's friends and pupils paid the singer's fee.

The first performance of *Don Giovanni* was given on May 23, 1826, with Garcia as Don Giovanni (baritone, though he had sung the tenor role of Almaviva a little while before), his son as Leporello and Maria Felicita singing Zerlina. Masetto and the Commandatore were sung by the same man.

By the way, prices of admission were: Box seats, two dollars; pit (orchestra), one dollar; gallery, twenty-five cents!

The performance could hardly have been extraordinary. Kobbe (in *The Complete Opera Book*) says: "At the first performance, during the finale of the act, everything went at sixes and sevens despite the effort of Garcia in the title role to keep things together. Finally, sword in hand, he stepped to the front of the stage, ordered the performance to be stopped, and exhorting the singers not to commit the crime of ruining a masterpiece, started the finale over again, which now went all right."

The New York papers did not employ regular music critics at the time.* I have been unable to find any review of the performance in the Public Library files in New York. The New York Daily *Advertiser* carried this notice on the day of the performance: "The preparation of the new piece of *Don Giovanni* having been completed, it will be brought out this evening. It is the most celebrated of Mozart's compositions and has been very successful in London. The story is uncommonly interesting, and as the whole troupe is to perform, it is predicted it will be the most successful piece yet given."

The opera was, according to Da Ponte's memoirs, an immediate success. Though familiar only with excerpts from Mozart's operas, people took the whole of *Don Giovanni* to heart. Da Ponte tells the story of one man who had slept through performances of other operas but who now not only could not sleep through *Don Giovanni* but could not sleep after it. The success of *Don Giovanni* was so great that Da Ponte sold "an enormous number" of the translated libretto which he had published at his own expense.

We might think Da Ponte's testimony prejudiced. However, I found in a magazine entitled *The Albion-British, Colonial and Foreign Weekly Gazette* (published in New York) an article which shows that the performance was indeed an important and popular event.

What is extraordinary about this article is the understanding of *Don Giovanni* which it demonstrates. Remember that opera was just beginning in New York and that nothing like *Don Giovanni* had ever been heard here. Yet this article could almost be a contemporary review:

---

*After the first performance of *The Barber of Seville*, one newspaper said: "We have been disappointed at not having a scientific critique from a professor of Italian music."

"This exquisite offspring of the greatest musical genius of any age was produced for the first time on Tuesday. Through the want of time for preparation some imperfection was apparent, and through the want of strength some parts were allotted to incompetent artists. . . . But the simple and deep beauties of the opera carry it triumphant over all the difficulties it has to encounter in this theater. It is a casket of precious jewels of the purest and highest taste. They have been transplanted to other cabinets and have become a sort of public property but nowhere do they emit so bright and penetrating a radiance as in their own proper sphere. Every note of this effusion of Mozart is familiar to the musical world.* It is like the rich quotations of Shakespeare so naturalized to the genial mind that we almost forget whence they were originally borrowed. The great characteristics of *Giovanni* are its beautiful simplicity, its dramatic effect, its deep and tender pathos and its bounding sparkling glee. . . .

"Signor Garcia is not much at home in this simple melody of Mozart. He must have a wide field for display, he must have ample room to verge enough for unlimited curvettings and flourishes. It is a maxim with Garcia that no one can ever be a great singer until the voice be a little impaired, that is, that a singer should depend more on his science than on his natural gifts. So explained the maxim is not particularly extravagant as has been exemplified in his own case. By his extraordinary skill he has contrived to hide many vocal defects. . . . His Giovanni is inferior to his Almaviva, yet who with a spark of musical knowledge will compare the music of the two parts? . . .

"The only person whose performance can be praised without any exception is Mlle. Garcia. Her Zerlina though not so simple and rustic as Fador's (the great Zerlina of Europe) is

*But hardly in New York!

much more pleasing and fascinating. It was admirably acted, which for a singer is high praise. The duet "*La' ci darem la mano*" was full of feeling and beauty. The celebrated "*Batti batti o bel Masetto*" was never better sung. It was the gem of the whole although the audience did not appear to think so. Some fears had been entertained for the purity of Mlle. Garcia's taste. It is manifest however that it is not yet impaired by faulty example. But in proportion as she is excellent must we regret that a few nights longer, and she will disapper from the public gaze." (She disappeared from the public gaze to marry the French merchant Malibran, who was more than twice her age but was reputed to be very rich. A year later, her husband became bankrupt, and Maria Malibran, after singing in Grace Church and in ballad operas on the Bowery, returned to Paris.)

This appreciation of *Don Giovanni* in a magazine which came out four days after the performance is, I submit, one more proof that great operas have found comprehension and success quickly. They did not always have to wait for the wiser public of a later age.

12. *A Musical Comedy by Mozart*

MOZART's *Abduction from the Seraglio* is usually labeled "a youthful work." What do we mean by that adjective? Is it youthful—meaning that it is full of life and sparkle and exuberance? Or is it youthful—meaning that it was written when the composer was young and that it is immature?

What is a youthful work, anyway? Is the polished Overture to *A Midsummer Night's Dream*, which Mendelssohn composed at the age of seventeen, youthful? Is Stephen Crane's *The Red Badge of Courage* youthful because he wrote it at the age of twenty-two? Is *Buddenbrooks*—a portrait of decline—youthful because the novel was published when Thomas Mann was twenty-six, exactly as old as Mozart was when he composed *The Abduction*? On the other hand, if we did not know musical history, would we call *Falstaff* the work of a man eighty years old? And aren't those paintings which Renoir did in old age his most youthful ones?

It is important to make the definition in the case of *The Abduction* because although Mozart wrote it in his youth, it is not a youthfully immature work. It is as successful and as mature as are his later operas. That it has never been as popular as the others, that it contains no music which stirs the emotions as deeply as do the great later operas is due chiefly to the fact that Mozart here was writing not a grand comic opera like *Figaro*, nor a *dramma giocoso* like *Don Giovanni*, but a *Singspiel*, a German musical comedy. Mozart wrote *The Abduction* because Emperor Joseph II was interested in promoting the German *Singspiel* as against Italian light opera. In executing his Emperor's commission, Mozart quite naturally kept the music within the framework of a musical comedy—light and gay, not too profound. . . .

In the Vienna of the late eighteenth century, the Turks

were as intriguing a subject for the stage and the novel as spies
are today for the movie and the comic strip (though Mozart's
Blondchen is not a forerunner of Blondie). Vienna had with-
stood two sieges of the Turks, and the Viennese playwrights
of the time liked to put the Turks on the stage and show them
as powerful brutes and terrific with the ladies. Mozart, as a
practical man of the stage, chose a topical subject for his
musical comedy: the Turks were almost surefire.

But as Paumgartner points out in his book on Mozart, the
plot of *The Abduction* goes back to a time long before Mozart;
it goes back to an ancient fairy tale about two lovers, Flos and
Blancflos, flower and white flower. Flos, the son of an Oriental
king, is the child companion of Blancflos, the daughter of a
captured vassal. They are children, but are in love. The king
disapproves of this love and banishes his son. Blancflos is sold
to the sultan of Babylon. Flos, wandering and seeking his
darling, comes to the harem, bribes the porter and is smuggled
into the room of Blancflos in a basket, hidden under flowers.
She is overjoyed when the youth emerges from the petals.
She keeps him with her. But one day the sultan finds him asleep
in the arms of his beloved and, furious, the potentate orders
them both burned at the stake. Flos and Blancflos possess a
magic ring, with the help of which one or the other can be
spirited away. But neither of them wants to die alone, so they
throw the ring away. The sultan, hearing this, pardons the
lovers and gives them safe conduct back to their home. They
both die on the same day, when they are a hundred years old.

This exquisite fairy plot became, in the services of the stage,
less symbolic, more realistic and, since we are dealing with the
eighteenth century, a good deal more sophisticated. Stephanie,
the man who prepared Mozart's libretto, simply helped himself to the latest and most convenient version of the story:
this was a drama by Friedrich Bretzner called *Belmont und
Konstanze*. Though Bretzner's work wasn't original either,

and though such borrowings were usual among the play-wrights of the eighteenth century, Bretzner was highly indignant. He inserted an advertisement in the *Leipziger Zeitung* which read: "A certain individual by the name of Mozart in Vienna has had the impudence to misuse my play, *Belmont und Konstanze*, for a libretto. I herewith solemnly protest against this violation of my rights and reserve the right to further action."

Around this appropriated plot Mozart wrote music which is as original and as fresh as are all his best works, as sparkling and bright as the wonderful *Haffner* Symphony which he composed in the same year. The beauty of this music is a beauty of gaiety. It moves fast and happily. It wears wings. Though the lovers grieve, nothing is really serious; all is in the realm of pleasant make-believe. Mozart's music lifts the plot from the purely topical and foolish into which it had sunk and lifts it again to the plane of the ancient fairy tale. Yes, *The Abduction* is a fairy tale set to music. And it is the kind of tale in which we know from the beginning that everything is going to come out all right. In fact, Richard Wagner said of the gay overture that it is impossible to hear it without realizing at once and with utmost certainty the character of the play which follows it. Mozart himself was proud of this overture. He wrote to his father, "It is quite short, alternating always between forte and piano, and when it is forte the Turkish music begins . . . and I believe it will be impossible to sleep when it is played, even if one hasn't slept at all the previous night."

In the sense that it bubbles and shimmers, *The Abduction is* a youthful work. Carl Maria von Weber said of it: "With the best will in the world, he could never have written another *Abduction*. I see in it the quality that everyone has in his joyous, youthful days, days the bloom of which can never be recaptured."

The première of *The Abduction* took place on July 16, 1782. That it was a considerable success can be deduced from the fact that in the same year the opera was given fifteen times more. The Emperor was present at the first performance, and he is supposed to have said to Mozart, "Too beautiful for our ears and a great many notes, my dear Mozart," to which Mozart is reputed to have answered, "Exactly as many as are necessary, Your Majesty."

One of the performances in the first year was given because the famous Gluck wanted to hear the opera; he was charmed by it and invited Mozart to dinner. Another special festival performance was given in honor of the Grand Duke of Russia. At that occasion Mozart found it politic "to go once again to the piano and to conduct myself, partly to wake up the somewhat drowsy orchestra . . . partly to make an appearance as the father of my child."

The Abduction was the first opera which spread Mozart's fame beyond Vienna. Many of the major German opera houses gave the work in the next two or three years. So did many of the smaller houses. We know of one performance given in Baden, the resort near Vienna, where Mozart sneaked into the orchestra incognito and began to play the 'cello. He was so incensed, however, by the execrable playing of the other 'cellists that he ran away cursing.

13. *The Politics of a Libretto*

THE MARRIAGE OF FIGARO is one of those rare works of art in which everything seems right. Every glittering song and every matchless melody in it possesses that peculiar kind of beauty which is absolutely independent of time. It seems always to have been here, and we may well assume that it always will be here—perfect, unaging.

It is an amusing paradox therefore that this music is welded to a libretto of sharp timeliness, a story which was in Mozart's day the last word in revolutionary bravado and actually should not have been touched with a ten-foot pole.* That Mozart did touch it shows that he had a sense for the theatrically topical. He may even have sensed the value of a controversial and argumentative subject. For he knew as well as everyone else that the Beaumarchais comedy on which the libretto is based was dynamite, and that it was therefore likely to attract customers to the box office. He did not and could not know that this comedy was to play a part in the mightiest upheaval of his time. *Le Mariage de Figaro* was the *Uncle Tom's Cabin* of the French Revolution.

I would guess that half the people who now listen to and thoroughly enjoy *The Marriage of Figaro* have not a very clear idea of what goes on in the plot and that they would be greatly surprised to learn that what they are seeing on the stage is an indictment of government by, for and of aristocrats.

The fabulous comedy had a fabulous author. Pierre Augustin Caron started out in life as a watchmaker, the son of a watchmaker. Desiring to change the merchants' quarter of Paris for the more floral atmosphere of Versailles, he became a harpist and, as such, charmed with his playing Mes-

---

*See chapter entitled *Immoral Operas*.

dames de France, the four daughters of Louis XV. From an old and invalid courtier he purchased, on the sly, a title and an office and became *controleur clerc d'office de la maison du roi*, which meant that he headed the parade of the kitchen personnel when the meat of the King was served. The invalid courtier soon thereafter died, and Caron married his widow, thus recoving his investment. Not a bad scheme! He then formed a friendship with a financier of Paris whom he supplied with certain royal decorations, for which his friends supplied him with loyal financial tips. In just a few years Caron became wealthy, achieved the title of *Sécrétaire du roi* and bought himself, for 85,000 francs, a diploma of nobility. He changed his name to Beaumarchais and climbed to the role of *lieutenant général des chasses à la capitainerie de la varenne du Louvre*, which translated means that he was a sort of super-forest-ranger. (He ended his life as *Citoyen* Beaumarchais.)

In turn he was banker, speculator, paper manufacturer, publisher of fine books (including an edition of Voltaire), wholesale wood dealer, secret agent of Louis XV, and ship outfitter, in which capacity he furnished forty merchant vessels and one battleship to a revolutionary colony across the Atlantic which was at war with England. He founded an early union of stage writers in France, and he had built under his personal supervision several Parisian edifices, among which was his own splendid palace on the Boulevard Beaumarchais.

He also found opportunity to be three times arrested in Paris and once in Vienna, to be exiled to Hamburg, to have his fortune confiscated, and to carry on a series of involved lawsuits which ranged from the protection of a youthful invention for a watch movement to defense actions in adultery, bribery and a poison case involving two married ladies. All of these processes of law were documented and publicized by him through witty and polemic pamphlets.

He also became the most popular dramatist of Paris, and through *Figaro* probably of Europe. He wrote for the stage "for fun," *par délassement;* he first wrote *The Barber of Seville,* and completed *Figaro's Marriage* in 1780. But *Figaro* was held in quarantine for three years and was turned down by five censors. Beaumarchais used to read the piece privately to princes and princesses, to dukes and duchesses, and finally to Louis XVI, who declared it *"détestable."* The very fact that the King disliked it made it popular with the court and with all of the inner circle.

At any rate, *Le Mariage de Figaro ou La folle journée* was finally performed on April 27, 1784, in the *Théâtre Français.* It was probably the most spectacular première Paris had witnessed. The entrance to the theater was beleaguered from early morning and the gendarmes had to be called out. Nevertheless, the people stormed the doors, broke the iron grating and filled the aisles long before the beginning of the performance. The ladies of the aristocracy spent the day in the dressing rooms of the actresses, just to be sure to be able to get into the theater. The enthusiasm and the success of the performance were truly *foux.* *Figaro* was given almost in succession sixty-eight times, and the people came from the remote provinces of France to see it.

Less than a year after *Figaro* appeared in Paris, there were twelve German translations being handed around in Vienna. The idea of setting *Figaro* to music was Mozart's. He broached this idea to the court poet of Joseph II. This poet, Lorenzo da Ponte, was another fabulous character not unlike Beaumarchais, one of those extraordinary adventurers of the eighteenth century, a compound of Casanova, Ahasverus and Wilson Mizner. He was a Jew who became a Jesuit priest. He was a professional gambler, teacher of rhetoric, musician, political writer, librettist and poet. As such he was a favorite of Joseph II, who enjoyed his sharp wit.

From Beaumarchais and Da Ponte Mozart inherited a plot that is impudent, colorful, gay and fast moving. Mozart alone, however, endowed *Figaro* with perfectly proportioned beauty. He alone clothed it with permanent aristocracy, for he gave it the kind of elegance that makes the listener feel elegant when hearing it. Mozart alone invested the opera with a delicate eroticism which in Cherubino created the most captivating character of opera.

So when you listen to this wonderful and young music, it might be interesting to remember that you are also hearing what was once an inflammable political tract, in which the servant becomes the master and the Count becomes the dupe. How was this bright jewel received? Let us turn, in the next chapter, to the account of a man who was there.

14. *Michael Kelly, "Composer of Wines"*

THERE ARE NO poor parts in *The Marriage of Figaro*. Every role is, or should be, a singer's delight. Mozart distributed his music with so just a theatrical sense that not one of the principals can complain of the lack of a beautiful and grateful aria. However, if there is one minor character who has not much to do, it is the lawyer who takes part in the complicated business of the promise-of-marriage contract which Marcellina holds. This character's name is Don Curzio; a good many people who know *Figaro* well would not, I dare say, recognize his name.

Yet, by the perverseness of history, it is the original interpreter of this role who has left us the most satisfactory account of the première of that great opera. The singer also played Don Basilio—but it with the role of Don Curzio that his account deals.

This tenor was Michael Kelly—a strange name to meet in Vienna in the eighteenth century! Kelly was the son of a wine merchant of Dublin. The boy showed great talent at an early age, and at seventeen he made his debut in Italy. He sang in all the principal opera houses on the continent; this brought him in the natural course of events to Vienna.

Late in life Kelly wrote a book of reminiscences. That is, the book was actually written by Theodore Hook, from material supplied by Kelly. Thus it must be a fairly early example of ghost writing, and as is frequent in this kind of collaboration, the supposed author was extremely displeased with the real author. "That rascal Hook," said Kelly, "omitted things he had no right to leave out."

At any rate, Kelly (or Hook) tells us this of the meeting with Mozart: "I went one evening to a concert of the celebrated Kozeluch's, a great composer for the pianoforte as well as a fine performer on that instrument. I saw there the composers Vanhall and Baron Diderstoff, and, what was to me one of the greatest gratifications of my musical life, I was there introduced to that prodigy of genius—Mozart. He favored the company by performing fantasias and capriccios on the pianoforte. . . . After this splendid performance we sat down to supper. . . . After supper the young branches of our host had a dance, and Mozart joined them. Madame Mozart told me that great as his genius was, he was an enthusiast in dancing and often said that his taste lay in that art, rather than in music. . . .

"He gave me a cordial invitation to his house, of which I availed myself, and passed a great part of my time there. He always received me with kindness and hospitality. He was remarkably fond of punch, of which beverage I have seen him take copious draughts. He was fond of billiards and had an excellent billiard table in his house. Many and many a game have I played with him, but always came off second best. He gave Sunday concerts, at which I never was missing. . . ."

In Vienna, three operas were being considered for production, one by Regini, one by Salieri, and one by Mozart. All three operas were ready, and the Emperor had to decide which was to be produced first. "Mozart was as touchy as gunpowder and swore he would put the score of his opera into the fire if it was not produced first; his claim was backed by a strong party; on the contrary, Regini was working like a mole in the dark to get precedence.

"The third candidate was *maestro di cappella* to the court, a clever, shrewd man, possessed of what Bacon called crooked wisdom, and his claims were backed by three of the principal performers, who formed a cabal not easily put down. Every one of the opera company took part in the contest. I alone was a stickler for Mozart. . . . [We may believe this or not!]

"The mighty contest was put to an end by His Majesty's issuing a mandate for Mozart's *Nozze di Figaro* to be instantly put into rehearsal; and none more than Michael O'Kelly (he was called both Kelly and O'Kelly) enjoyed the great little man's triumph over his rivals." (As Jahn points out, Kelly's recollection was faulty, for Salieri's opera was given first.)

Of the performance itself Kelly writes this: "All the original performers had the advantage of the instruction of the composer, who transfused into their minds his inspired meaning. I never shall forget his little animated countenance when lighted up with the glowing rays of genius; it is as impossible to describe it as it would be to paint sunbeams.

"I called on him one evening, and he said to me, 'I have just finished a little duet *"Crudel perche finora farmi languire così"* (sung by Almaviva and Susanna) for my opera; you shall hear it.' He sat down at the piano and we sang it. . . .

"I remember at the first rehearsal of the full band Mozart was on the stage with his crimson pelisse and gold-laced cocked hat, giving the time of the music to the orchestra. Figaro's song, *'Non piu andrai, farfallone amoroso,'* Bennuci (the original Figaro) gave with the greatest animation and power of his voice.

"I was standing close to Mozart, who, *sotto voce*, was repeating, 'Bravo! Bravo! Bennuci;' and when Bennuci came to the fine passage, *'Cherubino, alla vittoria, alla gloria militar'* . . . the whole of the performers on the stage and those in the orchestra, as if actuated by one feeling of delight, vociferated *'Bravo! Bravo! Maestro. Viva, viva, grande Mozart.'* Those in the orchestra I thought would never have ceased applauding, by beating the bows of their violins against the music desks. . . . The same meed of approbation was given to the finale at the end of the first act. . . . In the *sestetto*, in the second act (which was Mozart's favorite piece of the whole opera), I had a very conspicuous part as the stuttering judge. All through the piece I was to stutter; but in the *sestetto* Mozart requested I would not, for if I did, I should spoil the music. I told him that although it might appear very presumptuous in a lad like me to differ with him on this point, I did, and I was sure that the way in which I intended to introduce the stuttering would not interfere with the other parts, but produce an effect; besides, it certainly was not in nature that I should stutter all through the part, and when I came to the *sestetto* speak plain, and after that piece of music was over return to stuttering. And, I added (apologizing at the same time for my apparent want of deference and respect in placing my opinion in opposition to that of the great Mozart), that unless I was allowed to perform the part as I wished, I would not perform it at all.

"Mozart at last consented that I should have my own way but doubted the success of the experiment. Crowded houses proved that nothing ever on the stage produced a more powerful effect; the audience (at the performance) were convulsed with laughter, in which Mozart himself joined. The Emperor repeatedly called out 'Bravo!' and the piece was loudly applauded and encored. When the opera was over, Mozart came on the stage to me, and shaking me by both hands, said, 'Bravo, young man. I feel obliged to you and acknowledge you to have been in the right and myself in the wrong. . . .'"

Maybe Mozart was just being amiable; it is certain that his first view was the right one. In modern performances, Curzio does not stutter in the ensemble number, because the stuttering would interfere with the musical effect. As a matter of fact, to be realistic about it, a stutterer does not stutter when he sings.

Kelly reports that the opera was a big success, and this is corroborated by other contemporaries. "At the end of the opera, I thought the audience would never have done applauding and calling for Mozart; almost every piece was encored, which prolonged it nearly to the length of two operas and induced the Emperor to issue an order on the second representation that no piece of music should be encored."

Kelly tells us of the "numerous overflowing audiences." Yet in spite of this great success *Figaro* was withdrawn after nine performances, probably because of court intrigues against Mozart.

Approximately nine months after the première of Figaro, Kelly left Vienna for England. He stopped off in Salzburg to see Mozart's father. In London, Kelly eventually became acting manager of the King's Theater and also tried his hand at composing. (Mozart had warned him against this.) Making no great mark as a composer, he then engaged in the wine trade as his father had done before him. Richard Brinsley Sheridan, who knew the quality of Kelly's compositions, suggested that Kelly should hang a sign over his shop reading: "Michael Kelly, Composer of Wines and Importer of Music."

15. *Tale of The Tales*

IT IS A TRUISM to say that a work of art is timeless, that it walks down the line of years. But it is less obvious to observe that it does not walk in a straight line. It moves up and down. It moves up and down in affection. Some generations find it more sympathetic than others and enter into personal and friendly relation with it. To other generations, though they may acknowledge its eminence, it says little. It is not suitable to their immediate wants. If it is a truly durable work, it can wait for a succeeding generation to come along and hug it again, revivify it and give it new youth. A work of art does not age as a man does. It grows older and then younger and then may repeat the process.

At the moment *Tales of Hoffmann* is not a popular opera. A couple of seasons ago the Metropolitan revived it, but audiences did not respond to it.

I do not know why this is so. It would seem as if the fantastic and romantic qualities of the opera should be welcome to a generation which delights in the fantastic and romantic in its entertainment and its reading. Certainly the opera's hero, Ernst Theodor Wilhelm Amadeus Hoffmann, was in real life as well as in the opera an early exponent of the lost week-end and is an interestingly disillusioned fellow. He ought to appeal to present-day audiences. Perhaps Ernest Newman has hinted at the correct explanation for the opera's lack of popularity by pointing out that unfortunately the opera has come to be regarded in the main as comic. I have always felt the opera to be a tragic one, though a tragedy enveloped in satin. It is the mood of soft sadness which attracts me to the work, a mood consistent throughout and created skillfully by music which has more to it than a few obvious melodious hits.

If Mr. Newman's explanation is the appropriate one, then

we have here a fine example of historic irony. For Offenbach suffered throughout a great part of his later life from the fear that he would never be taken seriously. International though his fame was, he came to despise it because it was founded on operetta music. He longed to fulfill another and loftier ambition. He longed to get away from the cancans and the waltzes and to enter the serious opera house.

The idea of writing a grand opera was to Offenbach certainly not only a case of catering to changed tastes or merely an attempt at recapturing popularity. It was a deeply felt need; he had carried that need with him from the days when he was at the height of his fame. Even the idea of setting the fantastic *Tales of Hoffmann* to music was not entirely new to him. He was familiar with the works of the German author, E. T. A. Hoffmann, who at the period was especially popular in France because his highly fanciful tales were a pleasant memento of morbidity to the gay Second Empire. Hoffmann's writings were then compared to the work of a man from another strange land, a man who was influenced by Hoffmann and who also knew how to make the flesh creep and the dark night seem ominous—Edgar Allan Poe. The French, who like ourselves gobble up tales of mystery and imagination, considered that Hoffmann wrote as well as Poe. This notion was perpetuated by the popularity of the opera, so that the real Hoffmann is as a writer and poet famous beyond his deserts. Henry E. Krehbiel, for example, almost half a century later, declared that these two men were much alike: "Both were possessed of a genius of a high order." Actually this is overestimating Hoffmann or underestimating Poe by a great deal.

The Tales of Hoffmann had already been produced as a play (without music) at the Odéon in 1851. Its dramatists were Jules Barbier and Michel Carré, two gentlemen who live on in dubious but perennial reputation as librettists of *Faust* and *Mignon*. By the time Offenbach got around to setting the play to music, Hector Salomon, the chorus master at the Opéra, had nearly finished the score for an opera on the same subject. However, when Salomon heard of Offenbach's great desire to use the libretto, he withdrew his own score. It is therefore to the unselfish kindness of this forgotten composer that we owe *The Tales of Hoffmann*. Extraordinary man this Salomon must have been! Think of giving up one's own work and all the many months of effort it entailed as a friendly gesture to another!

Offenbach was a very sick man when he started the opera. Its composition was literally a race with death. He allowed himself no rest or distraction. He was deeply moved by Antonia's death in the opera and felt in it some connection with his own, which he knew to be close upon him. By May of 1879 he had finished enough of the work to play excerpts to several important guests, among them Carvalho, the director of the Opéra-Comique, who immediately accepted the work and promised that it should be the first production of the coming season. Offenbach was feverish with impatience. "Make haste and produce my opera," he wrote to Carvalho. "I have not much time left, and my only wish is to see the première." However, this première had to be delayed; things went wrong with the scenery and the costumes. While the rehearsals were going on, the sick man was carried to the foyer of the Opéra-Comique so that he might hear parts of the opera.

On October 4, 1879 Offenbach held in his hand the complete piano version of the opera. (He never scored the opera. The actual scoring was done by his friend, Guiraud, after Offenbach's death.) There it all was, his first and last grand opera, finished. "I believe tonight it will be over," he said. He was right. He died at three o'clock that night.

Thus he never did witness the première. He looked on the promised land of grand opera, but he never entered it.

16. *Foreign Correspondent, Style 1876*

AS LATE AS March, the festival seemed an impossibility. Where was the necessary money? Of the thirteen hundred patrons' shares which needed to be sold in order to procure sufficient cash to pay at least the living expenses of the musicians and singers (most of whom received no salaries), only 450 had been taken up. And the Emperor had denied a request for funds. But Wagner was certain of his way and certain in his belief. He wrote to a friend, "Everything will be got ready (on credit)", setting down in that sentence the leitmotiv of his practical philosophy. And everything was ready, or almost everything was almost ready, in August 1876, when the first Bayreuth Festival began.

So much had been said and written in advance of this festival, so tempestuous had been the controversies around Wagner, that it was to be expected that the leading musicians of Europe should wend their way to Bayreuth to see and be seen at what promised to be the most spectacular musical event of the decade—even if none of them liked music. Not all the musical celebrities of the time were there, of course. It was as natural for Verdi to be far from the madding crowd as it was for Liszt to be in its midst. But the little town did in one week play host to Saint-Saëns, Grieg, Cui, Rubinstein, Gounod and Peter Ilyich Tchaikovsky.

These were men of music with an interest born of their profession. But what about the general public? Particularly what about the non-German public? Did the first festival arouse any interest in our own country? The answer seems to be yes. The event was considered sufficiently important for the leading New York papers to send their correspondents all the way to Bavaria well in advance of August 13. Some of the magazines (*McMillan's*, *Scribner's Monthly*, *Fraser's*, etc.) did likewise. Altogether there were about 150 Americans present at the first festival. This fact was noteworthy enough to be reported to Wagner himself.

How did these correspondents take to Bayreuth? What impression was made on them by their first meeting with that operatic colossus, the *Ring*, which was soon to bestride our narrow world? I shall tell you what I have read in the old publications, and thus report on the reporters:

First, like all good tourists, they seem to have been more concerned with the material problems of lodging and food than with the philosophical problems of the new art form. This was not solely an American characteristic, I hasten to add. Almost everyone there seemed to be preoccupied with getting enough to eat.

Long before the festival started and the main public arrived, "the seats at the tables d'hotes and beer gardens were filled by artists, Wagner's friends and musicians and conductors from all over Germany. Indeed, the number of Kapellmeister who seem to be drawn at this time to a focus in Bayreuth is something alarming. One trembles for the existence of German orchestras with all their leaders away." Each new train brought more Kapellmeister. To address anyone at a table d'hote as Herr Kapellmeister was to cause a dozen heads to turn at once.

And then "the golden multitudes" arrived. Bayreuth, called by most of the correspondents the dullest town in existence, woke up with a start. "People and prices have undergone a change. Under ordinary circumstances, the civility of mine host of the hotel, with possibly six new guests to provide for, would have expressed itself in a series of bowing, scraping and gesticulating movements which long habit had taught him to perform with dexterity suggestive of grace. But now his six guests are sixty; and the increase in the number to be received has necessitated such rapidity of motions of polite reception that they have become nothing less than a series of contortions painful to look upon. Other cases of deranged natures may be found in almost every house where one applies for rooms."

The charge for a hotel room before the festival was a mark and a half a day. This price was raised during the eighteen festival days to five marks a day. The private families which had rooms to let followed suit, but with some timidity. If the room-seeker refused to pay the price and left, the house-keeper would send a boy running after him, offering the room at half the price. Barbers charged double for a shave during the festival, and hotel keepers, of course, short-changed on transferring dollars into marks. However, the town did spend a little of the money that the strangers brought within its gates. It spruced up. "There has been an eruption of firs. Great branches are stuck in the ground, festoons cover the fronts of the house and line the pavements. Wreaths with paper flowers are stuck on doorways."

On the first Sunday of the festival, "the mental excitement and its consequent interference with the course of habit reached its climax when all the peasant folk of the town appeared with shoes, stockings and washed faces." This particular occasion was the supposed arrival of King Ludwig of Bavaria, who however arrived not as a king but dressed in dark traveling clothes, and not in the light of day but at 2:00 A. M. His train stopped at a siding, and there Wagner had to meet him in the dead of night and whisk him away to the Bayreuth palace. It was the first time he and Wagner had seen each other in eight years, and the meeting was in the nature of a reconciliation. Ludwig hid in the comforting darkness of the theater during the final rehearsals. Even though royalty was present, the 113 musicians rehearsed in their shirt sleeves. And the carpenters kept on hammering while the cast rehearsed. . . .

On the day of the opening, around 4:00 P. M., the streets were alive with people taking the road to the theater. There were no cabs to be had. Altogether Bayreuth had only seven hacks, and almost none could be procured in the neighboring towns. "Two large wooden restaurants with balconies had been erected next to the theater, from which one could sit and drink beer and watch the crowds arrive. It was frightfully hot and everyone complained of the weather. Notices were posted around the theater requesting no applause until the end of the act, and sentimental feelings received rather a rude shock at discerning not very far from these commendable signs the more familiar 'Bass and Co.' and 'Jameson's real old Irish.' " The performance began at 7:00 P. M. The trumpets sounded a fanfare (the sword motif), the Emperor William stepped into his box, there were plenty of cheers—and then attentive silence!

Of the thirteen hundred seats in the theater, a thousand were reserved for the patrons and three hundred for visitors. In addition, every inhabitant of Bayreuth who provided a member of the orchestra with free lodging was entitled to a seat in the far rows for one series of rehearsals. Most of them did a thriving business selling these seats. In fact, in spite of all precautions, the ticket speculators had plenty of seats to offer.

One of the correspondents tells how he obtained a ticket for a *Siegfried* rehearsal. Having been unable to buy one, he was standing in front of the theater when he saw two men pass and heard one of them say: "One must be a regular Wagnerite to be able to stand any more of that." The correspondent immediately offered to buy one of their tickets. The men replied: "Where is the best beer in Bayreuth?"

"Angermann's."

"All right, take the ticket."

The Tribune correspondent was enormously impressed with the audience and with all the royalty present. The most illustrious of the non-German aristocracy was the Emperor of Brazil. However, there was also another kind of audience. At least, one critic wrote: "Never have I seen so many shortsighted people with long hair and loud hats gathered together in one place. Why is it that the Art Work of the Future goes in company with spectacles, long hair and funny headgear?"

Naturally, the town was full of Wagnerian souvenirs. Wagner's picture was to be had on pipebowls, tobacco boxes, toilet ornaments, album covers; it was displayed in every shop window and restaurant. Wagner's music filled the streets. Here some soprano declaimed at the top of her voice, there a tenor's voice floated down from his room, across the street a bass practiced. "As I sit here, I hear Wagner motives being hummed, sung, yodeled and bellowed from the garden," wrote Grieg. But there were other sounds, too. One night a brawl broke out in a restaurant when a Berlin critic said something derogatory about the *Ring*, whereupon a Wagner defender hit him with a beer mug and broke his nose. The Wagner champion was taken to jail. There were plenty of enemies of Wagner in the town. In the Hotel Sonne sat Eduard Hanslick, full of ink and venom.

After the first performance most of the audience met at the Hotel Reichsadler for a festival supper. The city was brilliantly illuminated, and a torchlight parade was held in honor of the Emperor.

On the days when there were no performances, guests were received at Wahnfried from 8:00 P. M. until 10:00 P. M. Liszt was there, charming the ladies and everyone else. Of course, what the visitors desired most was a glimpse of

Wagner. Few of them could crash the gates of Wahnfried, and even if they succeeded, the exhausted Wagner made himself scarce. He usually retired at ten o'clock, sleeping all night with the gaslight burning. The people did sometimes catch sight of him on rehearsal afternoons as he drew up to the theater in his carriage with Cosima and Liszt. One correspondent who watched him at rehearsals described him as "short, wearing spectacles, nervous in his movements, but his manner of directing is the most determined I have ever seen, stamping his foot if the least fault is detected, singing the part as it should be sung, and every five minutes taking off and putting on his black velvet cap."

Here are one American's comments on the performances themselves:

"The music (of *Das Rheingold*) on first hearing had rather a disappointing effect; with the exception of the prelude and the Rhine Maidens' song, which have all the romantic beauty and grace of Weber, it is more or less an orchestral accompaniment to a play in which the speeches are declaimed rather than sung. . . . The characters in the play had nothing about them to attract one's sympathy or interest—heathen gods and goddesses with all the lowest propensities of man and without any of his redeeming qualities." This critic regretted that Wagner's extraordinary powers were thrown away on such unworthy objects. He also thought that the mental strain of listening to *Das Rheingold* without a break was too severe to be productive of unalloyed pleasure. "Thoughts of ices and cool air dwelt uppermost in the mind."

He liked *Die Walküre* better because the characters were men and women, "a more interesting study than the inhabitants of Valhalla." However, he found the romance of Siegmund and Sieglinde "so entirely revolting to modern ideas that its ill-fated hero and heroine meet with little or no sympathy from us." He called it "a degradation of a noble art to employ it in connection with subjects which it is to be hoped will ever be deemed unfit for dramatic treatment."

Siegfried fared better in his opinion, but the music of the last act shocked him. "For the first time the true nature of Wagner's music stands clearly revealed. It is essentially materialistic and may not improperly be compared to the paintings of a Rubens, exhibiting animal life in all its beauty and luxuriance, but lacking the ideality and refinement of a Titian." He called the music "passionate but not refined."

He was pretty exhausted by the time he reached *Götter-dämmerung,* but stuck it through. "We are finally relieved of gods and other supernatural beings, whose ultimate conflagration in Valhalla is now heard of with unmixed satisfaction."

Another American critic, who liked most of the music, was offended by—one would hardly guess this!—the closing scene of the first act of *Götterdämmerung.* "In spite of the great musical effectiveness of the closing scene, I cannot but regard an open struggle between men and women as shocking to all sense of beauty. In the presence of the Siegfried and Brünnhilde parting scene, we fancy we are living in a land of chivalrous heroes; in the presence of the other, we remember we are in Germany."

But, all in all, the American correspondents did very well. Considering the newness of this music and in comparison to some of the nonsense written by native critics who could be expected to have more understanding of Wagner, the reports of our press representatives showed remarkable judgment.

17. *Another Correspondent Reports*

IN THE PRECEDING CHAPTER, I have brought you some excerpts from the reports of the American newspaper men who attended the first *Ring* cycle. Among the correspondents of the various nations there was also present a Russian correspondent, a cultivated man of music. He sent back to his newspaper a series of five articles. They seem to me interesting enough for partial quotations.

Shortly after his arrival in Bayreuth, the reporter, who was fond of his comfort, said: ". . . . The little town received and sheltered all the guests, but it couldn't possibly feed them. Thus, on the very first day of my arrival, I learned what struggle for bread meant. There are few hotels in Bayreuth, and most people stay in private homes. The existing dining-rooms in the hotels can't possibly hold all the hungry guests. Each piece of bread, each glass of beer has to be fought for and is obtained only after a terrific struggle, many tricks and an iron patience. And when you do get a place at a table, it still isn't a short wait until the coveted dish reaches you in a more or less undestroyed condition. The most chaotic disorder always reigns at the table. Everyone shouts at the same time. The tired waiters don't pay the slightest attention to your most legitimate requests. The getting of this or that dish is a matter of pure chance. Adjoining the theater, there is an open-air restaurant promising everyone a good dinner at two o'clock. But to get there and obtain anything in this pool of hungry humanity requires the greatest heroism and a limitless courage. I describe all these things on purpose in order to show the readers the main characteristic of the Bayreuth society of melomaniacs. During the whole first series of the Wagner tetralogy, food was everyone's primary interest, with artistic concerns considerably behind. There was much more talk about steaks, chops and fried potatoes than about Wagner's music. . . . I met a lady in Bayreuth, the wife of one of the most important people in Russia, who, during her whole stay in Bayreuth, didn't have dinner once. Coffee was her only food."

The new theater impressed him not too favorably: "I must confess that the Wagnerian theater attracts one's attention not by the grace of its lines but by its colossal size. It has much more the look of an enormous hangar hurriedly erected for some industrial exhibit than that of a building that has to house a mass of people gathered from all the corners of the world to seek artistic pleasure. In this harmonious union of all arts toward which Wagner is striving, architecture was given too modest a place."

Of the festival itself he wrote: "First, I must say that anyone who believes in art and in a civilizing force, any believer in an artistic endeavor outside of its utilitarian purposes, must experience a feeling of delight in Bayreuth at the sight of the enormous artistic undertaking which achieved success, and which reached the importance of an historic epoch because of its colossal size and the strength of the interest it awoke. . . . The Bayreuth festival is a lesson for those obdurate persecutors of art who have a proud contempt for it and feel that civilized people should not deal in anything but matters which bring them a direct practical benefit. From the point of view of a materialistic benefit to mankind, the Bayreuth festival has, of course, no meaning; but from the point of view of artistic ideals, it is destined one way or another to have an enormous historic significance. Whether Wagner is right in pursuing his idea to the limit, or whether he stepped over the boundary of esthetic conventions which can guarantee the durability of a work of art; whether musical art will progress further on the road started by Wagner, or

whether the *Ring* is to be the point from which a reaction
will be set in, remains to be seen. But in any case what happened in Bayreuth will be well remembered by our grandchildren and our great-grandchildren."

Of the music—that new, strange and shocking music—he
wrote: ". . . . His music has been deeply thought through;
it is always interesting music, sometimes splendid and captivating, sometimes a little dry and difficult to understand, a
music incredibly rich from the technical point of view and
provided with an exceptionally beautiful instrumentation.

". . . . Wagner shows an astonishing wealth of harmonic
and polyphonic technique. This wealth is too great. Constantly forcing your attention, Wagner finally tries it so that
at the end of the opera, particularly in *Götterdämmerung*,
your fatigue becomes such that the music ceases to be a harmonious combination of sounds and gets to be some kind
of tiring noise. Is this what art is supposed to achieve? Since
I, a professional musician, was nearing a complete moral and
physical exhaustion, then what must have been the fatigue
of the unprofessional listener?"

He summed up: "I am ready to admit that through my
own fault, I have not yet reached the point of completely
understanding this music, and that if I study it carefully, I
too shall some day belong to the large circle of admirers.
For the present, however, speaking quite frankly, the *Ring*
impressed me not so much by its musical beauties, of which
there may be too generous an amount, as by its lengthiness,
its gigantic size. And now I'd like to say what I finally got
out of the *Ring*. I have a vague remembrance of much extraordinary beauty, especially symphonic beauty, which is very
odd, since Wagner meant least of all to write an opera in a
symphonic style; I have an astonished admiration for the
enormous talent of the author and his incredibly rich technique; I have my doubts as to the justice of Wagner's view

on opera; I have a feeling of great fatigue, but along with it I have a desire for further study of this most complicated of all music ever written."

The name of the Russian correspondent was Peter Ilyich Tchaikovsky.

18. *Elsa*

LOHENGRIN is more than a hundred years old—to be precise, Wagner completed *Lohengrin* in March of 1848. It is indeed a famous and hardy centenarian. It is famous not only with operagoers and music lovers in general; millions of people who have never heard either opera or concert know that Lohengrin was responsible for the Bridal March. In this respect Lohengrin resembles the Mona Lisa and Shylock.

Wagner had begun the composition of *Lohengrin* in 1846, when he was thirty-three years old. After the opera was finished, there was little immediate prospect that it would be accepted by any of the leading German opera houses. It took two years more before *Lohengrin* was given its first tentative and timid world première. Liszt performed it as a labor of friendship in the little theater at his disposal in Weimar. He did what he could, but since his orchestra consisted of only thirty-eight musicians, the representation of the new and difficult opera could hardly have been adequate. Wagner could not be present. He was a political exile at the time, shuttling uneasily between Switzerland and Paris. It took another eleven years before Wagner was able to hear a performance of his work. This was in Vienna; by that time *Lohengrin* had become a solid success, and the particular performance which Wagner attended was turned into a personal triumph for and tribute to him.

Since then the sun has hardly set on *Lohengrin*. But it would be useless to deny that the opera has aged. The aging is least noticeable in the music, for that is so strong that a little rheumatic touch here and there doesn't do much harm. It has aged most in its philosophy, the symbolism and moral purport so dear to Wagner's heart, but which few non-Germans take seriously any longer.

Wagner, with his passion for philosóphical explanation, "explained" *Lohengrin* on several occasions, one of them being his essay, *Music of the Future*. A quotation from this essay suffices to make us realize how turgid, indeed how incomprehensible, Wagner's work behind the work has become. Here, for example, is what Wagner said about the Prelude: "The ethereal sphere from which the god is yearning to descend to men had stretched itself, through Christian longing, to inconceivable bounds of space. To the Hellenes, it was still the cloud-locked realm of thunder and the thunderbolt from which the lusty Zeus moved down to mix with men in their own likeness. To the Christian, the blue firmament dissolved into an infinite sea of ecstasy, in which the forms of all the gods were melted, until at last it was the lonely image of His own person, longing Man, that alone was left to greet Him from the ocean of his fantasy." Can you hear any of this in the Prelude?

Liszt said of *Lohengrin* that with it the old operatic world came to an end. This is a pardonable exaggeration, considering how new the music must have sounded to him. But it is exaggeration nevertheless. For *Lohengrin* is by no means a break with the old. It is hardly the beginning of the new. *Lohengrin* is rather the old romantic opera brought to culmination, the last link of an old chain rather than the first of a new. To be sure, the elements of romantic opera are here expressed in the musical language of a genius, and this language possesses many new figures of speech. Still, the materials of the old are used in *Lohengrin*. The set numbers—arias, duets, choral pieces and the unaccompanied quintet—are clearly recognizable through the disguise of the continuous web of music. It is significant that at the festive performance in Vienna the audience applauded the arias and ensemble

numbers as they had been used to doing in the older operas.
Nor is the classic recitative absent. Though Wagner called
it something else, it is still there and in some places is of
entirely traditional quality. Wagner was not to create his
new language of singing declamation until he sat down to
compose *Das Rheingold*. Several times in *Lohengrin* the long
recitatives are so little more than what one might call talented
clichés that the music seems merely to be coasting. Such an
old-fashioned recitative is the opening of the opera, the whole
scene until Telramund steps forward.

Dramatically the opera ought to be called *Elsa*. As a character Lohengrin never comes alive. He remains a messenger
though accoutered in the shiniest armor. It is Elsa who gives
the opera whatever interest it has as a play. Wagner based
the play on the old French fables which centered around the
tale of the Holy Grail. But the dramatic theme of the woman
who is consumed by tragic curiosity and who consciously
destroys herself is a universal and oft-occurring subject
which one may find in the literature and tales of all nations.
It is a human theme, and Wagner managed to make Elsa a
human, interesting woman, a visionary and mystic creature
but one not beyond the bourn of credibility. It is not
Wagner's fault that she seldom seems so in performances;
that, in fact, she usually appears as a simpering goose. If one
hears a really great Elsa, one realizes that the character is a
believable and pitiable character. Anyone who has ever heard
Lotte Lehmann knows the truth of this. Lehmann in the
very first phrase—that wonderful soft sigh, *"Mein armer
Bruder"*—evoked Elsa's mystery and laid claim to our sympathy. Lehmann made Elsa real. On the other hand, even if
a great singing-actor were to portray Lohengrin, although
we might have occasion to admire his art and to be excited
by the music, we should probably remain unmoved by any
interest in the Knight as a character.

But, though we are bound to admit certain musical and dramatic faults of *Lohengrin,* the total impression of its music is still glorious. Is there anything else like this music? Like all major works of art, it has a specific aura of its own. Wagner took over into the *Lohengrin* style many devices he had used in *The Flying Dutchman* and in *Rienzi,* things that he had learned from such diverse composers as Beethoven, Bellini and Meyerbeer. On the other hand, certain reminiscences of the *Lohengrin* style are to be found in Wagner's later works. Yet Wagner never wrote another *Lohengrin.* It is a unique creation. And at its best it is still astonishingly beautiful. The music is full of glitter. It is music that shimmers. Its color remains on the high side of the spectrum constantly, except for the opening scene of the second act, the scene at night between Ortrud and Telramund. Perhaps it is not too fanciful to say that the music, like the knight, is clad in a shining armor. Yet it is not metallic music, though Wagner was supposed to have said in later years that he thought he used too much brass in the *Lohengrin* orchestration. Elsa's appearance, with the pianissimo chorus and the remarkably suggestive question by the King, "Is it you, Elsa of Brabant?"; Elsa's answer which follows and her prayer in the first act; the chorus which heralds the appearance of Lohengrin (to me the finest moment of the first act); then in the second act the scene between Ortrud and Elsa, coming after a most conventional "operatic" end of the duet between Ortrud and Telramund; and the enormously effective though theatrical close of the second act; further, the entire love scene of the third act with its floating poetry; and finally, in the last scene, the overly familiar but nonetheless thrilling Narrative of the Grail—all these are high spots none of which have lost their luster.

After almost a century, however, dissension is still possible on the worth of *Lohengrin.* Curiously, two recent

Wagnerites disagree on it. Ernest Newman, in *Wagner as Man and Artist*, wrote that the Wagner of this period reaches the supreme height of his powers in *Lohengrin*. Lawrence Gilman, certainly no less an enthusiastic Wagnerite, dissented. He says in *Wagner's Operas*: "Save for the lovely, unrivaled Prelude—in which the chief thematic material of the score is developed with a concentrated power and a splendor of genius that are never equalled in the opera itself— *Lohengrin* marks the decline in musical vitality from its immediate predecessor, the Dresden version of *Tannhäuser*."

If I may add my opinion, I am with Mr. Newman. I prefer *Lohengrin* to *Tannhäuser;* very much so.

19. *Some Controversial Thoughts*

WORKS OF ART defy the law of specific gravity. It is a common occurrence that heavier and more formidable works rise in popularity beyond easier, lighter and more immediately appealing ones. Frequently a work which by all the rules should be above the heads of the ʾcrowd turns out to be a general favorite. The explanation that the weighty works are the better ones and that their public favor is due to their worth does not entirely hold water although it often seems true. Take the case of the Beethoven symphonies, the nine old aristocrats of the symphonic world: numbers three, five, seven and nine are the weighty ones and they are also the popular ones. Their "Hooper rating" outdistances numbers six and eight, which are equal though "easier" masterpieces.

I shall not attempt to analyze why the popularity of a work stands neither in direct ratio to its worth nor, as esthetic cynics claim, in indirect ratio. Perhaps—and this is merely a suggestion—the difficult work of art offers a challenge, and therefore we attack it with a greater will and expend more of our imagination on it: its very difficulty is its advantage.

Parsifal, Wagner's most formidable work, now enjoys greater popularity than even its creator—not an overmodest man—could have envisaged for it. It has surpassed in esteem others of Wagner's works such as *Siegfried* and *Das Rheingold*, either of which is a more stageworthy opera.

Undoubtedly part of the preference for *Parsifal* stems from the fact that it is a religious work, and that many people consider a performance of *Parsifal* tantamount to going to church. *Parsifal* has moral value; it is "good for you." At least part of the audience regards *Parsifal* as an exercise in uplift and an assertion in piety. At a time when people turn toward the spiritual, when books and plays on religious themes are in vogue, *Parsifal*, one of the major expressions of religious feeling in music, naturally gets the benefit of the trend.

Parsifal's popularity is nevertheless something of a paradox. For the truth is that *Parsifal* is formidable, long, difficult —and has its faults.

If we look at *Parsifal* without being overcome by the radiance of its subject, if we regard it simply as a work of art and not as a religious festival, it can be seen that this last work of a very great but perhaps weary genius combines some of his best music and some mediocre patches with a drama which is both repetitious and circumlocutionary.

Here we are confronted by a play in which a single natural and sensible question asked by its hero (whom James Huneker called "that formidable imbecile") would have made the plot dissolve at the end of the first act. Furthermore, an Oriental villain is expelled by the Brotherhood in contradiction to its own policy of forgiveness and love for everyone and disappears at the end of the second act without our ever knowing what becomes of him. There is also Gurnemanz with his beautiful white beard, who, like the *raisonneur* in the old-fashioned French drama, talks interminably and tells us in unmerciful detail the story of the theft of the spear, which is the real dramatic conflict but which has taken place before the play begins. Moreover, Gurnemanz, supposedly the symbol of wisdom and kindliness, treats Parsifal in summary and rude fashion, though he has previously rebuked his boys for similar treatment of Kundry.

And these are not all the contradictions and weaknesses of the play. The third act is dramatically (though certainly not musically) dull. Only the second act—the very secular seduction scene—is really dramatic, and only Kundry seems to me to be a really fascinating character.

Yet *Parsifal* is obviously a great work. Its true greatness lies not in its ethics or sentiment but—also obviously—in the music, which at its best is a consummate symphony written by a wise old man. It is church music, yes, in the temple scenes, but much of the time it comes outside the church and down into a world of both beauty and sadness. The humanity which the characters lack is to be found in the music. When Kundry speaks of Parsifal's mother, the music is as direct, and as poignant as the music in *Siegfried* when the young boy muses and longs for his mother. Indeed, the passage in *Parsifal* is better music. The "Good Friday Spell" is a *Pastoral* Symphony in itself; in it are contained the natural thrills that most of us have received from the spring, the sunshine, and good feeling toward other people. The Transformation Music in the third act is an *Eroica* of tremendous force. The Flower Maiden scene is plainly seductive music, enchanting and sensuous, and there is nothing wrong with that either.

Well, if *Parsifal* is music performed in an opera house, then let us not treat it as if it were a religious rite in a church. I am referring to the custom of not applauding after acts one and three, and of applauding after act two. This is now a tradition, and like many other theater traditions it seems to me to make little sense. I can well understand that one may not feel like applauding after the temple scene, but this ought to be something everyone decides for himself. The practical result of the present custom is simply that after act one there are always a few people who do clap their hands, and the ensuing outraged shushing is more disturbing to the illusion than applause could be.

Wagner himself, who thought of all his work in excessively devout terms, who regarded his theater as a temple, who set aside *Parsifal* from the contagion of the ordinary German opera house of his time and clearly marked it a "sacred fes-

tival play," was yet too experienced in the ways of audiences
to confuse the theater with the church. We know that at the
première of *Parsifal*, given for an audience which consisted
almost exclusively of the Bayreuth patrons, the audience did
applaud and that Wagner saw nothing particularly sacrilegious in that. After the second act he rose in his box and asked
the audience not to force the singers to take curtain calls at
that point. But he had no objection, he said, to the audience's
applauding and calling out the performers at the end of the
work. He himself left his box and went on the stage with the
intention of appearing with the singers and acknowledging
the applause. As it turned out, this was impractical because
some of the singers (Klingsor and others who sang only in
the second act) had already changed into street clothes. After
the second performance he did appear on the stage with the
singers. It was only at the first public performances that the
tradition developed which was followed for many years at
Bayreuth, that is, silence after the first act, applause after the
second and third, with the curtain being raised once more
after the opera was over to show again the last tableau. We
have gone a step further than Bayreuth by not applauding the
third act!

Ernest Newman says that Wagner himself applauded at
later performances. At the eighth performance he was seated
in his box at the back of the auditorium. After the Flower
Maiden scene, he clapped his hands and shouted "Bravo." The
Flower Maidens must have been exceptionally good because,
as Wagner wrote to the King, the parts were sung by artists
who were the stars of other opera houses and who had sung
Elisabeth, Elsa, Sieglinde and Brünnhilde in other cities. Did
Wagner, Newman wonders, think that he could applaud
without being heard?—for between himself and the spectators there were some rows of empty seats at that performance. He was heard, however, and some of the people in the

front seats "turned around angrily and hissed the unknown disturber of the peace." This did not prevent Wagner from repeating his tribute to the Flower Maidens at subsequent performances.

20. *Bel Canto at its Best*

NORMA is a perfect example of the grand in opera. It is
serious, heroic, mythical, opulent in canvas and in pageantry.
And it is stellar. The most famous divas of all time have been
attracted by the role of the unhappy Druidess. Norma is
truly a star role. In novels about opera stars, it is as Norma
that the heroine usually triumphs and usually on the very
night when the man she really loves leaves her forever or for
another.

Thus *Norma's* fame extends beyond those who have act-
ually heard the opera; and this fame pops up in unexpected
places. It is not generally known that the illustrious William
Schwenk Gilbert "began as a playwright by making burlesque of opera; he ended by making opera of burlesque"
(Isaac Goldberg). He wrote these early operatic buffooneries
for a real burlesque theater. One of them was *The Pretty
Druidess, or The Mother, the Maid and the Mistletoe Bough.*
It was a knavish piece of travesty in which what passed in the
Victorian era as a scantily-dressed Norma appeared and
called for

"A cup of tea, my customary fluid,
And the last number of the *Daily Druid*."

As a prelude to the enjoyment of *Norma*, it may be well to
quote a music critic of some astuteness who said that Bellini
in this opera "climbed to the summit of his power," and that
the composer "in these days of romantic extravaganzas and
overstimulation is a phenomenon who could not be too much
appreciated." Of *Norma* itself he says: "The action, bare of
all theatrical coups and dazzling effects, reminds one of the
dignity of Greek tragedy. . . . Can you tell me a picture of

the soul better executed than that of the wild prophetess, whom we see endure all phases of passion on to the final resignation of an heroic death? Is not everything we feel with her true and great?" Of the music he says: "Those who can hear in *Norma* only the usual Italian tinkle are not worthy of serious consideration. This music is noble and great, simple and grandiose in style. The very fact that there *is* style in this music makes it important for our time, a time of experiments and of lack of form."

Be careful not to use these words as an indictment of modern opera. For they were written in 1836, and they come from a little known and (as far as I have been able to ascertain) never-reprinted newspaper article. Their author was Richard Wagner.

He was young then, only twenty-three. But even later in his life Wagner admired Bellini. In this article young Richard accurately brings into focus what is both the thrill and the difficulty of *Norma*. "It is a difficult opera to give because its first requirement is singing, and we have as a rule only—voices."

Yes, *Norma's* beauty is first and last the beauty of song. It is conceived solely as melody—the kind of melody to which only that most flexible of all musical instruments, the human voice, can do justice.

How exquisite those melodies are! They are long-breathed, legato and lyric at one moment and in the next they are contrasted with exquisite vocal tracery. *Norma* is like the painting of a dark blue twilight landscape in which the flowers are painted with attention to every leaf. *Norma* is the triumph of bel canto, "beautiful song."

But though bel canto is an old art, it is by no means a distant one. For all its vocal trickeries and for all of Bellini's classic style, the *Norma* melodies are decidedly human. They are not so austere as Gluck's arias, nor so classically cold. Bellini had warmth, even a good deal of lushness. Later music inherited this Bellini lushness; it can be found in Liszt and in Chopin, in Puccini, and even in *Tristan*. It is a quality which the least initiated can enjoy.

It is only fair to add that not all of *Norma* is equally interesting or good. The overture to *Norma* is discouraging. It is loud and meaningless. There are arid spaces between the arias and the great ensemble numbers. But the high spots are so frequent and so high that we don't mind waiting. And early in the opera comes the "*Casta diva*," that miraculous apostrophe to the moon, that "peerless outpour," perhaps the most glorious single aria in all opera. (Bellini rewrote it eight times before he was satisfied.) It alone would keep *Norma* alive.

Norma has had a most romantic history. The composer himself was an improbably romantic figure, a Lord Byron of music. Heinrich Heine, the German poet, left us a description of Bellini:

"Bellini was a tall, up-shooting, slender figure, who always moved gracefully; coquettish, looking as if just emerged from a bandbox; a regular but large delicately rose-tinted face; light, almost golden hair worn in wavy curls; a high, very high marble forehead, straight nose, light blue eyes, well-sized mouth, and round chin. His features had something vague in them, a want of character, something milk-like; and in this milk-like face flitted sometimes a painful-pleasing expression of sorrow. It was this shallow sorrow that the young maestro seemed most willing to represent in his whole appearance. His hair was dressed so fancifully sad; his clothes fitted so languishly round his delicate body; he carried his cane so idyl-like, that he reminded me of the young shepherds we find in our pastorals, with their crooks decorated with ribbons. His whole walk was so innocent, so airy, so sentimental. The man looked like a sigh in pumps and silk stockings."

With all this charm Bellini possessed plenty of meanness

and would do almost anything for money. That *les femmes* should have been strongly attracted to such a man (and vice versa) is to be expected. His life follows a scenario pattern. All the elements are there: the seamstress who adored him, the wife whom he mistreated, the beauty who left her wealthy husband to follow the composer; and even the woman whom Bellini loved and who broke his heart (temporarily) by marrying another. She was the legendary singer, Maria Felicitas Malibran, the daughter of Manuel Garcia, composer, singer and impresario, who had so great an influence on New York's early operatic life, and who besides Malibran had two other famous children, Pauline Viardot Garcia, the singer who could sing Norma one day and Rosina the next; and the younger Manuel Garcia, the discoverer of the laryngoscope.

Bellini, like Donizetti, was a protegé of Rossini's. Rossini was most generous and helpful to him. This did not prevent some scandalmongers from whispering that Rossini had poisoned Bellini when the latter died of intestinal fever at the shockingly early age of thirty-four. Like Mozart, Schubert and Mendelssohn, Bellini should have lived longer.

When *Norma* was given for the first time, Bellini was already a famous composer. La Scala Opera House staged *Norma* with the kind of singers he could and did demand. Bellini knew that without great singing his operas meant nothing. Pasta sang the Druidess, Grisi was the Adalgisa, and Donzelli played the faithless Pollione. Yet in spite of these augurs of success, the première was a spectacular failure. Bellini sat in the orchestra pit, pretending to play the 'cello. But it was a transparent incognito; everyone knew that he was there, and everyone hissed him.

Bellini wrote to a friend: "I am writing you under the impression of grief, of grief that I cannot express to you but that you alone can understand. I have just come from the Scala; first performance of *Norma*. Would you believe it?

Fiasco! Fiasco! Serious fiasco! To tell the truth, the public was perverse. It seemed that it had come for the precise purpose of passing judgment on me and eagerly wished to subject my poor *Norma* to as sad a fate as that of the Druidess. . . ."

But the public changed its opinion. The second performance was successful. In the same season *Norma* was given forty-three times, and thus it started on its career as the most celebrated vehicle of the most celebrated singers of the world. Grisi, the first Adalgisa, became one of the greatest Normas. Malibran sang it. And so did Jenny Lind. It was one of her favorite roles. Lilli Lehmann was Norma, and it was she who remarked that Norma was more difficult to sing than all three Brünnhildes.

Difficult it is. We have to wait for a singer who not only understands but can handle Bellini's lyric line. But if one comes along—what an experience in beauty is *Norma* then!

Fidelio....

21. *A Misunderstood Opera*

IMAGINE THE UNLIKELY event that Mexico were to conquer the United States and that Mexican soldiers were to occupy New York. Imagine further that during this occupation a serious and thoughtful new work—a *Strange Interlude* or an *Our Town*—were to have its première. The New Yorkers would of course stay home, and the audience would consist mainly of Mexican soldiers with little or no knowledge of English. Such a state of affairs will give you a fair picture of the circumstances under which *Fidelio* was first performed.

On November 13, 1805 the French army, headed by Murat, had entered Vienna. Two days later Napoleon was already quartered in the summer castle of the Hapsburgs in Schönbrunn and was issuing his commands from there. Vienna was headquarters for the general staff. With troops in the streets and in the houses, even the theater-mad Viennese didn't feel like going out. All theaters were sparsely attended. Thus it happened that *Fidelio*, when it was given for the first time on the twentieth, was heard by a half-empty house and that most of the audience consisted of French soldiers.

The cast was not an unskilled one, though the first interpreter of that most exacting of all *Hosenrollen* was a young girl of twenty, Anna Milder. Haydn had said to her, "My dear child, you have a voice like a house," but the dear child could hardly have had enough stage experience to be convincing in the part. Pizarro was Sebastian Meier, who was Mozart's brother-in-law. (There exists an amusing anecdote about this Meier. He is supposed to have boasted to Beethoven that he could sing anything at all, that nothing was too difficult for him. Beethoven—who would take no nonsense from singers, performers or ducal patrons—wrote an accompaniment to one of his declamations causing the voice to

[170]

move over a series of scales, a trick which makes it extremely difficult for the singer to find the key. This was further aggravated by the musicians, who emphasized the off-notes. Meier fumbled, become angry, and said: "My brother-in-law would never have written such damned nonsense!")

Well, the French soldiers could not understand the German dialogue. And since in *Fidelio* most of the necessary explanation is given in the spoken dialogue, and since, anyway, the music is not as "tuneful" as French soldiers expected music to be, the fate of *Fidelio* was to be expected. It failed.

Other good operas have failed at first and suffered no harm in their later life. But the curious fact about *Fidelio* is that it has never been—and certainly not in our country— an unqualified success. Curious, too, is the fact that this work, which caused Beethoven more trouble than any other and which he called somewhat melodramatically "my crown of martyrdom," is still the one major composition of Beethoven which troubles quite a few people, which still causes controversy and about which critical opinion is still divided. Some, and by no means ignorant, opera lovers find it a bore; some, and by no means foolish, critics say that Beethoven had no real feeling for the stage. In that otherwise tolerant book, *The Opera*, Brockway and Weinstock devote a long chapter, called "The Beethoven Heresy," to an attempt to prove that "an unsurpassed creator of dramatic music was unable to evolve a successful music drama."

Yet a good performance of *Fidelio* is a tremendous experience. Given with a great conductor and a fine Leonore, the opera becomes uplifting and exciting, as anyone who has heard one of the Salzburg performances with Toscanini and Lotte Lehmann will testify.

Perhaps the reason we sometimes misjudge *Fidelio* is that we expect it to be what it is not intended to be. It is certainly not a legend drama in the Wagnerian sense of the word, nor is it a fast-moving blood-and-thunder creation like *Rigoletto*. It is a bourgeois and simple play dealing simply with lofty and moral feelings. That is the reason Beethoven was attracted to it in the first place. He preferred literature with high moral feelings. *Fidelio* belongs to a category in which German playwrights had already produced some notable examples, such as Schiller's *Kabale und Liebe* or Lessing's comedy, *Minna von Barnhelm*. I am not, of course, comparing the libretto of *Fidelio* in quality to these classic plays; I am noting its family relationship. We are unused to such bourgeois subjects in our opera-going experience. And that is why *Fidelio* may strike us as too simple and naive.

But grant it naiveté: grant that Pizzaro, the villian, is all villain, and quite a Desperate Desmond. Grant that Marcelline and Jaquino, the two characters inherited from the *Singspiel* and added for comic relief, are insipid. But after these defects have been admitted, there still remain dramatic situations of great pith and moment. The faithful wife is a genuine character and not a stock operatic figure. Indeed, the libretto has its moments; what is more exciting than the Dungeon Scene in the second act?

Furthermore, I believe that *Fidelio* contains some of the most beautiful music in all opera. I think that the quartet in the first act, with its andante introduction, the kind of slow, inward introduction that only Beethoven could write, is one of his magic creations. It is a Beethoven *Dankgesang* of the kind found in the last movement of the *Pastoral*, or in the lento assai of the String Quartet in F Major. It is interesting also to note that the *Fidelio* quartet is so eminently singable, because according to some critics Beethoven did not know how to write for voices! In the second scene, there is Leonore's famous aria. There is the beautiful Prisoners' Chorus, again a magnificent piece of voice composition. Finally there is the Dungeon Scene, a perfect fusion of drama and music. Here is Beethoven with his surest power as he takes us from the ice cold, dark, subterranean atmosphere of the duet between Rocco and Leonore to the intense, puissant shocks of the quartet with its tremendous climax, "*Töt erst sein Weib*," and finally to the jubilant allegro vivace of the duet between husband and wife. Even as the stage lighting goes from "gruesome dark" to brightest sunshine, so does the music rise from the darkest to the most exultant emotion. How can anyone listening to this music with unprejudiced ears fail to move with it or to be uplifted? Sometimes I think that an underground operates in the world of opera, or that audiences absorb opinions through osmosis. There must have been at one time prejudice built up against *Fidelio;* this prejudice still militates against it. I am convinced that someday the opera will come into its own.

In the meantime, I can only back up my own fondness for it by citing more celebrated authorities. One of these is Hector Berlioz. Berlioz wrote some illuminating essays on Beethoven and the nine symphonies. These are justly famous. His article on *Fidelio* is less known. He wrote it as a review of a production of the opera in Paris at the Théâtre Lyrique. He says: "The more I hear and the more I read Beethoven's work, the more I find it worthy of admiration. The general effect and the details of it appear to me equally beautiful; for everywhere energy, grandeur, originality and a sentiment as profound as it is true is to be found revealed.

"It belongs to that powerful race of calumniated works upon which are poured the most inconceivable prejudices and the most manifest falsehoods, but the vitality of which is so intense that nothing can prevail against it. Like those vigorous beeches, born amid rocks and ruins, which finish by splitting the rocks and piercing the walls and which rise at last proud and verdant, all the more solidly implanted on account of the obstacles which they have had to overcome in order to emerge; whilst the willows which grew without any trouble upon the river bank fall into its bed and perish forgotten."

Of the often voiced accusations—expressed before and after Berlioz and to this day—that the orchestra has the only worth-while music and that the opera is not singable, he says that these reproaches will always be made to composers who give an interesting part to the orchestra. He recalls Grétry's comment on Mozart's operas: "he has put the pedestal on the stage and the statue in the orchestra." "Truly, the people who are so prompt to blame the great masters for a pretended predominance of instruments over voices do not much esteem their learning or discretion; for we have seen, every day for the past ten years, the orchestra turned into a military band, a blacksmith's forge or a brazier's shop without startling the critics or causing them to bestow upon these enormities the least attention. So that, on the whole, if the orchestra is noisy, violent, brutal, insipid, revolting and exterminating for voice and melody, the critics say nothing. But if it is fine and intelligent—if it attracts a certain attention to itself by its vivacity, grace and eloquence—and if, notwithstanding all this, it still plays the part assigned to it by dramatic and musical exigence, it is blamed."

He then discusses the specific musical pieces. "The sixteen numbers of Beethoven's *Fidelio* all have a beautiful and noble physiognomy. But they are beautiful in different ways; and that is precisely what appears to me to constitute their principal merit." About the most famous aria, the "*Abscheulicher, wo gehst du hin?*" he writes: "I find the recitative a fine dramatic movement; the adagio sublime by its tender accent and melancholy grace; the allegro exciting ... opinion; but I am quite happy not to be of theirs.

"The theme of the allegro of this admirable air is proposed

by the three horns and the bassoon alone, which confine themselves to sounding, successively, the five notes B, E, G, B, E, during four bars of incredible originality. If these five notes were given to any musician who does not know them, I'd wager that in a hundred combinations there would not be found one to equal the proud and impetuous phrase which Beethoven has drawn from them, so entirely unforeseen is the rhythm employed. This allegro is considered by many people to have one great fault; it does not contain any little phrase they can easily remember. These amateurs, insensible to the numerous and striking beauties of this number, look out for their four-bar phrases as children look out for the prize in a Twelfth-Night cake; or as people in the country look out for the high B when a new tenor appears. The cake might be exquisite and the tenor the most delightful singer in the world; but neither one nor the other would have any success:

> There's no prize inside the cake!
> Where's the high note?

"The air of Agathe in *Der Freischütz* is almost popular; but then, *it has the note!* How many pieces, even by Rossini, that prince of melodists, have remained in the shade because they lacked the note! . . .

"Who knows whether light may not come sooner than we expect, even to those whose hearts are closed at present to this fine work of Beethoven, as they are also closed at present to the Ninth Symphony, the last quartets, the great piano sonatas of the incomparable master? A thick veil seems to be sometimes placed before the mind's eye as it glances toward one particular region of the heavenly expanse of art. It is thus prevented from perceiving the great planets by which the portion is illumined. But all at once, from some unknown cause, the veil is torn away. Then, at last, we see; and blush to have been so long blind."

PART III
SOME COMPOSERS

1.*A Little Known Document*

MOZART WAS SO extraordinary a child prodigy that he immediately attracted the attention not only of the general public, both music loving and sensation seeking, but also of professional musicians and scholars. For example, when he was in London, at the age of eight, he was examined by Daines Barrington, a philosopher and jurist. Barrington then wrote a long, scientific report to the Royal Society of London. Published in the sixtieth volume of *Philosophical Transactions*, Barrington's paper deals in detail with the child's astonishing power in extemporizing (while Barrington watched, Mozart had composed on the harpischord a love song and a "song of anger"), his sight reading (of a five-part manuscript score), his mastery at modulation, etc. Barrington was so impressed that he doubted the age of the boy (as given to him by father Leopold) and took the precaution of verifying Mozart's birth certificate before releasing his report. Incidentally, little Mozart was serious throughout the long examination and completely co-operative; only when a favorite cat entered the room did he slide off the piano stool, nor could he be brought back for a considerable time.

Barrington's document is well known. But there exists another report on the child prodigy which is almost unknown. At least I have not been able to find mention of it either in Jahn, nor in W. J. Turner's book, nor in the recent work by Paumgartner.

On their way back from London, father and son made their one and only sojourn in Switzerland. Among other cities they visited Lausanne, where lived a celebrated physician, Dr. S. A. A. Tissot. Dr. Tissot heard Mozart play, talked to him, studied him and then wrote a report which was published in the periodical, *Aristide ou le citoyen*. I happened to come across a copy of this article in Switzerland. While some of the article consists of general metaphysical speculations on the nature of the artist (*Aristide* was a metaphysical journal), it also contains certain specific observations which, as they are made by a trained observer and physician, are well worth noting. They do not, of course, explain the miracle of Mozart. They are only a contemporary description of that miracle. Here are excerpts from the article:—

"Gentlemen, without doubt you have heard the young Mozart. I am convinced that he made the same impression upon you as he does on all human beings to whom Nature gave the faculty of being able to appreciate manifestations of art. You have seen with astonishment a nine-year-old child who plays the piano like the great masters. You have heard with greater astonishment the testimony of trustworthy persons that he played finely when he was three years old. You will recognize that everything he plays is composed by himself and that all pieces played by him, including his free fantasies, show that power which is the telltale mark of genius, as well as that diversity which proves a fiery imagination and that agreeableness which shows a sure taste. Finally you have seen him execute even the most difficult pieces with a facility which would astonish us in a thirty-year-old musician. Perhaps you yourselves have posed the question, which, I take it, many people have already asked: that is, 'Do you understand it all?'

"It seems to me that it betrays as much stupidity to be astonished by nothing as to be astonished by everything. It is a sign of feeblemindedness to observe phenomena without trying to explain them. I have seen our young musician often.

I have observed him carefully. And when I now take the liberty to express a few thoughts about him, then perhaps these thoughts are not so far removed from your world of ideas as they at first appear to be. For the explanation of the young Mozart is intimately connected with the general question of the relation between the moral and the physical characteristic of a man.

"The same force which did not permit the child Ovid to talk prose to his father and constrained him to ask his father's pardon for the many verses he was writing, the same force which made the young Molière write comedies instead of upholstering chairs, impelled the young Mozart. They were born poets; he is a born musician. Is it then possible that one can be born a poet, a musician or a painter? Metaphysics must teach us the answer to that question. . . .

"But to return to our little Orpheus. He was born with an extremely fine ear and with an intellectual equipment which predisposed him to the influence of music. He is the son of a great musician and the younger brother of a sister whose playing has likewise excited admiration. The first noises he heard were harmonic noises. His susceptibility was aroused from his earliest childhood. He was able to reproduce the tones he heard immediately, and it is said that he made music from the moment when he heard it. . . .

"The musician receives at his birth such a precise and fine ear that the least false tone gives him pain, just as the ear of the true poet is offended immediately by a bad verse; whereas the man who makes verses only by rule and not by divine inspiration wastes most of his time in examining whether or not he has written any bad verses. The sensitivity and precision of young Mozart's ear are so great that false tones or those which are too sharp or too heavy cause tears to spring to his eyes. His imagination is quite as musical as his ear. In his brain there are present a whole series of tones at one and the same moment. A single tone awakens in him immediately all those tones which form with the first a melodic series and out of which a whole musical thought can be built. In human beings who have an extraordinary talent, all ideas appear only as they are connected with that talent. This was extremely noticeable in our young man. Sometimes he was drawn to his piano as if by a secret force and there, in playing, he gave vivid expression to those ideas which occupied him at the moment. One could have said that in such moments he was the instrument in the hands of music. One could have imagined him as a series of strings harmonically tuned and so arranged that it was impossible to touch one string without setting all the others in motion. In his playing there were to be found the same pictures which the poet puts into verse and the painter into colors.

"This still very young child is quite natural and utterly charming. He has extraordinary knowledge of music, but if he were not a musician he would probably be a very ordinary child. . . .

"*One can predict with a good conscience that he will one day be one of the greatest masters of his art.* But is it not to be feared that he who has blossomed so soon would soon wither? It is only too true that precocious children become burned out in the heyday of their youth, that the overworked tissues of their bodies lose their suppleness and make them unfit for further achievement. Yet has it happened that talented people were able to conserve their talent. Because the intellectual equipment which accompanies their talent performs the work so easily, the talent is hardly spent by use. It is to be observed that the work does not at all fatigue young Mozart. . . .

"Gentlemen, I have discoursed a long time on the childish musician. I should be remiss in my duty toward you if I did not call your attention for a moment to the moral characteristics of the child, a side of him which, quite naturally, will interest you more. . . . His heart is as sensitive as his ear. He has a modesty which is unusual for our age. . . . It is really uplifting to hear how he ascribes his talent to the Giver of All Things and how he remarks—with the most charming sincerity and with an expression of deep conviction—that it would be unpardonable to boast of such a talent. Not without emotion does one perceive all his signs of love for his father. His father seems worthy of such love, for he has devoted even more care to the development of Mozart's character than to the nursing of his talent. The father speaks of Mozart's education as sensibly as about music. What a satisfaction it is for him to observe that both his charming children are more flattered by an approving look from him, a look for which they search with tender uneasiness, than by all the applause of the public! . . . It would be most desirable if all fathers whose children showed exceptional talents were to imitate Herr Mozart."

2. *On Opera*

WHEN MOZART WAS twenty-five years old, he wrote to his father: "In opera, willy-nilly, poetry must be the obedient daughter of music. Why do Italian operas please everywhere, even in Paris, as I have been a witness, despite the wretchedness of their librettos? Because in them music rules and compels us to forget everything else...."

These opinions of the young composer were written before Mozart had produced any of his great operas. At the time, *Idomeneo* was the only major work for the stage he had finished.

The first sentence of this letter has often been quoted. I referred to it in the chapter, "Forgotten Man of Opera." The thought is true, if we apply it rightly. But it has contributed to a certain misunderstanding of Mozart's operatic art, to a certain lack of valuation of Mozart's ability as a dramatist. No argument remains about Mozart's music. But there are still those people who believe that he strung together arias of exquisite melodies and wonderful ensembles without worrying himself too much about the play for which he was writing them. The very power and loveliness of the music lead one away from any examination of the way the music fits the play.

Actually, Mozart was a superb dramatist. He was a true composer for the stage. He thoroughly understood its requirements. And he was concerned with all that happened on the stage; this meant to him—and means to us—words and action as well as song and music. The plays he set to music were of course eighteenth-century plays with eighteenth-century conventions. Some of these conventions may have grown strange to us. But any theatergoer with a little good will and a little imagination is able to accept strange conventions.

Susanna and Cherubino stopping for a hurried chat when in reality he ought to be making a getaway is a typical device of eighteenth-century comedy. At that, it probably places no more strain on credulity than the usual farewell-before-flight scene in a modern melodrama. Anyway, it is not believability which counts on the stage, but interest. And I feel sure that if either *Figaro* or *Don Giovanni* were given as a play without the music before a modern audience unfamiliar with the plot of either work, that audience would be interested. This would be less true of *The Magic Flute* because its action is naive, symbolic and at times confusing. And *Così fan tutte* is a special case: it is a piece of typically eighteenth-century fooling with implied erotic derision. But I'd gamble that *Figaro* and *Don Giovanni* would get good reviews as plays on Broadway.

Surely the fact that *Figaro* and *Don Giovanni* are good plays is due not only to the skill of Da Ponte but also to the interest which Mozart took in the fashioning of the librettos. We know from his letters and other sources that he did take an interest. However, the evidence of the opera itself is the most convincing testimony to Mozart's stage skill. With all the heavenly music, these operas would not be so popular as they are today had Mozart simply clothed words with melodies. As a stage craftsman he knew not only how to weld both together in such a way that the words help the music and the music helps the words, but he knew also how to intensify and accelerate the play's action through the music. There is instance after instance in these two operas in which, far from poetry's serving as the obedient daughter of music, music is the obedient daughter of the action on the stage. These moments are not only the "big" moments, they can be found not only in the climaxes of the play, but they are distributed throughout the entire evening to "keep things going." The recitatives, for examples, have a rich stage life of their own; they contain wonderful and subtle accents which highlight the action and give the words additional dramatic suppleness.

It is a combination of musical genius and stage ability which gives us the scene at the beginning of *Don Giovanni* where the Commendatore is slain, and the ensuing short andante trio of Don Giovanni, Leporello and the Commendatore. The music of the duel is exactly ten bars long, but this music, culminating in the bar-long chord which announces the deathly thrust, packs in its ten measures an incredible amount of dramatic underscoring and stage excitement. In the short trio which follows it, Don Giovanni is to sing "frivolously"; yet the music communicates not only his bravado but also his guilt. There are undertones of the shock that accompanies all death. The trio seems to me to foreshadow the end of the opera, the punishment of its hero. Yet it is only a brief moment; it passes quickly and unimportantly. But what genius in creating a mood on the stage is here revealed! ...

In later years, when Mozart was composing *Figaro* and *Don Giovanni*, he no longer wrote many letters which might throw light on his method of working. But from the days of *Idomeneo*, when he consulted his father about each step, we have correspondence which shows how much Mozart was concerned with the fitting of the music to the dramatic action. These are some quotations from the letters: —

"The second duet will be cut out entirely—more for the good then the harm of the opera. You shall see for yourself, if you read over the scene, that it would be weakened and cooled by an aria or duet, which, moreover, would be extremely annoying to the other actors who would have to stand around with nothing to do."

"It will be better to write a recitative under which the instruments can do some work; for in this scene, which is to be the best in the whole opera, there will be so much noise and confusion on the stage that an aria would cut but a sorry figure. Moreover there will be a thunderstorm which is not likely to cease out of respect for an aria."

"Don't you think that the speech of the subterranean voice is too long? Think it over carefully. Imagine the scene on the stage. The voice must be terrifying—it must be impressive, one must believe it real. How can this be so if the speech is too long—the length itself convincing the listener of the fictitiousness of the scene? If the speech of the Ghost in *Hamlet* were not so long it would be more effective."

These few quotations tend to show—though less convincingly than the operas themselves—that Mozart deeply interested himself in the drama on the stage.

Long before *Don Giovanni* and *Figaro*, he knew what he wanted both in the drama and the music. His father recommended to him "not to think in your work only of the musical public but also of the unmusical. . . . You know that there are a hundred ignorant people for every ten true connoisseurs; so do not forget what is called popular and tickle the long ears." Mozart replied: "As to the matter of popularity, be unconcerned; there is music in my opera for all sorts of persons—but none for long ears."

3. *Two Men in a Fog*

THE PATHS OF Berlioz and Wagner crossed on several occasions. But only once were they drawn to each other, only once did they really like and understand each other. And that was when both of them were away from home and thoroughly miserable.

In the spring of 1855, both Berlioz and Wagner were in London. Both were there as guest conductors, to earn a few pounds which they sorely needed. Both had come with certain stipulated conditions which, had they been fulfilled, would have given them a chance to present fine concerts. Different as these two were in their musical outlook, they were yet alike in their ability to interpret orchestral music in a way which shed new light on old scores. But before they were through with the concerts, both had reason to complain of the English fog, not only of the fog which lay over the streets, but also of the fog that lay on the musical life of London.

Wagner's London stay has been fully covered in Ellis' biography, which devotes a whole volume to it. The visit of Berlioz also has been described by himself and by his biographers. Nevertheless, because this double visit still makes a good story and because I have discovered a few sidelights on it in articles published in the *Musical Times* of London in 1903 on the occasion of Berlioz' centenary, and also in a book called *Half a Century of Music* by Francis Hueffer — we might briefly sketch these events once more:

It appears that Wagner's invitation to conduct the Philharmonic Society of London was actually one in which he played second fiddle (if I may use that expression about a conductor). The man whom the Philharmonic really wanted as a successor to Sir Michael Costa, who had resigned the year before, was Berlioz. In England Berlioz was considerably more famous than Wagner. That was only natural, since London concertgoers were well acquainted with Berlioz in person, while Wagner was a stranger. Berlioz had been to London three times before: once as a conductor of opera, when he had presented not only *Figaro* and *Lucia di Lammermoor* but also Balfe's *Maid of Honor* (imagine Berlioz conducting Balfe), once as a judge in a musical prize competition and once as conductor of the New Philharmonic, the young rival orchestra of the older organization which now sought him. But Berlioz was unavailable because he had just agreed to return to the New Philharmonic Society.

Wagner was suggested to the directors of the old Philharmonic by M. Sainton, a French violinist. Sainton himself had no personal knowledge of Wagner's capabilities; neither had any of the other directors. Sainton proposed him because "a man who had been so much abused must have something in him. This sentiment was received with acclamation and it was unanimously resolved that a leap in the dark should be made."

Wagner stipulated two conditions, first that there would be a second conductor for the "fiddle-faddle" (as he described in a letter to Liszt the minor popular works which were then always part of an orchestral concert), and second, that he could have as much time for rehearsal as he needed. As it turned out later, neither condition was met. His fee for eight concerts was to be two hundred pounds.

Wagner found London not only a depressing place—he undoubtedly missed Mathilde Wesendonck and his Asyl—but also expensive beyond expectation. Wagner was particularly frightened by the high prices of meals in the restaurants, the fact that coal cost him a shilling a day and that he had to spend a good deal of money on cabs. He had no top hat, which in formal England was indispensable for official calls; so he had to go out and buy one, and he seems to have had difficulty finding a hat that would fit his enormous head. So convinced was he of the extreme formality of the English at all times, that a day or two after his arrival he made his first official call on M. Sainton immaculately attired in full evening dress—at nine o'clock in the morning!

Though the length of the proposed programs reminded Wagner of the cry of the London bus conductors, "Full inside!", he went to work with a will. At his first rehearsal he conducted the *Eroica* without a score — at that time an almost unheard-of-fact—and "the orchestra and the few persons present were at once astonished and delighted at the new reading given to the familiar work, the delicacy of the nuances insisted upon, the intelligence and fire with which the melodies were phrased. After the rehearsal the musicians broke into a storm of applause such as has been seldom heard in an English concert room."

But troubles came quickly. The English critics almost unanimously attacked Wagner, and furiously. If these attacks seem incomprehensible to us now, we must remember first that Wagner's music was indeed novel to people whose current god was Mendelssohn, who had died eight years before; secondly, that they judged Wagner's conducting by the standards of that very idol, Mendelssohn, who had so long held musical sway over England's concerts, and Wagner's new, freer and more expressive style of interpreting music seemed to them just so many liberties taken with the scores; and finally that Wagner, never particularly gracious with the critics, made no effort to cater to them in London and failed, in fact, to make even the usual courtesy calls.

The most powerful critic in London was G. W. Davison of the London *Times*. Of the first concert Mr. Davison simply reported that "the result on the whole was by no means satisfactory." In his opinion this was due at least partly to the fact that "Herr Wagner conducts without a score before him, which says more for his memory than for his judgment."

Wagner suspected the critics to be in the pay of Meyerbeer, and while it is true that Meyerbeer used to invite critics to an exceedingly opulent dinner before the première of each new opera and that he used to send them more or less valuable "baubles," this accusation is probably without any more specific foundation. It is certainly true, however, that the London critics were exceptionally ill-tempered toward Wagner. Chorley, the famous critic of the *Athenæum*, even fumed against him for the singular reason that Wagner was not only a foreigner but also that he disliked "all such music as the English love."

Sainton relates that at the first rehearsal for the second concert, not a hand was raised to welcome Wagner when he entered, the musicians receiving him in absolute silence.

Nor did matters improve with subsequent concerts. At the fifth concert the overture to *Tannhäuser* was played. This is what Davison of the *Times* thought of it: "A more inflated display of extravagance and noise has rarely been submitted to an audience; and it was a pity to hear so magnificent an orchestra engaged in almost fruitless attempts at accomplishing things which, even if really practicable, would lead to nothing." Later he summed up by saying, "The engagement of Herr Wagner has not proved fortunate. No foreign conductor ever came with such extraordinary pretensions and produced so unfavorable an impression."

The public was not quite so hidebound as were the critics. (The public usually is not.) After the eighth and final concert they gave him (according to Wagner) "a storm of applause so continuous that I really felt awkward. . . . In this manner my absurd London expedition finally took the character of a triumph for me." One member of this approving public was Queen Victoria, who attended the seventh concert with Prince Albert. She and the Prince Consort talked with Wagner during the intermission, and she was so affable toward him that Wagner was almost moved to tears. He was, you will remember, at the time a political exile; he wrote to his wife, Minna, that after this expression of royal favor perhaps "the German police might let me pass in peace."

There was also one critic who disagreed with the rest. George Hogarth of the *Daily News* took a much more sympathetic view of Wagner than did the others. Perhaps he had acquired tolerance by reading some books written by his son-in-law, among the latest of which were *The Cricket on the Hearth, Dombey and Son* and *David Copperfield*. At any rate, he wrote this of the concerts: "Whatever differences and controversies may exist as to the doctrines and tenets of the musical school to which Herr Wagner is said to belong, and as to his own character as a composer, disputes into which we do not enter because we are as yet unacquainted with their merits, on one point he has left no room for question—his consummate excellence as an orchestral chief. . . ."

If Wagner had been most reluctant to leave Mathilde Wesendonck to go to London, Berlioz also had not been over-eager to make this particular trip. In fact, after signing the contract, he wrote a letter begging for his release because he had "a number of very advantageous propositions . . . from various quarters for next season which on your account it will be impossible for me to accept." The New Philharmonic was unwilling to free him from his promise, but the two concerts were arranged for the very end of the season so that Berlioz could fulfill some of his other engagements. He therefore arrived in London later than Wagner and knew before leaving Paris that, as he wrote his friend Auguste Morel on June 2d, "Wagner is sinking beneath the attacks of the entire English press. But he remains calm and unmoved, so I am told, convinced that fifty years hence he will be master of the musical world." (Wagner was then forty-two years old!)

The reception of Berlioz by the London critics was quite the opposite of Wagner's. Davison wrote: "Happily, M. Berlioz is a vast favorite with the Exeter Hall public and could not be easily swamped. He came and was received as before. He was not swamped but achieved a new triumph. Yea—'by Abs and by Adam'—he roused up his hearers to enthusiasm, and their applause made the walls tremble."

Wagner was present at the first of the Berlioz concerts, which included among other selections Mozart's G minor Symphony and the conductor's own *Romeo and Juliet*. (Berlioz did not, however, succeed in getting a chorus to sing the vocal parts.) Wagner liked Berlioz' playing of *Romeo* but was astonished, as he says in *Mein Leben*, "to find a man who conducts his own works with such energy sinking into the commonest rut of the ordinary time-beater" in the conducting of the G minor Symphony. In turn, Berlioz heard Wagner's last concert. His comment: "Wagner conducts in free style, as Klindworth plays the piano."

A few days after Berlioz' first concert, the two met in Sainton's home for dinner. They were the only two guests. Wagner writes of this and a subsequent evening to Liszt: "He was lively and the progress in French which I have made in London permitted me to discuss with him for five hours all the problems of art, philosophy and life in a most fascinating conversation. In that manner I gained a deep sympathy for my new friend; he appeared to me quite different from what he had seemed before. We discovered suddenly that we were, in reality, fellow sufferers, and I thought upon the whole I was happier than Berlioz. After my last concert he and the other few friends I have in London called upon me; his wife also came. We remained together till three o'clock in the morning and took leave with the warmest embraces." In the same letter Wagner also says:

"One real gain I bring from England—the cordial and genuine friendship which I feel for Berlioz, and which we have mutually concluded." And Berlioz, also writing to Liszt, says: "Wagner is splendid in his ardor, and I confess that even his violence delights me. He has something singularly attractive, and if we both have asperities, these asperities dovetail with each other."

It must have been quite a dinner! I wonder, was M. Sainton bored? Did he follow the conversation? What subjects the two discussed we shall never know. We do know that Wagner indulged himself in his usual "metaphysical flights" and that Berlioz, smiling, said, "*Nous appelons cela 'digerer.'*" It is perhaps not too fanciful to suppose that Wagner in deadly seriousness discoursed on the theme of "the folk" in art and on the regeneration of art through the people, and that Berlioz, ten years older and having lived his musical life in Paris, was a little skeptical. It is my guess that from the beginning of dinner at eight until they went home at one, Wagner monopolized most of the five hours.

Though the two met in later years, they never again were real friends. But that is another story.

4. *As Conductor*

WHEN MY GRANDCHILDREN grow up they will undoubtedly have their own favorite conductor. And undoubtedly, in discussing this new conductor with them, I shall assume that tolerant, wise, patient and superior smile which is so irritating in a member of the older generation, which in fact I find most distressing when it is applied to me by people who have heard Mahler and Nikisch. My grandchildren will be at a disadvantage, though. I'll be able to play them Toscanini's records and have the goods on them.

Since no such proof exists of the performances of past ages, I am free to form my own images of the singers, conductors and musicians whom I know only by name. I suspect I should not have liked Jenny Lind. I imagine I should have enjoyed Chopin's playing and disliked Paganini's. I believe that Schröder-Devrient, whom Wagner adored and whose portrait hung at Wahnfried, must have shown as an artist certain similarities to Lotte Lehmann. Schröder-Devrient did not have a great voice, but what voice she had she used so eloquently, so convincingly that the music glowed and lived. Her Fidelio probably had the same qualities of high-charged drama and womanly beauty that we used to admire in Lehmann's performances.

I like also to imagine that Wagner as a conductor was a little similar to Toscanini. This is not entirely romantic day-dreaming: the accounts of Wagner's methods of interpreting music do disclose evidences of this similarity. That is, they can be seen if one likes Wagner. And Toscanini.

Needless to say, Wagner did not have at his command the perfected virtuoso orchestra that we take for granted today.

What poor orchestras he actually had to work with, how meager were the resources of German music-making, can hardly be realized. Ernest Newman's *The Life of Richard Wagner* contains an illuminating chapter on this subject called, "The State of Music in Germany." Wagner not only had to deal with orchestras much inferior to ours, but he had no examples of fine earlier conductors on whom he could model himself. At the time of which I speak, Felix Mendelssohn was the only musician who had applied himself seriously to the development of the art of conducting. And the obstinate Richard was hardly likely to learn from Mendelssohn, whom he considered merely a salon musician.

Like Toscanini, Wagner came to conducting in concert halls by way of the opera house. When Wagner was twenty, he got his first theater job, as choral director in Würzburg. He then became conductor in Lauchstädt, Rudolstadt, Magdeburg, Königsberg and Riga. And after the miserable interval in Paris, he was appointed conductor of the Dresden Opera House, which post he held for six years.

As might be expected, he was an uncomfortable man to have around the opera house, even when he was setting forth other men's operas rather than his own. For he was intent on changing conditions which every man of sense had taken for granted. He was particularly difficult with singers who, having learned their parts, could see no reason whatever for relearning them. He was not, and could not afford to be in those early days, the venerable tyrant of the later Bayreuth days. But he got what he wanted by exercising his unique whirlwind charm, charm which he could turn on and off at will, with which he wheedled and coaxed, and which worked almost as well with the male singers as with the female singers. He had a frightening amount of industry and energy. He had absolute musical sincerity and a fanatical devotion to the work which was to be performed.

One of his great performances was supposed to have been Weber's *Der Freischütz*. In *Mein Leben* he tells us how much he admired this music and how as a young man he used to play the overture on the piano with many errors but with a good deal of feeling. *Der Freischütz* was already fairly well established as a classic and was beginning to share the fate of classics: all kinds of mistakes, false interpretations and general slovenliness had crept into its performances. Wagner restudied it in Dresden from the bottom up. He made particular changes in the tempi, using after careful study of the score those which seemed to him to "express the meaning of the melodies." The result was that a certain old 'cellist in the orchestra said, "Yes, these are the tempi that Weber himself used to take; for the first time I hear them again correctly." Weber's widow, who heard the performance, was enchanted by it and wished that Wagner "remain in his fruitful work with the Dresden orchestra." She could hardly have foreseen that Wagner could achieve anything more important than to be the interpreter of her husband's masterpiece.

Another work he thoroughly restudied and coached and partly rearranged was Gluck's *Iphigenia in Aulis*. He was not satisfied with the version of the opera then generally accepted in Germany but took recourse to the original Paris score. He was thus able to correct many misapprehensions which in the course of the years had clustered around the ordinary German performance of *Iphigenia*. He also took particular care with Gluck's *Armide*. Edouard Devrient, who had heard this opera conducted in Berlin by Meyerbeer, was delighted with the finer, more melodic interpretation under Wagner in Dresden, and commented on the "delicate movement and declamation of the music."

Wagner also restudied Mozart's *Don Giovanni*, paying particular attention to the neglected recitatives. He took these at a pace which made them into living dialogue and, as Hans von Bülow wrote to his father, thereby gave the dramatic action form and reasonable continuity.

In another letter Bülow said, "Wagner conducted the *Eroica;* he worked a miracle, incomprehensible! Nowhere have I heard the symphony performed like this. It was magnificent and exciting."

Perhaps more convincing than this testimony from a friend is the testimony of Hanslick, certainly not a friend. He wrote in 1863, after Wagner had performed the *Freischütz* Overture at a concert in Vienna: "An excellent conductor is this man, a conductor full of spirit and fire. . . . We do not wish to argue that all the practices which Wagner used for the rejuvenation of a work which after all is essentially young and healthy are necessary. Yet beneficial it was to hear the overture, which is usually run off in even slovenliness, now played with a new dash and exceedingly fine nuances. The gradual crescendo and decrescendo of the horns in the introduction, the tempo of the song in the allegro, which was a restrained tempo, and the broad singing of the two fermatae near the end—all these made the most beautiful effect."

Wagner's most important conducting deed was his interpretation of Beethoven's Ninth Symphony, which he presented in Dresden in 1846, '47 and '49. In none of these three performances, incidentally, did Wagner put his name on the program.

The Ninth Symphony was as good as unknown in Dresden. It was regarded as incomprehensible music. Wagner chose it for a concert for the benefit of the pension fund. The musicians were highly alarmed at this choice, and wanted to take up the matter with the King. Everyone felt that the house would be empty and the receipts poor with so obtuse a program.

But Wagner insisted. For the Ninth Symphony, which he had long loved, the score of which he himself years ago had copied out (for no printed full score was then available), meant a great deal to him; more, in fact, than any other music. In that winter of 1846, when he was plagued by the visions of *Lohengrin* and by his own despairs and doubts, he found in the music of the Ninth the mystic consolation his nature needed. He writes: "I sat before the open score. I pondered over the best means of performing this music, and as I did so, I sobbed and I shed tears. If anybody could have seen me, he might well have questioned whether such behavior was worthy of a Royal Saxonian Hofkapellmeister."

He worked like a fiend. The sculptor Kietz, who saw him often during those days, relates that Wagner came home completely exhausted from every rehearsal, that he had to change his clothes, and when he sat down to eat he sat with a silk cap pulled down over his ears because he was so afraid of catching cold.

First Wagner marked all the orchestral parts with exact dynamics and expression marks. Then, at rehearsals, he insisted that the orchestra observe these exactly and that they sing the melody. He demanded an even legato tone, equally important, he said, to a singer and to an orchestra.

He had his quarrels with the chorus, particularly because he demanded a portamento at the point where the chorus sings, "*Seid umschlungen Millionen.*" This the chorus said was impossible, but after repeated rehearsals they discovered that they could do it, and very well, too.

He held twelve special rehearsals for the 'cellos and bass 'cellos in order to coach them in his idea of the proper playing of the beginning of the last movement. He wanted a true recitative style, and he succeeded in producing a free declamation at once tender and energetic. This is, of course, the way it is done in every good performance of the Ninth Symphony today, but what a job it must have been to teach it first to a bass 'cellist used to playing oom-pahs!

He told the basses of the chorus that certain portions, particularly the *"Brüder überm Sternenzelt,"* could not be sung at all if they attempted to sing it in the usual way. It had to be almost exclaimed, almost invoked. "I was able," he relates, "to transport everyone into a really unaccustomed state of mind, and I didn't let go (shouting at them and singing with them) until I myself couldn't hear my own voice. I felt myself drowned in a warm ocean of sound."

Finally, he published at his own expense in the local paper anonymous reader notices which discussed the forthcoming concerts. And in order to make the symphony less frightening to the public, he wrote some program notes in which he illustrated the work with quotations from Goethe's *Faust*.

The result was a popular success so great that the receipts were higher than at any previous Pension Fund concert, and the symphony became the committee's safest drawing card for similar future occasions.

What Wagner must have been like during this concert you can glean from another description, that of Anton Seidl: "Though he was really small, he looked like a giant when he faced the orchestra. I shall never forget his huge head with the uncommonly sharp features, nor his wonderful, penetrating eyes, now full of life, nor his facial muscles with which he could command such clear expressions of emotion. He stood motionless, only his eyes flickered, glowed and pierced. His fingers twitched nervously. He communicated through the air with every single musician, and thus an unseen force penetrated the heart of every participant. Everyone felt this force, for no one could escape the look of this man. He held all the orchestra captive in magic chains; the musician could do nothing else: he had to accomplish the extraordinary. At the first rehearsals, his impatience, which wanted to have everything correctly performed immediately, seemed to turn matters topsy turvey. The men were confused and taken aback because of his strangely illustrative movements with the long baton. But then they understood that it was not a question here of the division of bars, but it was a question of the phrase, the melody, the expression. . . . Soon they were all in Wagner's hands. The weakest orchestra under him grew and played beautifully. The notes achieved life and meaning. The most exact rhythm and the noblest expression of emotion reigned. . . ."

5. *And as Coach*

IN THE FIELDS of athletics, college courses and opera the word "coach" has a special meaning: it is an instructor who "carries you along." The imaginative conversion of the original meaning of a word to describe something which is different but performs a similar action is known in the science of language as "figure" transference. This useless bit of philological information leads me to a point: namely that Wagner, when he undertook the task of setting the *Ring* on the Bayreuth stage, choosing the singers for it and teaching them his ideas of interpretation, had to be a coach in the original as well as the transferred sense of the word. He drew his singers from all parts of Germany, and having assembled them, he then had to teach them an almost entirely new method of singing and miming. It was uphill work and Wagner carried his artists most of the way, even though the performers he had assembled were exceptionally serious and well-disposed and eager to make the undertaking a success.

Wagner had remarkable qualifications as a coach. He was at home not only on the cloud-capped towers of Valhalla but also within the wooden O of the opera house. He was a practical and experienced man of the theater, adroit at getting his ideas across to singers and musicians, a diplomat when he wanted to be a diplomat, a panjandrum when the occasion required. He could cajole or threaten his workers into accomplishing what he wanted to have accomplished.

The best detailed description of Wagner's working methods is to be found in a book by Julius Hey called *Richard Wagner als Vortragsmeister*. The book is known to Wagnerian scholars, but it is unknown to general readers. It has, as far as I know, never been translated into English; even in German it has long been out of print.

Julius Hey was a singing teacher in Munich whom Wagner had met some years before Bayreuth and in whose abilities Wagner had great confidence. Now, in the summer of 1875, when it was rehearsal time in Bayreuth, Wagner urged Hey to give up his position in Munich and to join him in order to help coach the singers. As usual when he wanted something, Wagner recognized no difficulties in the way of his request, and in spite of Hey's pleading that he was needed at the final examination of the Munich music school, Wagner insisted that he come right away. As was also usual when he wanted something, Wagner had his way.

The book is the result of Hey's stay in Bayreuth, his conversations with Wagner, and the extensive correspondence between the two. In addition to describing the details of the rehearsals, Hey sets down some of Wagner's general principles by which Wagner chose his interpreters. Wagner's remarks are scattered through the book, and I have attempted to cull them and set them forth in some order:

Curiously enough, one of the things that concerned Wagner most—at least he speaks of it first to Hey—was a singer's appearance. "How," he asks, "can the spectator receive an impression of the courageous Tannhäuser or the idealistic Lohengrin if these roles are incorporated in singers of small, thickset stature, with a fat head without a neck?" One of Wagner's chief considerations in choosing a relatively unknown tenor, Georg Unger, for the role of Siegfried was Unger's heroic build. Wagner could not always fulfill his wishes—there were several homely singers in Bayreuth—but it is interesting to find that stage illusion was so important to him.

His second criterion for a singer was ability to handle the text. In German opera houses, said Wagner, there existed a most flagrant incomprehensibility of the text. In France it was different. Because Paris was the center of theatrical life, a rigorously clean language was cultivated at the Paris Opéra. Frenchmen in general had a developed sense for beautiful sounding, articulated language. The German singers not only lacked a natural capacity for mellifluous speech, they lacked even the instinctive desire to perfect themselves in this respect. They also lacked schooling. Wagner was delighted with Materna, the first Brünnhilde, chiefly because of her fine diction. She had learned it in the field of musical comedy, where she had begun her career.

His third requirement for a singer was ability to change the color of the voice. Wagner insisted that voice color must be flexible and must be suited to the particular emotion or situation in the drama. "What good is it," said Wagner, "if an intelligent singer manages to understand that the Elsa of the first act of *Lohengrin*—the heavily pressed and timid creature with her dreamy and visionary soul—is in reality a different Elsa from the woman in the third act who rushes to her doom with open eyes? I still despair of finding a singer whose understanding reaches so far that she can find for those two Elsas the appropriate expression of voice color and phrasing. . . . Instead of dark shadows in the voice at her appearance in the first act, one hears light tones. The chief intention of the singer is to sing as loud as possible, so that the audience can hear right away how much voice she really has. Then in the finale of the first act she screams. The delicate, mimosa-like Elsa of the first act, who can as yet hardly understand the happiness of her love and who, moved by her sudden change in fortune, thankfully joins the general jubilation—this Elsa suddenly becomes a conceited prima donna who steps, head high, to the prompter's box intent on outdoing the others and to make sure of sufficient applause. Now, if Lohengrin too succumbs to this temptation and

King Henry, the third of the triumvirate, places himself in the middle with utmost power of voice and drawn sword, then we have a real operatic effect and Meyerbeer . . . could well have accused me of plagiarism."

Long ago, Wagner added, he had expounded his theories of coloring the text to Tichatschek. The tenor had laughed and said, "Well, perhaps if you could throw those horrible consonants out of the German language. But the Italians are right when they say that German is *la lingua per i cavalli*—the language for horses." Only gradually was Wagner able to convince Tichatschek, and never with complete success. For example, in *Tannhäuser*, in the apostrophe to Venus, when Tannhäuser sings, "*O Königin, Göttin, lass mich ziehen*," Wagner insisted that Tichatschek pronounce his ö's in a dark voice. In vain. The tenor sang with the clear, light, usual tenor voice. The *clair obscure* of the voice for which Wagner strove was incomprehensible to Tichatschek. They quarreled, the tenor screaming, "Those damned ö's and ü's are and remain unnatural vowels, and you are not going to change that even if you stand on your head." "That," said Wagner, "can happen easily"—and stood on his head! But the tenor did not think it was funny.

We must not misunderstand Wagner: the stress he laid on clear diction and voice color—that is, the dramatic side of the singing—does not mean that he slighted the musical, the purely beautiful aspect. We know that he believed in beauty of sound, in a continuous and songlike melody. Wagner would have disliked any growling, forcing, pushing or oversharp accenting, the kind of "expressive" stressing that many Wagnerian singers have indulged in and called dramatic. Speaking of Tichatschek, whose art he admired despite some shortcomings, Wagner declared that the tenor caused the revival once more of hope that a German bel canto could be accomplished. Wagner drew a distinction between the Italian and German treatments of a text and noted the paradox that although Italian opera regarded the text as something incidental, the Italian singer considered it his duty to make that text understood in a distinct phrasing of word and sentence. And this in spite of bel canto! Not so the German singer. Wagner was, of course, talking of the older Italian opera; there is no evidence that he so much as knew of the existence of *Aïda*. Nor is the text in even the older Italian opera as unimportant as Wagner thought it was. Nevertheless, Wagner's insistence that both the instrumental and the sung melodic line must be spun in a continuous and "lovely" thread proves that he wanted beautiful singing both from the orchestra and the vocalists.

His fourth criterion for a singer was the one which may be most surprising. He expressed it when someone made a derogatory remark about Materna, who, as has been mentioned, started her career as an operetta singer, and who seemed to some of the pundits gathered in Bayreuth to have had "insufficient education" to essay so lofty a role as the three Brünnhildes. Wagner said, "Should I entrust my female roles only to singers who are capable of cogitating deeply—with every sentence that they sing—on the moral cause and appropriateness of my intentions? No. I wish for a natural talent musically endowed, with sufficient voice and made secure by sensible schooling. Temperament, in my experience, is the essential. It is the most valuable basis for all that the drama demands of an opera singer, both dramatically and musically. . . . Anyway, what need has a healthy instinct for the byways of reflection? . . . How often does it happen that a highly educated 'Herr Doktor' crammed full with university study sings miserably and without understanding while an erstwhile cigarmaker or wigmaker moves the audience to tears with his song? I won't deny that personally I find an educated man more sympathetic than an uneducated one—

especially if he can sing." We see, therefore, that Wagner considered temperament and not intellect a singer's requisite.

Wagner desired Hey's co-operation particularly in the coaching of the singer whom he had tentatively chosen for his Siegfried. This was a tenor by the name of Georg Unger, whom Wagner had met in Mannheim. Unger was then thirty-eight years old and had not particularly distinguished himself as an artist. But Wagner, seeking someone whom he could mold and, acting on intuition, felt that Unger had latent qualities just right for Siegfried. He persuaded the tenor to take a leave of absence from the Mannheim theater and to devote a year, a full year, to the study of the role.

Unger arrived in Bayreuth in the summer of 1875, a year before the festival was to take place. He was a colossus of a man, bodily an ideal Siegfried. Wagner felt happy when he thought of Unger as Siegfried and the equally resplendent Niemann as Siegmund.

At the first meeting of Wagner, Hey and Unger, the composer got down to business. "Let's have a few samples," said Wagner to Unger, "from *Tannhäuser* and *Lohengrin*. These two roles make different demands on voice and interpretation. Let's begin with the Venusberg." After Unger sang the first hymn to Venus, Wagner interrupted. "Well," he said, "now we know how things stand between the low E and the high G-flat. We also know that you sing a very comfortable Saxon and careless phrases. Now a different tack! Sing '*Inbrunst im Herzen, wie kein Büsser noch sie je gefült* (from the Rome Narrative in the third act).'" Unger did not go far. Interrupting him peremptorily, Wagner demanded "a supreme effort of all his vocal powers of expression" in singing the last two words.

How fortunate for Wagner that Unger was a sensible man! How fortunate that Unger did not lose his temper and that he wasn't famous enough to be conceited! For Wagner

minced no words. He spoke as if Unger had been a backward
schoolboy. No doubt he wanted to show Unger the difficulties of the task so that if he wished to quit, he could do so
at the beginning. He told Unger that he had much, much to
learn and that he was only at the threshold of being an artist.
"You will have to pay closest attention and will have to be
rebuilt thoroughly if you ever are to amount to anything.
You will also have to take care that Hey (whom Wagner
called his Don Basilio) doesn't run away. There is so much
new to be learned in so little time. This afternoon we will
hold the first rehearsal at Rubinstein's (the young pianist who
played the piano at the preliminary rehearsals). *Auf Wieder-
sehen* at five o'clock." Hey and Wagner were left alone, and
Hey began to voice his fears. For Hey perceived that Unger
had the typical German tenor's palate tone, a pressed, unfree
voice, "a voice in chains." Nor had he the faintest notion of
how to phrase a text properly. But to all objections Wagner
had an answer, and he expressed his arguments in such persuasive language that poor Hey could do nothing but say Yes,
he would see what could be done.

At the afternoon rehearsal, Wagner said to Unger, "Now
please sing without hesitancy and quite naturally, just as you
like, so that our friend can form his own opinions and will
know which way to guide you." By the way, this is characteristic of Wagner's rehearsing method. Later, in going over
the *Ring* with his artists, he usually rehearsed a large portion
without interrupting or correcting, in order to give the artists
an understanding of the whole. Then he went back and began
the bar-by-bar careful corrections. Here, while Unger strug-
gled with Siegfried's music, Wagner sang Mime. Hey writes
that compared to Wagner's interpretation Unger's singing
sounded forced, colorless, even incidental. Wagner not only
sang the cues but the entire part. He wanted to show Unger
by actual example what was required. It was a plastic model-

ing of tone and word, yet of a purely musical nature. Without "acting" Mime, without using hands or body, but purely by voice and words Wagner created a character which, Hey says, was indescribably vivid and real. It *was* Mime that stood before them. In spite of the fact that Wagner had no "voice," no particle of dramatic expression remained unfulfilled in the score. This example did not fail to make an impression on Unger. Through the mass of conventionality there appeared, here and there, a tone, a phrase that was new and alive.

Wagner's face was an open book. Looking at him, Hey could tell when the tenor did well, when he did badly. Sometimes Wagner's countenance was sunny, his lips moved and sang silently with the artist. At other times there passed over his face the shadow of a cloud, darkening when he had to repeat the same passage several times. When there was a short pause, Wagner noticed that Unger was in a depressed mood. Wagner then turned on his famous charm. He knew how to humor and encourage Unger. Without making any false compliments, he still was able to point to those passages which Unger had sung well, and he voiced his hope that he would be able to learn everything. Unger stood there "like a young student after his first duel," half courageous, half afraid, and heaving a deep sigh.

It would lead too far to recount all the details which Wagner taught Unger, all the admonitions which he imparted to his Siegfried. It is possible to get a feeling of Wagner's work in coaching a singer by giving only a few of the many nuances:

In the song of the forging of the sword, when Siegfried exclaims, "Hei-a-ho," with descending notes, the instruction was to sing as if it were a glad exclamation, almost a yodel. Regular "artistic singing" was here out of place, said Wagner.

When Siegfried enters in the second act and asks Mime whether it is here that he is to learn fear, Wagner wanted the voice to express a stubbornness, a hidden temper. The entire scene was to be given in a subdued voice, and not until Siegfried answers Mime's question as to what he would do with the dragon by saying that he would sink Nothung into him, was Siegfried to resume the victorious tone of the first act.

For the next scene, when Siegfried is alone under the tree, Wagner asked for a sweetly tremulous voice. Unger failed here; he gave the conventional tenor tremolo. The high point of this scene, musically as well as dramatically, was to be Siegfried's phrase, "Ah, if I, the son, could see my mother." Here Wagner appealed to the actor's intelligence, feeling, warmth, imagination and understanding. At the bottom of his voicing of the phrase was to be all the knowledge of singing he could summon. But of "studied technique" nothing was to show in actual performance.

For the ensuing dialogue between Siegfried and the bird, Unger was to find a new voice color. "Here," said Wagner, "you must find a childish tone, one full of curiosity. You must, so to speak, sing in a higher register, everything clear and friendly and with a pleasant chatter."

At the beginning of the Fafner scene his interpretation was to change and to assume a character of impudence and of cocksureness. The tone was to sparkle like Nothung in the sunshine. Hey reports that Unger tried so hard that beads of perspiration were standing on his forehead, yet the voice remained "Nothung in the sheath."

When Mime re-enters, something new was again to be added to the character of Siegfried. The song of the bird had awakened distrust in Siegfried against Mime. And this distrust was the root from which was to grow a new Siegfried. He was to develop from a boy to a young man who expressed his will seriously. His instinct of self-preservation aroused, it was to rise to the decision of self-defense. Siegfried's instinctive dislike of Mime, which had slumbered in him for long, was now to change into disgust, hatred and revulsion. To express this change Wagner demanded a noble and measured moderation, a holding back of the voice, a distance of bearing. Siegfried's last question, "In my sleep you want to murder me?" was to begin in a veiled voice, to change to a full voice in the third bar and to end on a note of deep emotion. . . .

These few examples convey, I believe, Wagner's consistently double conception, paying equal attention to music and words and welding the two without seams. We have since quite accepted this theory: it has become a truth which remains nonetheless applicable though everyone knows it and many have forgotten it. Whenever a singer comes along who gives a fine performance, he proves afresh that Wagner was right.

Wagner's work as a coach went, however, beyond words and music.

His concern for his interpreters went even beyond artistic considerations. Being a practical man of the theater, he knew what might be worrying a singer aside from his art. Wagner obviously had a problem or two on his mind in organizing the huge project; nevertheless he found the time to pay attention to the human side of his charges. He inquired of Unger whether he was satisfied with his lodging and whether the food in Bayreuth, which consisted every Sunday of roast goose and potato dumplings, was to his liking. He wanted to know whether Unger, who was over six feet tall, had found a bed long enough for him. Wagner remembered his own days in Riga when he, who was a short man, could never get a bed short enough, so that in spite of heaping all the clothes he possessed on the bottom of the bed, he always suffered from cold feet.

At the end of a particularly long rehearsal when Unger seemed completely exhausted—although Wagner, who was then sixty-two years old and who had been speaking and singing continuously during the rehearsal, still appeared quite

fresh—Wagner turned, linked his arm to Unger's, and spoke
to him with that combination of diplomacy, good nature and
truthfulness which a stage director must know how to employ. He said, "Perhaps we have demanded too much of you
today. Just think, we have worked almost three hours. It is
quite understandable that you are exhausted. But I want to
repeat what I have already told you on the first day of your
stay here. Your entire way of looking at life is too ponderous
and colored too dark. You must become more gay and sunny.
Please, no minor chords! The fresh and healthy love of life
of Siegfried you must never put aside. Don't think that your
way of life and your way of acting are separate entities and
that one has nothing to do with the other." Yes, it seems that
Wagner even attempted to change his singer's philosophy.

Wagner took like pains with his other interpreters, though
all of them did not need so thorough an overhauling as Unger.
Hill, for example, who was the first Alberich, understood his
part well, and the two Fräulein Lehmann, who were to
portray two of the three Rhine daughters, were also most
satisfactory though they trembled with fear of the strange
contraptions in which they were to be moved up and down
while they were supposed to be swimming in Wagner's
Rhine. Incidentally, the three assistants who were to direc.
the motion of these devices were Seidl, Fischer and Mottl,
two of whom became famous conductors later.

Though most of the singers believed in Wagner and were
devoted to their tasks, there were some doubting Thomases in
the group. Wagner needed all his patience and diplomacy to
hold the troupe together, and one or two bowed out, all the
same. One of the chief troublemakers was Niemann, the Siegmund. Hey tells the story of a *Die Walküre* rehearsal in
which Niemann, who was a more famous singer and therefore
less willing to take direction than Unger, did not come up
to expectation. Wagner kept correcting him and Niemann

became more and more nervous. Beet red in the face, Niemann suddenly burst forth in an anger which vented itself on Rubinstein, who had been accompanying at the piano quite faultlessly. Niemann, a huge man, grabbed the little pianist by the shoulder and shook him. There was a dead silence in the room. Wagner said nothing. He only looked at Niemann. After a short pause Wagner mumbled, "Please, let's go on." After the rehearsal Wagner invited his singers to the garden. While they were promenading, Wagner spoke to Hey of the incident. He told Hey how painfully Niemann's tantrum had affected him, particularly because Rubinstein, to whose endeavors Wagner owed so much, had been the victim. Wagner knew that the underlying cause of Niemann's behavior was his disappointment at not having been chosen for the coveted part of Siegfried. Wagner also knew that there were several members of the company who disapproved of this decision and made no secret of their disapproval to Niemann. Still, he felt that Niemann was eventually going to give a fine and manly interpretation of Siegmund, in contrast to "the pomaded and fatuous salon tenors."

While there were discoursing thus, Niemann came into the garden and joined a table at which sat Frau Jaide, who was to sing Erda. Niemann was moody and refused all refreshment. After a little while Jaide speared a piece of ham on her own fork and playfully handed it across the table to Niemann. This he took, and by and by he ate a little from Jaide's plate. Then he left. Cosima had watched the proceedings from her own table. It was characteristic of Cosima that she should be angered by such innocent bad manners. She sent a message with Wagner's servant, Schnappauf (a name which seems to come straight out of Carlyle's *Sartor Resartus*) summoning Jaide into the house. After a few minutes Jaide returned to the garden. "I am going," she declared and left immediately.

The consequence of the little scene was that Niemann, who of course heard the story promptly from Jaide, decided to throw up the part and quit Bayreuth instantly. Others planned to follow his example, and a meeting was called for the next afternoon in order to arrive at resolutions. Thus the entire project was threatened by the first-lady aspirations of Cosima. Etiquette undermined an epic. That day Hey had to leave Bayreuth to be present at the final examinations of the music school in Munich. When he returned three days later, he found matters still unsettled, the breach between Niemann and Wagner unhealed. Wagner was in a deep depression. That evening Liszt played to cheer him up, but when Hey bade him good night, Wagner said sadly, "We had been too lucky." Later the quarrel was patched up. Niemann returned to sing a superb Siegmund. Jaide was mollified and sang Erda. Unger, if he did not quite fulfill Wagner's anticipation, if he did not remember quite all he had been taught, was nevertheless a fine Siegfried and amply justified Wagner's faith in him.

6. *Conservative Revolutionary*

AS I WRITE this, in 1948, *The Barber of Seville* is 102 years old. More than a century is a long span of time in the relatively short history of opera; it is plenty of time for Rossini to have become a classic.

He has become a classic, though of a rather peculiar and special type. How many of his operas do we know? One—the *Barber*. How much of his other music do we usually hear? A few of the overtures. On so tiny a territory has Rossini grown to classic estate. As a matter of fact, his fame is built on hearsay—but more "say" than "hear." He is better known as a man than as a musician. He is famous as a prodigiously lazy fellow. And he is particularly famous as a prodigiously witty fellow. Almost everyone can repeat at least one good Rossini quip—such remarks as his reply to a pupil who brought him a funeral march composed in honor of Beethoven's death: "It would have been better if you had died and Beethoven had written the march." (This was one of Verdi's favorite anecdotes.) As to his legendary laziness, there is his well-known advice to a young composer that overtures should not be written until the last possible moment. Inspiration not only flows more freely at the eleventh hour but this procrastinating procedure has the additional advantage of driving theater managers crazy and making them tear out their hair. In his day, said Rossini, all the impresarios were bald at thirty.

The result of this and similar badinage is that we think of Rossini as the most carefree and casual of all the famous composers, a man who dashed off music without much thought or worry.

But was he really quite as slapdash in his work as he wants

to make us believe? Was he really so indifferent to it that he could—so the story is told—go to sleep while *The Barber of Seville* was being hissed and whistled off the stage?* Or was he rather one of those men who like to run themselves down, who belittle their own achievements, make light of their own importance? Perhaps this is a form of shyness, perhaps merely of coquetry. At any rate, the amount of work that Rossini did in his lifetime—thirty-nine operas and two major religious works—is more proof of *dolce far molto* than *dolce far niente*. Granted that he was able to compose quickly and easily, granted that he adapted, borrowed from himself and others, granted that he gave too little thought to the worth of his librettos, yet there is so much fine music in his operas so carefully and artfully worked out that the evidence of the music contradicts the evidence by the man. Why don't we hear more of this music? Because, as Francis Toye has pointed out, Rossini's was a tragedy of bad librettos. His music would be more widely known had he not coupled it with so many nonsensical plays. But even if we justly reproach him with carelessness in choosing texts, even when we know that he didn't rebel against the custom of accepting any libretto no matter how unworthy—"Give me a laundry list," said he, "and I'll set that to music"—we can more safely accuse him of lack of theatrical instinct or lack of force to break a tradition than of disrespect for his craft or indolence. Even the well-known story—once while composing in bed, he dropped a sheet of paper on which he had just completed a duet, but rather than climb out to pick it up he preferred to write an entirely new duet—simply points up the fact that if physically lazy, he was mentally industrious.

But the question goes beyond a matter of industry. I believe that Rossini, in spite of all those flippant remarks, took

*This story is at variance with Rossini's remark made to Wagner. See "Famous Failures."

his craft seriously. He jested about it. But he was no slipshod composer. His operas are products of a careful artist. Indeed, Rossini was so forceful and serious in his work that he insisted on and achieved certain important innovations and reforms in the opera house. He was not of course a teacher or a theorist. He did not speculate philosophically as Wagner did. Nor could he, like Beethoven, conceive of music as an ethical force. Rossini did not postulate. He knew, he said, only two kinds of music, good and bad. Yet this un-didactic man created a revolution in Italian operatic life, a conservative revolution perhaps, but one without which the work of Verdi and Puccini would have been impossible.

In order to understand this revolution better, in fact in order to understand Rossini better, we ought to go back and examine the state of opera in Italy when he came upon the scene. Italy at the beginning of the nineteenth century was a country where the operatic export trade far out-balanced the import trade. Italian opera was popular in the two major operatic capitals of the world outside of Italy: Paris and Vienna. But the reverse was not true. What was happening in those opera houses was virtually unknown in Italy. Gluck and Mozart were names which meant little to the Italian public.

Thus Italian opera was a home-grown plant and there were no visiting foreign bees around. The honey in the plant was of the lightest consistency. Opera was light music, light entertainment to be taken lightly—and to be forgotten promptly. An opera was as transitory a creation as is the ordinary radio script today.

There were four operatic seasons, the season of the Carnival, which was the most important and which commenced the day after Christmas; the season of Lent; a short additional season in the spring and one in the fall. An operatic composer was hired by the manager for the season; he was obliged to write a certain number of operas for that particular season without thought of carrying any of them over to the next season. When the composer joined the troupe, he usually had no opera ready in his portfolio. He first had to listen to the singers, learn who was available, find out what they could sing and what they *liked* to sing. Operas were tailored to fit the particular stars of the troupe. They were rewritten during rehearsals, much as early (and some current) movie scripts were rewritten while being photographed. Speed was of the essence; if an opera failed, it was necessary that another spring quickly into existence. Even if an opera succeeded, it had usually no more than thirty performances, after which the public demanded something new.

The thirst for opera was indeed enormous. Each major town in Italy had its own opera house, leased by a manager who usually operated with a subsidy granted by the local court or nobleman. Smaller towns were visited by itinerant troupes. Sometimes the opera house was run in connection with a gambling establishment. Barbaja, impresario of the San Carlo Opera in Naples and one of Rossini's first employers, had made his money from a gambling house in Milan and ran a similar establishment attached to the San Carlo opera house. If anyone grew bored with the music, he could take a few rounds at cards.

Since the turnover in new operas was so rapid, most operatic composers borrowed from themselves. If an opera had failed and something good had gone down with the rest of it, why not resurrect the worthy material? Rossini wrote a beautiful overture for an opera which failed. Very well, he used the same overture for another opera. This opera also failed. Rossini, however, still liked his overture. So he employed it once again, this time for—*The Barber of Seville*. Yes, the famous overture had served two operas before the *Barber!*

Most of the operas produced in such a hurry resembled each other as one Western movie does another. Operatic conventions were set in a mold. There were two kinds of operas, the serious type, called *opera seria*, and the musical comedy, called *opera buffa* when it had two acts, and *farza* when it had one. The *opera seria* was made up mostly of solo arias and duets; a trio was rare, a quartet or quintet most uncommon. The necessary business of the plot was explained by recitatives, and these were often exceedingly long. The two most important persons in the *opera seria* were the soprano and the castrato, later on the tenor. The bass almost never appeared.

Opera buffa allowed a little greater freedom for ensembles and combinations of voices. The bass voice was used for its comic effect. In both forms of opera the orchestra played only a meager part. The instrumentation had to be kept down to avoid overshadowing the singers. That is why few brass instruments were used.

As I have indicated, the Italian singer might well have said, and probably did say if not in these words, "I am the law." Since the customers came to hear him or her, the singer reigned supreme in the opera house. The composer was subordinate to the singer. The music had to be approved by the singers; they dictated how their entrances were to be staged and in some cases even the words they were to sing. Many of them had favorite "lucky" words which had to be used in the big aria. In the contract which Rossini signed for *The Barber of Seville*, it was stipulated—although he was by this time a successful composer—that "the said Rossini promises and binds himself to compose, and produce on the stage, the second comic drama to be represented in the said season at the theater indicated, and to the libretto which shall be given to him by the said manager, whether this libretto be old or new. The maestro Rossini engages to deliver his score in the middle of the month of January, and to adapt it to the voices of the singers; obliging himself, moreover, to make, if necessary, all the changes which may be required as much for the good execution of the music as to suit the capabilities or exigencies of the singers."

The singer of Rossini's day possessed a vocal skill incomparably greater than that of the modern singer. Whatever may be the modern singer's superiority in power of interpretation and musical feeling, the singer of Rossini's day was vocally a far better athlete. To show off the agility of his throat, the singer had become an improviser. He did not sing what the composer had written; he used the composer's melody as material which he could embroider. He improvised somewhat as does the jazz musician in a swing session. The singers of Rossini's day did swing their arias, and the more brilliantly they did it, the more they were applauded. The castrato led all the rest: in his aria the composer provided for a space of about twenty bars during which the castrato sang a cadenza of his own invention.

We must not forget that the art of improvisation which the singers practiced was in its way a most interesting one. Many of the singers were more than tricksters. Their cadenzas were often beautiful and of musical value. They must have been good, or how could they have held the audience's attention for so long? Actually, the evening's entertainment was longer than a Wagnerian opera. After the first act of the *opera seria*, a ballet was interpolated which lasted about an hour. After the second act, another ballet followed, so that the evening stretched from half-past seven until past midnight. The audience did not follow all the goings-on with rapt attention. During the less important scenes the people in the boxes visited each other, perhaps even made side excursions to the gambling house, or they ate refreshments. Berta's aria in the second act of *The Barber* was such a less important scene. Her aria was an *aria di sorbetto*, a sherbert aria, so called because people used to eat ices during it.

Into this world of entertainment, still brilliant but already cold-blooded, now stepped Rossini with his ebullience, his genius and his ambition. As I have mentioned, he was no theorist reformer. He would have found it ridiculous if anyone had suggested that the house which was connected with the gambling establishment was a temple of art, destined to uplift souls and make people better. Rossini wanted nothing more than to entertain his audience. But he wanted to do it in his own way, a way adequate to the expression of his richer melodies, his more flexible musical sense, his more refined feeling for comedy. One of his first improvements was to supply a more important role to the orchestra and to introduce into it certain instruments which, if previously employed at all, had been used sketchily. Mozart had done this too, had done it with far greater art. And both Rossini and Mozart were promptly accused of interfering with the singers and making opera thick and ponderous. To some *Don Giovanni* with its trombones was heavy noise. To some Italians *Tancredi* was tough going, though it did not take too long before Rossini's orchestration was enthusiastically accepted.

Rossini shortened the recitatives. In one of his first serious operas he used ensembles which had previously been allowable only in comic operas. And these ensembles took the place of recitatives. They carried the dramatic action forward. Here his innovation met with some opposition. One cultivated music lover, Lord Mount Edgcumbe (quoted by Edwards, one of Rossini's early biographers), objected to these "long singing conversations," and described Rossini's wonderful finales as "tedious succession of unconnected, ever-changing motives."

Rossini went further: he introduced the bass voice into *opera seria*. He introduced refinements into *opera buffa*, placing it nearer to comedy than to farce (a fact which some of the singers who appear in *The Barber of Seville* today forget). In short, he brought *seria* and *buffa* closer to each other, to the benefit of opera.

Important as these innovations were, they might have been merely the natural development of Italian opera and might have come along in due course without Rossini. Where Rossini proved to be a fundamental innovator was in his treatment of the singer. Here the change was sweeping. So sweeping, in fact, that he was accused of being the enemy of the singer. When he found that a celebrated castrato embellished his music to the point where Rossini could no longer recognize his own brain child, he decided that this had to stop. Henceforth in his operas there was to be no improvisation. And he began to write out whatever embellishments the singers were to use. Perhaps Rossini foresaw that the style would eventually become wearisome to the public, as singers were laying on improvisation thicker and thicker. He may also have realized that the singers were becoming less accomplished and that there no longer existed singing schools in Italy capable of producing the singers of the past. At any rate, he wanted his singers to sing what the composer had set down. It was brilliant, florid and often wonderful music that Rossini gave them. But what a commotion his demands must have caused! Not only among singers—even cultivated music lovers objected to the end of improvisation. They felt that opera would become static if no latitude were given a vocalist to vary the cadenza or coloratura according to the mood of the moment ...

So we see that Rossini was not altogether the casual composer he described himself to be. His operatic innovations were considerable, the most important being the halt to improvisation. Too bad he used all those poor librettos! Every time we hear snatches from his operas, we realize how irresistible, how enchanting his music is! Will the time come when we shall be willing to accept his librettos just to hear the music? Or is someone going to fit his music to new texts? Or are we always to continue to hear only the *Barber?*

7. *Feud*

IN EARLIER and more rambunctious days, the violent quarrel, the deadly enmity, the cut direct, the intrigue profound, in short, the well publicized feud, were standard equipment of the opera house. That one prima donna should get along with the other prima donna was unthinkable. And Rosina and Almaviva were either lovers off the stage as well as on, or they were not on speaking terms at all.

Voltaire's favorite prayer — Oh Lord! Make my enemies ridiculous—could have served as the motto for those operatic battles. The rivalry between Etelka Gerster, a famous Hungarian singer, and the divine Adelina Patti furnishes a typical example of the kind of duels that were fought. Patti hated Gerster so much that she ascribed all misfortunes and accidents to her rival. Once when Patti was singing in San Francisco and a slight earthquake occurred, she crossed herself and mumbled, "Gerster." Another time, when Patti was singing *Home Sweet Home* in a gala concert, the governor of Missouri, a spry, enthusiastic old gentleman, was so carried away by the song that he jumped upon the stage and kissed Patti. When this news was brought to Gerster, she saw no occasion for much comment. "Why speak about it?" she said. "There's nothing wrong in a man kissing a woman old enough to be his mother."

Less feline, but certainly no less scratchy, were the rivalries between operatic composers. Here, as you go back into history, you will find determined enemies: Puccini and Leoncavallo; Spontini and Weber; Mozart and Salieri.

Perhaps the best known of all operatic feuds is that between Rossini and Meyerbeer. Rossini was the most popular stage composer of Paris, the director of the Théâtre des Italiens, the father of more than thirty successful operas, when Meyerbeer appeared in Paris. Meyerbeer had started his career writing Rossinian operas. Then he proceeded to try his hand at a German opera, which failed. He then went on to produce another more spectacular work in Venice called *Il Crociato in Egitto*. It was this work which Rossini sponsored for production at the Théâtre des Italiens. So it was Rossini who introduced Meyerbeer to the Parisian public and thus set his own star to waning.

Five years later and two years after Rossini's ambiguous success with *William Tell*, Meyerbeer triumphed solidly with his *Robert le Diable*. And five years after that, in the year when Meyerbeer produced *Les Huguenots*, Rossini withdrew from any possible competition by leaving Paris altogether; he had remained that long only to pursue a lawsuit for money he thought due him from the French government. Now he retired to Bologna, where (according to him) he devoted himself to eating. Rossini returned to Paris only once more, nineteen years later. But he never wrote another opera; *William Tell* was his swan song.

Why Rossini, at the age of thirty-six, decided to give up the art which he had practiced with such apparent facility and which had brought him much money and fame, remains one of the major mysteries of operatic history. No one has come forth with a really satisfactory explanation, the least satisfactory being Rossini's own flippant answers. Was the popularity of Meyerbeer responsible? Was Rossini jealous of this grander practitioner of grand opera? We do not know for certain, but it is quite likely that if not Meyerbeer himself, then the swing of public preference to Meyerbeer's type of opera had something to do with it. Rossini's strength was his facility for beautiful, fast-moving melodies. He could not double in brass, the kind of brass which served the pomp and pageantry of Meyerbeer's grand operas.

The French always had a way of mixing music with politics. During the Restoration and until the Revolution of 1830, it was the sign of a good royalist to praise Rossini's music, which was classified with the romantic school of poetry and painting. And the romantic school, including Victor Hugo, Lamartine and Alfred de Vigny, began as royalists. Later on, when the trend turned toward stormy liberalism, Meyerbeer's heroic subjects and heroic music had more of an appeal. In 1837, Heinrich Heine wrote that the reason Rossini's vogue was declining was to be sought in the nature of his music: the predominant factor in Rossini's music was melody, which is the expression of man as an individual; while the predominant factor in Meyerbeer's music was harmony, which expresses man in his communal aspects. This shows that even a good poet can talk fruity nonsense about music.

It is probable that Rossini disliked Meyerbeer as a man. He considered him somewhat of a fraud. It is certain that Rossini disliked Meyerbeer's music. To a friend Rossini spoke of the brevity of Meyerbeer's musical ideas and his occupation with theatrical effects. He scoffed at Meyerbeer's slow method of working, and when he heard that Meyerbeer was taking "ten or twelve years to bring forth an opera," he said, "And I, insignificant person that I am, wrote *The Barber of Seville* in thirteen days." He called *Les Huguenots* a "voice breaker."

There were other darts, too, which were thrown by "Signor Crescendo" in Meyerbeer's direction, and these furnish the anecdotes which makes the feud interesting. Rossini was walking with a friend when he happened to meet Meyerbeer, who asked after his health. Rossini replied with a recital of various distressing symptoms, so distressing, in fact, that when Meyerbeer left, Rossini's friend suggested that they return home immediately. "Not at all," said Rossini, "I feel fine. But dear Meyerbeer would be so delighted to hear of my death tomorrow that I did not wish to deny him a little innocent pleasure today."

Meyerbeer, in his turn, used to send two elegantly dressed

gentlemen to every performance of Rossini's operas. It was the duty of these two gentlemen to sit in well exposed box seats and fall fast asleep fifteen minutes after the curtain rose. At the end of the opera, they had to be wakened by the usher. Regular opera subscribers were familiar with these *"sommeilleurs de Meyerbeer."* For a performance of *Semiramis*, Rossini sent two tickets to Meyerbeer himself. "Please do me the favor," he wrote, "of using these tickets yourself. The box is visible from all parts of the house. The chairs are comfortable. Shortly before the end of the performance, I shall have you waked. Your true admirer, G. Rossini."

8. *"Opera Guyed"*

CARL MARIA FRIEDRICH ERNST, Freiherr von Weber, composer of the sylvan *Freischütz*, was, like Wagner and Berlioz, a professional music critic at one point in his career. Weber's critical writings are not nearly so trenchant as those of Berlioz, nor so enthusiastic as Wagner's essays on Beethoven. (Weber rather disliked Beethoven.) But there is enough substance in them to show that Weber was a scholar, a gentleman and a judge of good music. He was most certainly not a judge of good librettos, and posterity has for this lack meted him out severe punishment by hardly ever performing more than the overture of *Euryanthe* or *Oberon*. Even *Der Freischütz* leads an uncertain existence outside its native country.

Though as a composer he could not select a good libretto for his own work, as a critic he could see the faults in others and was able to make fun of the stereotyped operas which came and went with great rapidity in the Germany of the early nineteenth century.

There is a little known piece of Weber's, never before published in English to my knowledge, which distills the standard libretto for each of three types of operas, Italian, French and German, suitable at any time in any opera house. These are a gift from Weber—any opera composer may use them.

Here is Weber's idea of grand Italian opera: "A long, emaciated and transparent figure appears. Her characterless face remains the same as heroine, as Seladon or as barbarian and continuously exudes an aura of exceeding sweetness. The figure wears a thin, flowing garment of an indeterminate color; on the garment are sewn little brilliant stones to attract the eyes of the public. As the figure enters, the orchestra makes a noise in order to induce the audience to keep quiet. In Italian this noise is called an overture. She begins to sing:

RECIT. *Oh Dio — — addio — —*

ARIOSO. *Oh non pianger mio bene*
Ti lascio — — Idol mio — —
— — — oime — —

ALLEGRO. *Già la Tromba suona — —*
Colla parte. Per te morir io voglio
più stretto — O Felicità — —
(On the syllable *ta* a trill of ten bars; the public applauds like mad.)

DUET *— Caro — —!*
— Caro — —!
A Due: Sorte amara — —
(On *amara*, on account of the *a*, the sweetest passages in thirds.)

ALLEGRO. *— Oh barbaro tormento —*
(Not a soul has listened, but a connoisseur shouts Bravo! Bravo! and the whole public follows suit fortissimo.)

THE END"

This is the classic French opera: "A well-born Parisian lady is promenading on the proscenium. She moves most decorously in a Greek gown which is too tight and uncomfortable. The corps de ballet surrounds her continuously while divers gods lurk in the background. The action takes place between twelve o'clock and noon.

FIRST ACT

LA PRINCESSE. *Cher Prince, on nous unit.*

LE PRINCE.   *J'en suis ravi, Princesse;*
Peuple, Chantez, dansez, montrez votre allégresse!

CHOEUR.   *Chantons, dansons, montrons notre allégresse!*

END OF THE FIRST ACT

SECOND ACT

LA PRINCESSE. *Amour!*

(Warlike noise. The princess faints. The prince appears, fights against his enemy, and is killed.)

Cher Prince!

LE PRINCE. *Hélas!*

LA PRINCESSE. *Quoi?*

LE PRINCE. *J'expire!*

LA PRINCESSE. *O Malheur!*
Peuple, chantez, dansez, montrez votre douleur!

CHOEUR. *Chantons, dansons, montrons notre douleur!*

A MARCH CLOSES THE SECOND ACT

THIRD ACT

Pallas appears in the clouds.

PALLAS. *Pallas te rend le jour.*

LA PRINCESSE. *Ah quel moment!*

LE PRINCE. *Où suis-je?*
Peuple, chantez, dansez, célébrez ce prodige!

CHOEUR. *Dansons, chantons, célébrons ce prodige!*

FIN"

For a libretto to serve the German opera, Weber wrote a most affecting tragedy called *Agnes Bernauerin,* "a romantic-patriotic play with music." This is too long to quote, but I can tell you that "the action takes place in the heart of Germany—with as many persons as necessary." And that the imposing first act finale is set in a mountainous forest landscape. "In the background to the left a castle; to the right a vineyard; in the foreground a hermit's hut, a cave, and an arbor, and in the center two hollow trees plus a subterranean passage." At one and the same time the hermit sings a prayer, Agnes sings an aria in the castle accompanied by a chorus of vintners; on the other side of the stage Albrecht, sleeping in the arbor, emits some disjointed tones in his dream; Caspar in the tree trunk is so frightened that he sings a Polonaise; a band of robbers hiding in the cave shout a wild chorus; and several genii float protectively above Albrecht. The noise of war is heard behind the scenes. A march is played far off. Of course everything simultaneously. Then two bolts of lightning crash on the stage from opposite sides and strike a few assorted objects. All sing "Ha!" and the curtain falls.

PART IV

OPERA IN AMERICA

When opera flourished
in New Orleans....

1. *The Devil's Synagogue*

THE FIRST American opera performance of which a record is extant occurred in Charleston, S. C., in 1735. Our operatic tastes—as all our tastes—were then influenced by the British. In England, a popular type of entertainment was the ballad-opera. It was a form more kin to the comic than to the grand, and it mixed English, Scotch or Irish popular ballads with disjointed music by Purcell and Handel. This particular ballad opera was *Flora or Hob in the Well*, and its announcement appeared in the South Carolina Gazette:—

> On Tuesday, the eighteenth inst., will be presented at the Courtroom the opera of *Flora or Hob in the Well*, with the *Dance of the Two Pierrots* and a new pantomime called *The Adventures of Harlequin Scaramouche*. Tickets to be had at Mr. Shepheard's in Broad Street. To begin at six o'clock precisely.

Another popular importation from England was the famous *Beggar's Opera* of John Gay. It was produced in New York fifteen years after *Flora*, and ran intermittently for a good number of years. One of its productions was described as a spectacle "with instrumental music to each air, given by a set of private gentlemen," which presumably means that an amateur orchestra played. The best of these productions were given in Philadelphia, which in those days was a considerably more sophisticated city than New York. In Philadelphia the Joneses tried to keep up with the Sir Joneses of London, and live their lives as nearly as possible in imitation of the fashionable overseas metropolis.

But these entertainments were merely light operatic forerunners. The heavy artillery of grand opera first came into play in New Orleans, the first city to give a regular season of French opera, which in our country preceded Italian and German opera in popularity. In 1791 a group of itinerant players fled from one of the frequent revolutions occurring in Santo Domingo and sought refuge in New Orleans. This was a weatherbeaten collection of troupers accustomed to playing under all sorts of conditions and to all sorts of audiences; they were quite as used to appearing in a tent as in a drawing room, in the open air as in a theater. Tabary, their manager, acquired a small theater in the Rue St. Pierre. It was hardly a setting of splendor; it was lighted by oil lamps and was uncomfortably damp—"a low wooden structure built of cypress and alarmingly exposed to the dangers of fire." But it served. There were no programs, Tabary coming out on the stage to announce the change of scenes. The repertory included French operas by Grétry, Monsigny, and others.

The theater prospered—Tabary called it Le Spectacle de la Rue St. Pierre—and became a popular meeting place of the townspeople. But as New Orleans grew, the "Spectacle" became inadequate, and Tabary then built a more elaborate opera house, the Théâtre St. Philippe, which had a parquet and two tiers of boxes and seated seven hundred people.

The St. Philippe was a show place but still not good enough for the operatic enthusiasm of New Orleans. Early in the nineteenth century, therefore, another enterprising impresario, one John Davis, also from Santo Domingo, erected a new house called the Théâtre d'Orleans. Like most of the old theaters, this one was soon damaged by fire. That was bound to happen, in spite of the tubs filled with water which were placed at strategic spots. But Davis managed to get enough money together to rebuild in 1817. The new theater had real boxes, galleries, and what were called "loges grilles," which were latticed boxes and which could be secured by persons in mourning, "who without being seen might witness the performance in comfort." I like the delicacy of this—

but perhaps it was merely an adroit circumlocution to tell people of quality that they could go to the opera incognito.

For in those days theatergoing was still considered *infra dig* by a good many good people. There was considerable objection also to the opera—not for sensible or artistic reasons, to be sure, but for moral reasons: the magic scene was judged too voluptuous and tantalizing for right-living ladies and gentlemen. A clergyman declared from the pulpit that the opera house was nothing less than "the devil's synagogue."

You will, I am sure, understand that such a pronouncement helped John Davis' business. More and more did opera captivate New Orleans. Families came from neighboring plantations, brought along their retinue of servants and put up at a hotel. Young Southerners fought serious duels over rival prima donnas, and young and old came to the Théâtre d'Orleans four times a week, twice for grand and twice for comic operas. The audience arrived at six and stayed until midnight when, possibly to salve their consciences, they left and went to mass.

Rules of the opera house were strict. Tuesday and Saturday were the fashionable nights, when the gentlemen were required to wear white gloves and full-dress coats, though in their choice of trousers they could follow their own inclination. No male spectator was allowed to enter carrying "a stick, cane, sword or saber"; these had to be checked at the entrance. There was, of course, no admittance without a ticket, "under penalty of fine or imprisonment." Neither noisy clapping nor hissing was permitted. No one was allowed to throw or pretend to throw oranges "or anything else" onto the stage. Operas became so important a part of the correct social life of that charming city that "all the fashionable young folks, even if they could not play or whistle Yankee Doodle, felt that the opera was absolutely necessary to their social success and happiness." During the 1830's the current manager used to go to Paris every year to recruit the season's casts. Then the chosen company would come over all on one boat, and New Orleans would turn out to meet them; the shops and schools would close, and the prima donnas would drive through the streets in open carriages. The Théâtre d'Orleans was still the fashionable house. In 1846 another gallery was added to this theater—reserved for slaves!

The performances must have been of good quality. A New Yorker visiting New Orleans in 1847 reported respectfully: "The French Opera at New Orleans is worth while; always good management, always good instrumentation; always an agreeable, fashionable and critical audience. The lobby was filled with critical young Creoles, whose family incomes or salaries as genteel clerks supplied the allowance for weekly visits to the opera. On simple benches sat the unwashed patrons of Auber, Donizetti and Halévy. There were no injudicious encores, no encores at all, in fact; no applause worked up at unseemly times; no snobbishness of look, action or language; no gross inattention." It can be seen from this that New Orleans had gone beyond the French repertoire. In fact, in the same year the management announced in the prospectus: "The first representation of the splendid opera in four acts entitled *Lucy of Lammermoor*, music by Donizetti. To be preceded by *My Friend Pierrot*, a vaudeville in one act. In Rehearsal: the celebrated grand opera, *La Favorite*, the last opera composed by Donizetti."

That was the golden period of opera in New Orleans—the time of Julie Calvé, a protegée of Rossini and a beautiful and intelligent singer, though prone to arbitrary fainting fits. Her era was succeeded by the reign of the young Adelina Patti, who made her New Orleans debut when she was eighteen.

Among the operas which had their American premières in New Orleans were *La Fille du Regiment*, *La Juive*, *Le Prophète*, *William Tell*, *Il Trovatore* and *Samson and Dalila*.

*Where to go in New York
on October 22, 1883....*

2. *When the Met Began*

"Situation wanted. Cook, good at soups, meats,
bread, biscuit, pastry; can serve course dinners,
do chambermaid work. Not afraid of washing
and ironing; city or country. Monthly wage $18."

THE NEWSPAPER which carried this attractive offer also carried the first advertisement of New York's Metropolitan
Opera House. It read: "Mr. Henry Abbey has the honor of
announcing that the inauguration of the new Metropolitan
Opera House will take place and the Fall season of Italian
operas will commence on Monday, October 22, 1883."

Aside from the fact that one could get a good cook for
eighteen dollars, New York offered many other attractions
on October 22, 1883. The great actor, Lawrence Barrett, was
appearing as Lanciotto, the Hunchback, in *Francesca da
Rimini*. At the Madison Square Theater a beautiful and edu-
cational spectacle, *The Rajah*, could be seen; at the Fourteenth Street Theater there was Miss Fanny Davenport—
billed somewhat uncomplimentarily as "America's Daughter
of Genius"—in Sardou's *Fedora*. At Daly's there was a farce
called *Dollars and Sense*. The Casino Theater was giving
Offenbach's *Princess of Trebizonde;* at Billy Birch's Opera
House the San Francisco Minstrels were holding forth; and
in the old Madison Square Garden, New York was able to
see its first horse show, "fully the equal of any in England."
The Thalia Theater, devoted to German plays, was running
the famous operetta, *Der Bettelstudent*.

Though one might think that the opening of the world's
most spectacular opera house was an event sufficient unto itself,
there actually took place three operatic openings on Octo-

[237]

ber 22. Colonel Mapelson, in irate and bitter competition, insisted on opening on the same night his season of grand opera farther downtown—or I should say not so far uptown— at the Academy of Music on Fourteenth Street. Colonel Mapleson, who had been serving New York with opera for a good many years, did not hide his displeasure over the fact that certain powerful and wealthy families, being unable to buy desirable boxes at the Academy, had finally succeeded in building their own better box to which the world now was beating a path. There was no nonsense in those days about being polite to your competition, and Mapleson let it be clearly understood that in his opinion the people who went uptown to the Met—such as Adrian Iselin, Cornelius Van- derbilt, James A. Roosevelt, J. P. Morgan or George F. Baker —were upstarts, misguided and uncultured. Still another opera company opening this same night was Maurice Grau's French troupe, in a presentation of Lecocq's *Le Coeur et la Main*, at the Standard Theater. Finally, if you did not care for opera you could nevertheless have attended a première on October 22, for Tony Pastor was opening his season of vaudeville.

The important serious dramatic entertainment in the offing was an engagement of Henry Irving and Ellen Terry. Their appearance in New York was being managed by the impre- sario of the Metropolitan, Henry Abbey. They arrived on the day before the Metropolitan opening. Abbey hired a tug to meet the boat, which was scheduled to dock at five in the morning. On this tug he placed a specially picked orchestra of players from the Metropolitan orchestra, conducted by the Metropolitan's conductor, Signor Vianesi. In the tug party were Lawrence Barrett, who brought the greetings of the Lotos Club to his famous colleagues, and Henry Irving's ad- vance agent, who had arrived previously. This was a young man by the name of Bram Stoker, who later achieved distinction as the most blood-curdling author in literature by writing *Dracula*. There is no way of knowing whether Irving and Terry liked their early morning Metropolitan serenade. It is recorded only that Miss Terry wore yellow "Bernhardt" gloves and that Irving dramatically climbed over the side of the boat and jumped into the tug.

Things were lively also in the literary line. The day of the opening Matthew Arnold arrived from Europe for a lecture tour. He remarked, with a fine sense of prejudice, that he feared he would never "get at the heart of real American life," and that there was no place like "dear old smoky London."

The Philharmonic season had not yet opened. (There was of course no Carnegie Hall—that came nine years later.) But the papers were discussing a proposal to give children's symphony concerts, and Theodore Thomas declared himself eager to co-operate.

Not all of New York's interests, of course, were occupied by matters musical or dramatic. The newspapers were much concerned because King Alphonso of Spain had been insulted on a visit to France, the reason for the insult being that he had previously accepted German hospitality. Maude S., the great trotting horse, was taken to winter quarters. There had been "Foul Work at Jerome Park Race Track. Rascally Conduct of a Jockey." Charley Ross was still missing, and his father had gone to Illinois to look for him. A man was arrested for driving his carriage too fast over Brooklyn Bridge. Stocks were "active and excited." A young lady in Wisconsin sat up in her coffin just as she was about to be buried. Chili and Peru signed a peace treaty. The French fashion forecasts for autumn had just come out. The new fans were of gray doves' plumage, and also of owls' feathers, with the owl's head as trimming and the owl's eyes made of rubies.

As the Metropolitan stars gathered from abroad, they gave out the traditional shipboard interviews. Italo Campanini, who was to be leading tenor, stated that he considered Christine Nilsson, with whom he was to sing, the greatest artist of the day and that, on the other hand, Patti, Colonel Mapleson's chief drawing card, was certainly not worth the five thousand dollars a night which Mapleson was paying her. There is no record that Patti sued him for slander.

Marcella Sembrich arrived on her first visit to the city which was to be her future home. She was scheduled to sing Lucia di Lammermoor in the second performance, on Wednesday. The press described her as a plump little woman, not strictly beautiful but pleasing, with luxuriant hair and perfect teeth. Mme. Sembrich had prepared herself for the crossing by living in a little cottage by the sea; the preparation proved ineffective: she was seasick all the way over. She said that "everything was so big in America," which could not have been news to the reporters. But then she startled them by announcing that she planned to give a concert at which she would not only sing but also play piano and violin solos. (This she later did do, in a concert for the benefit of Mr. Abbey, who lost heavily during his first season, and, as the program stated, "as a personal compliment to Mr. Abbey and on this occasion only." She performed in all three forms of music expertly and created quite a critical and popular sensation. Henry Irving and Ellen Terry also helped Abbey at this same benefit by appearing in the trial scene from *The Merchant of Venice*.)

As would be expected, there was heavy concentration of wealth represented by the first-night boxholders. According to statistics offered in the *American Art Journal*, a contemporary society paper of importance and standing, the occupational breakdown was as follows: "18 hereditary land fortunes, twenty-one bankers, five lawyers, twenty-one merchants and manufacturers, twenty-five Wall Street investors, five miscellaneous." This same paper commented with sanctimonious condescension, "Some of the fine people who now attend this opera owe their elevation to Florida Water, patent medicines, oleomargarine, lucky marriages. . . . Having money, they wish to spend it in a fashionable manner, hence the opera. It shows their good taste in selecting music which has a refining influence. In this democratic country, we do not stop to ask how fortunes are made if only the owners of them are polite, refined and gentlemanly. Society is so constructed even in America that there is no place in the upper circle for ignorance and vulgarity."

Most of the music critics commented sternly on the fact that the audience paid scant attention to the performance. Mr. Krehbiel wrote: "When the opening notes of the overture sounded through the house . . . everybody turned to his neighbor and began to chat in the liveliest manner." Succeeding writers describing the Metropolitan opening have retold this story and embroidered it. But in justice to the society of that day, we ought to remember first that the opening was intended as a social and not as a musical event, and second that there was not a great deal in that performance to command attention. The public of New York, which had its Philharmonic Orchestra and had heard good opera well presented, that public which was musically led by Theodore Thomas and Leopold Damrosch, was not quite so ignorant as we may think. In 1883 *Faust* was already thrice-familiar to this audience; it could probably have hummed most of the tunes. And Mr. Abbey's performance of *Faust* was in no way more spectacular or more modern or more newsworthy than the many performances the 3,045 auditors had previously heard.

The *Tribune* expressed this quite clearly. "The performance of the opera was on the average plane of performance of the same work by Colonel Mapleson and his artists, not better as a whole nor worse as a whole." The only things new about the performance were the costumes, which had been imported from Venice, and were said to have been very beautiful, and the scenic effects, including Faust's transformation and the flowing wine, which were "brilliant." The star of the occasion was Christine Nilsson, who was the original Marguerite of the Paris Opéra. She also was no stranger to New York. It is curious that she, one of the most bewitching, siren-like and soft French singers—like so many other great women singers, like Jenny Lind herself—came from the harsh climate of Scandinavia. At any rate, she sang Marguerite so well that it had unpleasant consequences for her. She was pursued by a man, eventually proved to be insane, who conceived the idea that Nilsson was in love with him and glanced on him alone when he was in the auditorium. He threw himself in front of her carriage and later burst into a reception given to her, threatening to carry her off. The affair finally went to court, and even there he escaped the policemen and tried to chase after Nilsson. He was locked up.

The tenor, Italo Campanini, was also a familiar artist to New York. His repertoire ranged from Lohengrin to Rhadames. He was a handsome, tall man and a good actor. His voice, however, at the time of the Met opening, had already lost some of its beauty, though "he gave off flashes of his old fire."

The conductor was Vianesi, who, to the admiration of certain critics, conducted without a score.

The opening performance began half an hour late, though today the Metropolitan is one theater which starts exactly on time. The first performance lasted five and a half hours.

The intermissions must have been exceptionally long, giving the people four occasions to become acquainted with the new house.

During the performance, Nilsson was presented with a

golden wreath. When she repeated the "Jewel Song" (the ban against encores did not go into effect until later), she used this wreath instead of the property jewels.

Justly, the chorus, which had been gathered and trained well in advance, received the most unstinted praise. The *Tribune* said: "The chorus is unquestionably the best chorus ever heard on an operatic stage in this country."

At 12:45 A.M. the première was done. The carriages were called. The people drove home, downtown and east. New York had an opera house which could vie with those of Europe. . . .

3. *Revelations of an Opera Manager*

THE NAME OF Max Maretzek probably does not mean much to you. It did not mean much to me until Erno Balogh, the pianist, who likes to rummage in second-hand book stores, found and gave me a little volume called *Crotchets and Quavers*. It is subtitled, "Revelations of an Opera Manager in America." It was written by Maretzek in 1855, almost a hundred years ago.

Max Maretzek was a violinist, a conductor and an impresario. As such, he managed the Astor Place Opera House for three seasons and did fairly well until the arrival of Jenny Lind who gave him competition which he could not meet. Historically he is noteworthy because he conducted the first New York performances of many operas which are now the staples of the repertory, including the three Verdi works, *Rigoletto, Il Trovatore* and *La Traviata*.

In *Crotchets and Quavers* he describes, with much vigor and some vinegar pressed from sour grapes, operatic conditions in the New York of the middle nineteenth century. For example, there is his description of a certain performance of *Norma*. It seems that the principal tenor of the company, Signor Benedetti, had quarreled with the impresario, a Mr. Fry, who had given the part of Norma to a singer who was not the tenor's mistress. Whereupon the tenor refused to sing Pollione, and it was now up to Mr. Fry to make him do it.

"It was on a stormy evening in December, that the operatic Napoleon entered the dressing room of our king of modern tenors. He found him painting his face. In the first place, the two monarchs glanced at each other. Their glances were such as a lion and a tiger might exchange, in measuring each other's strength. . . . The prince of tenors was literally burning with indignation and panting to avenge his blonde ally.

"After a moment of awful silence, the Napoleon of the Opera said, with that laconic brevity which distinguishes him:

" 'Friday, *Norma*. You, Pollio!'

"These four words were pronounced very slowly, and with an expression which would have caused a tremor in any other than the king of tenors.

"Passing quietly a damp towel over the rouge upon his cheeks and the lampblack upon his eyebrows, he calmly responded:

" 'Never.'

" 'Never?'

" 'Neve-e-e-e-e-r!'

" 'But the public wishes specifically to hear you with Madame Laborde.'

" 'Have the kindness then to inform the public that the principal tenor of this operatic troupe sings only with the queen of prima donnas.'

" 'That, sir, shall certainly be done.'

"Having registered this declaration, the Napoleon of the Opera rushed out of Benedetti's dressing room, and dashed upon the stage. He appeared before the astonished audience as unexpectedly as the ghost of Banquo rises through the trap at Macbeth's banquet, and *apropos des bottes*, announced to the public who had assembled in the Astor Place Opera House, to hear and quietly enjoy *Lucretia Borgia*, that Benedetti had positively refused to sing in *Norma* on the Friday following.

"Before anyone could understand what this extraordinary announcement might mean, he has vanished from the stage, and again stands before Benedetti.

"Waving his hand, he grandiloquently exclaims, 'I have now given you your deserts.'

" 'Then I will now give you yours, you puppy and liar,' replies the incensed royalty.

"So saying, he draws his sword and attempts with the flattened side of it (the edge was as blunt as stage swords invariably are) to castigate the manager.

"A fierce struggle ensued. . . . The prince of tenors soon found the Napoleon of the Opera entirely in his power. Turning him round, he administered a kick to his enemy. It took effect in that part of his body where the completed dorsal bone terminates, and the leg has not yet begun. With its force, he was sent three or four paces beyond the limits of Benedetti's dressing room."

Nevertheless, the performance of *Norma* was announced. And Mr. Fry, being more interested in revenging his own wounded feelings than in the welfare of his company, got an intrigue going among the public, to make sure that the assembled auditors would rebuke the recalcitrant tenor who had in the meantime decided to sing in *Norma* in spite of everything. When Benedetti appeared, "Screams, whistles, clapping of hands, hisses, trampling of feet, roaring, menacing outcries and gesticulations of every kind filled the theater. You might have imagined that the inmates of some half a hundred madhouses had broken loose and crowded it upon this occasion. To catch a note from the orchestra, was as impossible as to listen to the singing. After a brief time, chaos having roared itself hoarse, began to shape itself into some intelligible form, and a few cries of 'Order! Order!' were occasionally heard.

" 'What order?' retorted the friends of the manager. 'Off the stage with the rascal!'

" 'No! No! Go on and give us a tune,' roared the public.

" 'Order! Order!'

" 'Off the stage with him! He wouldn't sing when we wanted him. He shan't sing, now.'

" 'Apologize to Fry.'

" 'Fry be d——d! Apologize to Madame Laborde.'

" 'Never mind Laborde! Apologize to the public.'

" 'The public doesn't want an apology.'

" 'Give us a song.'

" 'Yes! Yes! *Yankee Doodle*. "Carry him back to Old Virginny." '

" 'Order! Order!'

"For some time Benedetti stood all this very quietly. Occasionally he would open his mouth in an attempt to sing. It was perfectly hopeless, and his lips would close again almost as quickly as they had separated. At length, he advanced a few steps and performed a curious specimen of pantomime supposed to be expressive of his desire to speak. As you and myself both know, the public is at all times a curious animal. Its curiosity at present, therefore, restored order. But this order menaced Mr. Fry's programme of proceedings. . . . He and those of his friends who were with him behind the scenes trembled lest by these means their own tactical arrangements might be turned by their astute enemy against themselves."

Mr. Fry has the curtain dropped and himself rushes out to the footlights:

"But what was his astonishment to find that the flattering reception indicated in his program was by no means accorded him! There must have been some unaccountable error committed by those to whom his arrangements had been entrusted. He gazed wildly around the house, but hisses, catcalls and objurgations couched in the most derogatory terms were all that could be afforded him. In his horror, he would not even have endured it as long as Benedetti had done but for the suggestions of some of the members of his orchestra. These, with a keen relish for his most unmistakable nervousness, encouraged him not to leave the battleground. At length, agitated and trembling, he was permitted to stammer out his speech, hissed by the friends of the tenor, applauded by his own and laughed at by the public, after which the performance was allowed to go on.

"Never, possibly, had Benedetti or Laborde sung better, and very certainly, never was there a greater amount of merriment elicited from its hearers by any farce than was then called forth by the lyrical tragedy of *Norma*."

*A composer visits New York
and finds a libretto....*

4. *Puccini's Visit*

OF ALL THE visits of famous composers to New York, Dvořák's was the most productive, Tchaikovsky's the most historic, Johann Strauss's the best paid, and Puccini's the most glittering.

The Metropolitan Opera House found it worth while to pay Puccini eight thousand dollars for a visit here in the winter of 1907. The contractual purpose of the visit was for him to rehearse the first Metropolitan performances of *Madama Butterfly* and *Manon Lescaut,* and to correct whatever errors had crept into the performance of *La Bohème,* that opera being already a well-established Metropolitan drawing card.

Puccini arrived here too late to do any rehearsing on *Manon Lescaut.* In fact, he arrived at six o'clock on the evening on which this opera was to have its première, and after getting through the customs formalities, was quickly rushed to the opera house. He entered the directors' box unobserved during the first scene. When the lights were raised at the end of the first act, the audience recognized him, the orchestra welcomed him with a big fanfare and the people cheered and waved handkerchiefs. "Extraordinary ovations," he wrote to Tito Ricordi. "I have never seen anything like it." He liked the performance, being pleased with Cavalieri's "temperament, especially in the moments of spiritual exaltation." She was indeed an amazing singer, an Italian who had climbed all the way from the Folies Bergère to eminence in the world's opera houses. Caruso, who was Puccini's personal friend, and whom (like most of his friends) Puccini alternately adored and damned, was "the usual marvelous **Des Grieux**."

Puccini then set to work rehearsing *Madama Butterfly*. He does not seem to have had an easy time of it. He didn't like Farrar at first—"she sings out of tune, forces her voice, and it doesn't carry well in the large space of the theater"— though he finally conceded that the role in which she gained so large a portion of her fame was finely interpreted by her: in fact, at his final interview he diplomatically or forgetfully told the press, "Oh, she is delightful. I had to tell her very little. It is all herself that she puts into the role."

Puccini was also displeased with the conductor and disappointed that Caruso had such difficulty in learning his part.

Between rehearsals, Puccini had time to have himself admired and lionized in New York's traditional manner toward celebrities.

He also had time to see New York. Puccini and his wife stayed at the Hotel Astor, "high up" on the tenth floor, which made him "dizzy." They roamed around and "walked across the old and the new Brooklyn Bridges very slowly." Later, as Johann Strauss and Arthur Sullivan and Dvořák and practically all the others had done, he visited Niagara Falls. He also had an opportunity to hear the Boston Symphony; he found it a wonderful orchestra. "Such warmth, such precision and vigor I have never heard. . . . I wish I could hear it play some of my things."

He also interested himself in a project for the education of Italian children in this city. A building fund for a school to be erected on the upper east side was being collected; Puccini sat for a special photograph and gave away autographed copies of this to anyone who contributed to the fund. He could be hard on autograph collectors, however. One man called daily and offered five hundred dollars for a line of music written in Puccini's hand. Daily Puccini refused, until one day he saw in a show window a motor boat he wanted (he was an enthusiastic sailor), whereupon he decided that it was worth writing out for his admirer the opening bars of the Musetta Waltz in order to help pay for the motor boat.

While he was here, Puccini concerned himself also with a new instrument which was to be of considerable importance to the consumption of his music. The popularity of the phonograph has so increased in recent years that we sometimes forget how old it really is. As far back as 1907 the phonograph was taken seriously by Puccini, taken seriously at least as a possible source of additional income. Puccini's friend Caruso had already given the phonograph respectability and impetus by making a number of records, including *O Sole mio*. Hence, during his visit Puccini published a letter in the *New York Herald* discussing copyright laws as affected by reproducing instruments. He observed that these laws were promulgated when "no such means of reproducing sound waves were dreamed of." And, he continued, "while I am heartily glad to note that eminent interpreters of my music, including fellow countrymen like Messrs. Caruso and Scotti, are not only paid princely honorariums for rendering solos from my operas into phonographs but are also allowed liberal royalties on the sale of those records, it seems strangely inconsistent that the composer of those very themes should not be granted slight pecuniary recognition. . . . I am sure that the American people, who are firm believers in the principles of justice, equity and square dealing, will join hands with Italy in the suppression of this form of musical piracy."

Furthermore, he wished not only to be paid, but also (and sensibly) urged: "If the music box manufacturers desire to reproduce my melodies, it seems to me that I should have the same liberty of selecting the medium and the method by which they shall be transmitted to the public as I have in choosing the managers and theaters to produce my operas...."

Madama Butterfly had its première on February 11. The
cast was a brilliant one; in addition to Farrar and Caruso, it had
Scotti as Sharpless and Homer as Suzuki. It was not only a
musical but a sensational occasion of first importance. Puccini,
leaning on his cane—he had suffered a serious automobile accident four years before—hobbled in front of the curtain to
acknowledge the applause. *Madama Butterfly* instantly captured the hearts of the Metropolitan audiences (it was already
familiar to most of them in an English version which had been
given the year before by Colonel Savage), though we might
have forgiven them had they shown some slight resentment
against Puccini for making Pinkerton so unsympathetic a representative of our navy. The newspapers also were enthusiastic; the *Tribune* said of Caruso, "No one would expect an
impersonation with even a tittle of dramatic illusion; but the
music is a perfect vehicle for his voice or his voice for the
music."

Since Butterfly was so successful, Puccini, always on the
lookout for his next libretto, now turned to another play by
the same David Belasco who was responsible for *Madama
Butterfly*. Puccini had seen the original *Butterfly* drama in
London and had been moved by the performance without
understanding much English. Now, not knowing much more
English, he went to see the Belasco play, *The Girl of the
Golden West*, which was then a great hit in New York.
Again he was attracted, and eventually he decided to aban-
don a projected opera on Marie Antoinette in favor of *The
Girl*. It is stated by at least one of Puccini's biographers that
Puccini saw the play only in the last days of his visit, and that
the idea of the new opera didn't come to him until weeks
later, when he had returned to Europe. I doubt that this is so.
I doubt it from reading the interviews which Puccini gave
during his visit. He, like many another composer, knew the
value of piquing curiosity; he knew the value of letting such

important news as the subject of a new opera slip gradually out of the bag. That he had something in mind, that in fact he may have seen the Belasco play earlier in his visit than is generally supposed, appears probably from the hints and half-denials he published while he was here.

About a week after his arrival, he said, "If I could get a good western American libretto, I would undoubtedly write the music for it. The Indian does not appeal to me, however. Real Americans mean much more, and there are costume effects to think of. I should think that something stunning could be made of the '49 period. I know the West only through Bret Harte's novels, but I admire them very much, as I have read them in translations. If I undertook a work with a Western subject, I should not necessarily visit the locality. Human nature is very much the same everywhere. . . ."

Then on February 18 (a month after his arrival) he wrote to Ricordi, "Here too I have been on the lookout for subjects, but there is nothing possible, or rather, complete enough. I have found good ideas in Belasco (so he probably already had seen *The Girl*), but nothing definite, solid or complete. The West attracts me as a background, but in all the plays which I have seen I have found only some scenes here and there that are any good."

He left New York February 28, 1908. In his final interview he said, "When I came to America, I visited the theaters a great deal, looking for something original. I wanted a subject for a new opera, not necessarily American, but something which had not been touched on in Europe, something which appealed to Americans. This being a new people, I thought it less likely to be bound by convention than European nations. I regret that I did not find what I looked for. What I do admire immensely is the American girl as portrayed in your plays. The naiveté of *The Girl of the Golden*

West is adorable. I was much impressed by the sincerity of your actresses. Your women are incomparable."

That sentence about "your women" is of course standard equipment of visiting politeness, but doesn't this statement sound as if he had already made up his mind, or at least was flirting with the idea?

Three years later Puccini returned for the world première of *The Girl of the Golden West.* The performance was a glittering one though the audience outshone the performance with a display of jewels and gowns unprecedented even for the Met. Caruso, Scotti and Destinn had the principal roles, and Toscanini conducted. The audience cheered and called out the composer and the dramatist. The critics were rapturous about the new opera. But the magic was in the occasion, in Toscanini's conducting and in Caruso's singing. The magic was not in the opera.

From that visit a grateful Met sent Puccini home in the Imperial Suite of the *S. S. Washington.* Said he: "A stupendous suite! Praise be to the Metropolitan."

5. *Visiting Fireman*

THE PHILADELPHIA CENTENNIAL EXPOSITION in 1875, whose management obviously had plenty of money to spend, offered Offenbach a regal sum to come over and conduct a series of concerts. (This same exposition had already spent five thousand dollars for what turned out to be a second-rate march by Richard Wagner.) The Philadelphians may have been guided by precedent, for three years earlier Boston, holding a musical festival in the cause of world peace, had paid Offenbach's competitor, Johann Strauss, a dainty $100,000 to conduct *The Blue Danube* next to the Charles River.

Offenbach did not want to come. His whole family disapproved of the idea. "It is madness," was their outcry. Not curiosity but cupidity finally tempted him. He was frightened at first. It was so long a trip for a Frenchman tied to a large family! He hoped until the last minute that the backers would default in their advance payment. But on the appointed day the cash was deposited. There was no way out but to take a solemn farewell of the family and to embark.

On the boat some traveling Münchhausen must have told him—by way of introducing him to the wonders of the new world—a fanciful story. Offenbach reports it, never doubting it. It concerns "two little islands known as Quarantine." It seems that there was a feud between Staten Island and Long Island. Neither one would take the sick people landed from the ships. "The authorities were puzzled. But in America it is not the custom to remain puzzled for long. The board met and resolved that since the two inhabited islands would not consent to receive the sick, two new islands should be constructed on which there should be no other inhabitants. A short time later the islands now before us rose out of the sea as if by magic. The whole spirit of the American people is revealed by this feat."

Of his reception he writes: "They had organized an excursion to meet me. Vessels decorated with flags and Venetian lanterns and a military band of sixty to eighty pieces waited at Sandy Hook, and when the ship was late, put out to sea to meet it. But as they got out, seasickness began to assert its rights and the musicians were not the last to feel its effects, which reproduced the same results as that in Haydn's comic symphony where the musicians disappear one after the other, putting out the lights as they go; but instead of giving forth sounds, they gave forth, one after another, their souls to the sea."

He stopped first at the Fifth Avenue Hotel, where for twenty dollars a day (they seem to have charged him a good price!) "you have a bedroom and a sitting room and the right of eating all day." He was much impressed by the hotel and its two hundred waiters, among whom, he said, he could find not one able to speak French. "When you are seated, the waiter, without asking what you will take, brings you a large glass of ice-water; for there is one thing worthy of note in America: it is that of all the fifty tables in the dining room there is not one upon which anything but water is drunk.

"After the glass of water, the waiter hands you a list of the eighty dishes of the day. You make your choice, selecting three or four, and the most comical part of the business is that all you have ordered is brought to you at once. If you have unfortunately forgotten to mention the vegetables you desire, then the fifteen vegetables down the bill of fare will be brought to you at the same time. So that you find yourself entirely surrounded by thirty dishes. All is arranged before you, bidding defiance to your stomach; the first time it makes you dizzy and takes away all appetite."

Later he moved to an apartment house and marveled that all the apartments were heated, that there were gas and hot and cold water at all times in all the rooms, and that he could have had, had he wanted it, a ticker tape machine. He approved of New York, approved of the fact that the streets were numbered instead of named, and of the bird houses in Madison Square for the homeless sparrows. He disapproved of the horse cars: "In case of necessity, the passengers would sit on the conductor's shoulders; as long as there is a projection free, a knee vacant, a step unoccupied, the car is not considered full." He also approved of the free lunches in the saloons. He called them "restaurants that serve meals gratis. One must really go to a progressive country to see such things."

But most of all he approved—in traditional fashion, but I think with perfect sincerity—of "our women." "Ladies and even young girls enjoy here the greatest freedom. I have an idea that when Lafayette went to America to fight for Liberty, he had only the ladies in view, for they alone are really free in free America. . . . It must be confessed that there are perhaps no women so fascinating as American women. Out of every hundred you meet, there are ninety who are lovely. . . . A strange fact for the depraved Parisian who is fond of following pretty women on the street is that no one in New York or in any other city in the United States would venture to take up his line of march behind a youthful Yankee maiden, and still less speak to her, even to offer her an umbrella. In order to be able to offer her this object, with or without your heart, you must be presented, or introduced, as they say."

Before going to Philadelphia, he played in New York at Gilmore's Gardens. Maurice Grau, later to become the impresario of the Metropolitan Opera, was then managing this attraction and did handsomely by Offenbach. He engaged 110 musicians, and the gardens were decorated with a cascade imitating Niagara Falls and with several Swiss cottages, which must have rather confused the geography but no doubt looked very pretty. At the first rehearsal he learned that "the musicians here have a vast and powerful organization, and have constituted a society out of which there is no salvation. Any one who wishes to join an orchestra must first become a member of the society." At the first rehearsal, Offenbach offered to join. Because of his eminence the musicians said it was unnecessary for him to join, but he insisted.

While he was in New York, he also visited the theater. Among his theatrical experiences was a minstrel show. He was enormously flattered when he noticed that the Negro orchestra, "playing tunes more or less fantastic," was pointing to him. He could not believe that he was known to so many Negroes. Returning after the first act intermission, he was amazed to see that the orchestra as well as the cast were all white, and he was quite incensed when he was told that these were the same men—with their faces washed. Blackface seemed to him cheating.

After giving rapturously received concerts in New York, he went to Philadelphia but had the misfortune to land there on a Sunday. "On Sunday the Exhibition is closed, the houses and taverns are closed, everything is closed in this joyous city; it is exceedingly gay. The few people one meets are coming from church with their Bibles and funeral faces. Should you be guilty of smiling, they look at you with horror. Should you laugh, they would have you arrested." He not only objected to the Blue Laws, but as a man of sense and sensibility he severely criticized the Jim Crow laws, and as a Jew he was angered by noticing that one of the hotels in which he stopped put out a sign saying "No Jews." "These excesses," he wrote, "increase greatly my respect for our effete governments."

Further, he marveled that Americans had such a passion for forming "associations with and without purposes; any pretext will do." He named the Temperance Society, the Masons, the Grand Army of the Republic, and others and made fun of their parades and honorary symbols.

But the most thrilling experience Offenbach seems to have had in America was an inspection of New York's fire department. He was, as a specially honored guest, permitted to sound a six-alarm. "All at once and from all directions the sound of bells is heard accompanied by a fearful rumbling noise. The engines arrive at full speed, roaring, hissing, puffing, emitting clouds of smoke and steam. Firemen and engines are on hand. 'Where, where?' ask the men. A sign stops this ardor. Each one returns to his post without a word of reproach or a sign of annoyance. All this in four and one-half minutes. . . . It is better than stage fairydom. It is real magic."

*When New York went
Parsifal-mad. . . .*

6. *Parsifal in New York*

THE HISTORY OF *Parsifal* in New York is a special one. New
York was the first city outside Bayreuth to perform *Parsifal*.
Wagner intended that his "Sacred Festival Play" be reserved
for Bayreuth. It is doubtful whether he really meant this res-
ervation to be a permanent one because there is evidence to
show that he was willing to give his favorite touring opera
company, that of Angelo Neumann, permission to include
Parsifal in the repertoire. There were no objections, either,
to concert performances of the opera outside of Bayreuth,
and Walter Damrosch gave such a presentation in 1886, seventeen years before *Parsifal's* New York première.

When Conried became the manager of the Metropolitan in
1903, he determined to give *Parsifal* as the second of the two
sensations he set before New York during his first season. The
first was the debut of a tenor named Caruso. The second involved him in a legal fight which was as lucrative to the
lawyers as it was productive of publicity. As soon as Conried
had announced his intention of giving *Parsifal*, Cosima, ful-
minating from the Wahnfried Valhalla, started the storm
which was followed avidly on the front pages of the world.
Cosima first declared that anyone who would have anything
to do with the New York production of *Parsifal* could never
again appear in Bayreuth. Felix Mottl, the conductor, therefore withdrew from participation in the New York production. Hertz took his place and conducted the New York
première. Cosima then took her case to court and tried to
obtain an injunction against Conried. This was denied by
the United States Supreme Court on November 24, 1903,
and Conried was free to proceed. But many ministers were
not of the court's opinion. They preached in the pulpit

against the production, and a delegation called on the Mayor of New York, Seth Low, to protest. The subject was debated in musical circles throughout the world, and it was by all odds the most popular subject for people who wrote letters to the editor.

It was also the favorite subject of the cartoonists. A Berlin comic paper published a picture of "The Rape of the Grail," in which a centaur with Conried's face carried off the struggling Cosima. *Kladderadatsch*, the popular German magazine, showed a sad and resigned Cosima dancing with Uncle Sam. And the cartoonist Arpad Schmidhammer gained wide circulation for a cartoon which showed Uncle Sam, marked Conried, standing before a grail represented as a safe filled with money bags, and holding aloft a rayonnant dollar which all the artists worshipped, while Richard Wagner from the grave of Titurel looked on.

You can imagine how all this pro and con drove up the temperature of excitement prior to the performance. Never was a première preceded by such garish publicity. The New York *Evening Telegram* published a "*Parsifal* Extra." Fanny Bloomfield Zeisler, pianist from Chicago, hired a special train called the "*Parsifal* Limited" to bring Chicago's curious to the occasion. From other points also special excursion trains came to New York.

The performance was scheduled for five o'clock on Christmas Eve, 1903, and people wrote letters asking whether they should or should not wear evening dress to a performance which started at that hour. They also gladly paid the special prices which were necessary, "owing to the unusual cost of this long-awaited production." An orchestra seat cost ten dollars.

New York went so *Parsifal*-crazy that even the staid New York *Times* allowed itself to publish a cartoon on the subject called "Parsifalitis." The cartoon shows a bewildered and wobbly-kneed Father Knickerbocker reeling in the streets while newsboys around him hawk their extras, all about *Parsifal*. One extra is marked, "*How To Dress for Parsifal*." An organ grinder stands in the middle of the street —all traffic has ceased—and he carries a sign, "*Parsifal* Selections Only." Every building in New York is plastered with signs announcing lectures about *Parsifal*. The biggest sign says, "Sermon Morning and Evening Denouncing *Parsifal* as Sacrilegious by Rev. Warn 'Em." Next to him the crowd is streaming into a lecture entitled "What *Parsifal* Means with Maps and Diagrams." But next-door a competitor announces, "Only Genuine *Parsifal* Lecture Here." He too has a competitor, a "Grand Musical Lecture Explaining *Parsifal* to Those Who Do Not Know by One Who Saw Wagner's Picture." All the advertising signs are completely devoted to the subject. There is a bargain sale of *Parsifal* hats; one can get *Parsifal* Cough Drops, a *Parsifal* five-cent cigar; the music store displays "Latest *Parsifal* Cakewalk"; there is a breakfast food called "Par-see-fall"; there is a novel, "1,000,000 Edition of the New Historical Novel, Parsifal Jr." And upstairs in one of the buildings is housed a Signor Parsifal, Mind Reader and Fortune Teller. In the background there is a beautiful new *Parsifal* Skyscraper advertising *Parsifal* flats. Finally, the smoke coming out of a factory chimney writes *Parsifal* on New York's sky.

On the afternoon of the performance, a few minutes before five, several trumpeters appeared at the Broadway doors of the Metropolitan and, no doubt to the astonishment of Christmas shoppers, stenographers and trolley conductors, blew several motives from *Parsifal*.

Thus was heralded the Christmas performance of the work which Wagner made believe he finished on another Christmas. For the score of Parsifal is dated December 25, 1881. Actually, *Parsifal* was not finished on that date. But Wagner wrote it thus on the manuscript because he wanted to present the score to Cosima on her birthday, which fell on Christmas Day. He had not had time to complete the orchestration of twenty-three pages of the final scene. So he skipped those pages, orchestrated the very last one, hid the uncompleted section, and laid the score under Cosima's Christmas tree. She never knew the pleasant deception until he confessed it to her.

In the first New York performance, Ternina was Kundry, Burgstaller was Parsifal, Goritz was Klingsor and Blass was Gurnemanz. Louise Homer sang the few bars of music allotted to "A Voice." Of the performance Richard Aldrich, writing in the New York *Times*, said: "A vast assemblage was gathered at the Metropolitan Opera House to witness it —an assemblage most brilliant in appearance and quality, following the drama with the keenest attention, with breathless silence, and submitting early to its spell.

"At the very outset it may be said that yesterday's production went far to justify the bold undertaking of Mr. Heinrich Conried, the new director; and that whatever else he may in future accomplish as head of the chief operatic institution in this country, he has made his incumbency long memorable by what he then achieved.

"The artistic value of the production was of the very highest. It was in many respects equal to anything done at Bayreuth, and in some it was superior. It was without doubt the most perfect production ever made on the American lyric stage. Those who wish to quarrel with the performance on esthetic, moral, or religious grounds have still as much upon which to stand as before; artistically it was nothing less than triumphant."

Financially as well as artistically, *Parsifal* was a success. It was given eleven times the first season, and these performances brought in nearly $200,000 in box-office receipts.

7. *Sculptor in Snow*

THIS IS the tale of a tenor.

He was the son of a mechanic. The mechanic had twenty-one children, of whom only three survived.

His first singing teacher thought little of the tenor's voice, which he described as "wind whistling through the window." His first full-fledged appearance in opera was rewarded by a payment of forty dollars, a pair of shoes, a suit of underwear and a handkerchief. His first real success came when he sang in Leoncavallo's *Bohème* in Milan. He was slender then and wore a curled-up moustache and gaudy clothes—just a tenor, just a man "holding a plume and a dagger and waving his arms about," singing in any opera house that would pay him, and singing any role which he could master without inquiring too deeply into its meaning. And yet, when a few years later he sang in *L'Elisir d'Amore* at La Scala, the conductor of the performance, who knew something about singing, said, following "*Una furtiva lagrima*," "By heaven, if this Neapolitan continues to sing like this, he will make the whole world talk about him." This conductor was Toscannini.

Conried engaged him for the Metropolitan without having heard him; the tenor's reputation was already considerable when he came here to sing in *Rigoletto*.

The critics received him well but not rhapsodically. He made an instant hit with the public. The Italians especially adored him and hung around outside his apartment waiting to catch a glimpse of him. After he had sung Rhadames and Canio, it was certain that opera lovers had found a new idol and that he was to become one of the Met's great stars.

Later, when other opera houses tried to charm him away, Gatti would hand him yearly a blank contract and let him fill in his own figure. Gatti used to say, "No matter what you pay him, he is still the least expensive." But he had a certain fixed top fee for his Metropolitan appearances, $2,500 per performance. When Otto H. Kahn offered him more, $4,000, he declined because so high a figure would mean "too much responsibility." Yet he did accept as much as $9,000 a performance from other opera houses. He used to write one-word criticisms—ranging from "fair" to "magnificent"—on the back of his pay checks when he endorsed them. His income from his records was also not paltry. Before he died he had earned $1,825,000 in royalties.

This money he loved to spend. He was almost foolishly generous, and at one time he was supporting one hundred people, for one reason or another, or for no reason. He was always handing out gifts, gold watches or bracelets, or medallions. He was also a collector who collected everything from amulets to zebra skins. He had an extraordinary, instinctive knowledge of art. He knew values and was rarely cheated. But he also collected gaudy waistcoats, impressive clothes (he changed his suits three or four times a day), good-luck pieces, anything he had ever used in any opera—and all his clippings.

Yet with all the spending he did, he was neat, almost fussy about his "budget," and knew quite well where his dollars went. He even jotted down an expenditure incurred on a day when most men lose their heads. He marked down "$50 for my wedding."

He never pampered himself or "took care of himself" as opera singers do. He once sang six major performances in eight days. He ate what he liked, and a very great deal of that. He smoked cigarettes incessantly. But with all the assurance he had, with all his certain resources, he never lost his stage fright. On the day of the performance, his accompanist would come to the Knickerbocker Hotel to play over the opera. (He himself could not play an instrument, nor did he know anything about the theory of music, about harmony or counterpoint. But he did know every part in the operas in which he sang, every word of every part, not only his own.) He arrived at the opera house two hours before the performance, intensely irritable and nervous and ready to throw things. He then fussed with his make-up and got himself into an even darker mood. Just before curtain time, the call boy would come around and say, "May we begin now?" That deferential phrase was used to no one else. The tenor then would step into the wings, flanked by his two valets; one handed him a sip of whiskey, the other a sip of sparkling water. Then he ate a quarter of an apple—and was ready.

As he grew older and as his voice darkened, he undertook more of the heroic than the lyric roles. He never sang Wagner, but he knew and loved the music of *Tristan* and *Parsifal*. He knew more than fifty parts. His only failure was *L'Amore dei Tre Re,* which he sang three times and then gave up. Two of his great dramatic roles were Samson and Eleazar. Unused as he was to reading, he spent hours in the public library, studying the history and background of these operas. He had a Jewish friend, a Mr. Scholl, who was head of the opera claque, and who adored the tenor devotedly. He went to Scholl for advice on the costume that Eleazar should wear, and learned *Eili Eili* from him.

The older he became, the more he grew in mastery. He was not a good actor at the beginning of his career, and he had many of the annoying Italian mannerisms; even his singing was not free of that Italian tenor sob which he had inherited from another tenor and which, in turn, has left a curse on later Canios. He said, and justly, that he had different voices for different roles, keeping each voice locked away in a secret compartment.

Though he showed real humor in the caricatures which he drew everywhere, including the backs of the scenery, his practical jokes, which were his pride and joy, were abominably unfunny. He could not resist putting a lump of ice into Farrar's hand during the first act duet in *La Bohème*, in order to give a realistic meaning to "*Che gelida manina.*" He could not resist sewing up Colline's coat nor doing tricks with raw eggs or rubber pigs on the stage. He also was passionate about cards. There was nearly always a poker game going on in his dressing room. He would finish the tenderest love song in that voice which Huneker called "gold swathed in velvet," and immediately rush backstage and ask, "Who deals?"

He always had customers, of course, for his card games. Everyone was his friend. John Drew, Ethel Barrymore, De Wolfe Hopper and George M. Cohan were his particular fans. He in turn never missed a Cohan show, and learned how to sing the words of *Over There* phonetically. During the first World War he also wrote a song, *Sempre libertà*. And for the country which he called his "good stepmother" he raised $21,000,000 in Liberty Bonds.

Booth said that an actor is a sculptor who works in snow. That impermanence is true equally of the singer. Yet somehow — and not through his recordings alone — this singing actor is an exception. He is as famous and as fabulous today as he was in his lifetime. To all those who heard him he is unforgettable. To millions who never heard him, to millions who have never been inside an opera house, his name is synonymous with the beauty of song, the ultimate in a voice, the ideal imagined but not experienced.

You will have guessed that this unique artist was Enrico Caruso, *b.* Naples February 25, 1873 — *d.* there August 2, 1921.

PART V

THE PUBLIC, PERFORMERS AND PERFORMANCES

*Opera has changed over
the years—but so have audiences....*

I. *Our Opera Audiences*

THIS IS AN AGE of large numbers and broad statements. We assert—with pardonable pride—that opera has an "enormous" audience and that "millions" listen to the radio presentations of opera on Saturday afternoons.

Though none of us can really picture what a million represents, we throw the figure about with a light hand. The Gallup polls and the national budget have accustomed us to strings of zeros. A "million" or "millions" is easily said. Then we get a look at the Hooper ratings, which measure the popularity of sponsored radio programs. The Hooper report says that last season (1947-48) the Saturday performances of the Metropolitan Opera had these average ratings: December 3.3. January 3.0. February 4.4. March 3.3. The figures mean that 3.3% or 3.0% or 4.4% or 3.3% of all the radio sets turned on Saturday afternoons are tuned to the Metropolitan broadcasts. This is about the same percentage as the New York Philharmonic captures on Sunday afternoons (though the N.B.C. concerts on Saturdays at 6:30 P.M. EST get a considerably higher rating).

Only 3% or 4%? The figures seem slim at first glance, particularly when we know that Jack Benny or Fibber McGee and Molly have an audience approximately ten times as large. But immediately we must consider that the leading programs are given at choicer times, in the evening, when more people can listen. Then we must ask ourselves—is it not natural that a comedian be more popular than an opera? Is it not to be expected that serious music have a smaller audience? Are the two entertainments, indeed, comparable, or are we comparing a joke book with a volume of poetry?

Let us shift our ground. Let us look at the statistics from a different point of view. Is it not remarkable that the figure is as high as three per cent? Consider how little contact most Americans had with opera before the advent of radio, consider how many people entertained the idea that opera was too exclusive, too difficult, too foreign for their enjoyment, and we must conclude that the popularity of the Saturday afternoon broadcasts is a double testimonial, a testimonial both to the people who listen and to opera itself.

For even three per cent represents a vast audience, one greater at a single broadcast than all the people who entered the Metropolitan Opera House in a span of ten years!

Whether the people at home listen to all of the performance, how intently they listen, whether the opera is but a background noise for the chores which have to be done Saturday afternoon, or whether the listening is done with quiet concentration, all these are factors which cannot be properly measured, at least not yet. But it is certain that many converts have been made, much curiosity has been piqued, and a great deal of enjoyment has been distributed. I repeat, it is little short of amazing that so wide an audience has been attracted to a form of entertainment which was originally meant to be seen as well as heard (for the spectacle is part of opera's allure) and which is now not only not seen but is also presented in a language unfamiliar to most of the listeners. If opera under these handicaps has pleased so many people, how many will it please when it is presented on television and, when as some day may happen, it is given in such a way that people can follow it completely? One does not have to go to the Delphic Oracle to prophecy a future for the opera.

The popularity of opera heard on the air has been reflected in the popularity of opera paid for. Without boring you with any further statistics, I can tell you that the Metropolitan audiences have increased in numbers over the past seasons. It is almost always difficult to get a ticket. When the Metropolitan goes on tour, it regularly plays to sold-out houses. The splendid season of opera given in San Francisco is equally popular. So are operatic enterprises like the New York City Center.

Why then do we not have more opera houses and more regular seasons? We have first-class symphony orchestras in many cities—why not opera companies? The Metropolitan still has, both by reputation and length of season, a corner on the market. Obviously such a unilateral state of affairs is not a good state. The answer lies in economics and not in the lack of demand. The demand for opera exists. But opera with a repertoire system is the most expensive form of entertainment. A deficit is inevitable, a large one is usual. There are traveling opera companies which avoid the deficit and even make opera pay. I believe that both the San Carlo Opera and Salmaggi's enterprise operate at a profit. But these are special cases.

Has the character of the opera audiences also changed? It is claimed that opera used to belong only to the rich, that its trademarks were the high hat and the diamond tiara, that people went to the opera because it was the socially correct thing to do. Today opera is a more democratic institution.

Such a generalization is both true and untrue. It is true that the high hat has gone out of fashion in the opera house. It is true that except for the opening night few people dress at the Metropolitan. The tuxedo and the full dress suit are more the exception than the rule. It is also true that most people who go to the opera now seem to go there to enjoy the opera. They go to see and hear, not to be seen and heard.

But before we draw too conceited a conclusion from that, we must remember that opera is still a high-priced entertainment, that society in the sense that it was known in the early part of the century no longer flourishes, and, most important, that a genuine music-loving public existed and went enthusiastically to the opera long before our own superior days. A true interest in music is of an older origin than some of the present-day historians would have us believe. The quantity of musical interest has vastly increased in the last generation. But musical interest of quality, of understanding and of appreciation has been in evidence in the Metropolitan Opera House for many more years than twenty-five. When we say today that the Wagnerian music drama has come into its own, when we observe that people sit in silence and absorption through a performance of *Tristan*, we who have an interest in music can be and are proud. But in fairness we should recollect that there was an enthusiastic audience for *Tristan* at the Metropolitan as long ago as 1886, when Lilli Lehmann sang Isolde and Niemann was the Tristan, and Krehbiel, then the critic of the New York *Tribune*, wrote a detailed criticism of the work which his paper thought important enough to be published in three successive issues. Wagner was the mainstay of the Metropolitan repertoire for seven seasons, from 1884 to 1891, and there is no question but that the audiences of these performances did not consist exclusively of social butterflies.

Perhaps it is true, however, that the opera has lost its importance as a meeting place for high society, that some of the snobbishness has been aired out of its loges, that it no longer is the showcase wherein the young lady from the finishing school can have the opportunity to meet exclusive suitors, and that in such a loss the opera has gained the strength of a theater for a broader public. The average age of the audience—I have observed in my twenty-five years of going to the Metropolitan—has certainly become younger. It has therefore become more American. Furthermore the differences of the various audiences are less marked. When I started to go to the opera, Verdi nights brought out an entirely different crowd of people than the Wagner nights. That is not so true today. Today also the Metropolitan attracts a great many sightseers. Perhaps because of the fame achieved through the radio, the Metropolitan has become one of the points to be included on a visit to New York, a sight only slightly less popular than Radio City Music Hall, but surely more favored than Grant's Tomb.

Changes in audiences do not come overnight. They are subtle and slow, and are to be observed more than to be measured. Even today, for example, a few of the Old Guard still exist. At most evening performances (except on the popular-priced Saturday nights) there are a few people who come in late and get up and waddle out before the close, who enjoy heart-to-heart conversations while the music is going on, and who in general behave as if they had come to the Metropolitan as a social duty and decidedly not for the music. It is to these few members of a fading tradition that I dedicate my next chapter.

*Practical hints for those who go
to the opera only because it is
the thing to do....*

2. *How Not to Enjoy the Opera*

FIRST AND FOREMOST, be sure not to clutter your mind with any advance idea of what the opera is about. If you know the story, if you know the dramatic reasons why the characters behave as they do, if in addition you know some of the words that are expressed in song, then there is danger that you might enjoy the opera merely as dramatic entertainment. So, 'tis folly to be wise. Be baffled! And be sure to stay baffled! If you have come to the opera house hardly knowing what opera is being given and not caring what happens therein, you must not weaken halfway through. I have seen people go staunchly into the opera without the faintest knowledge of what they were about to hear—and then during act one or two give up and hastily consult a synopsis. This is not cricket.

TIME OF ARRIVAL. Here the saddest change has taken place. Time was when every overture served as entrance march of the guests, when people drifted in unhurriedly throughout the first act. The Met treasures a letter from a subscriber of a past day who requested that the singing of the "*Celeste Aïda*," which Verdi placed at the beginning of the opera, be transferred to a later point as she couldn't possibly arrive in time for the aria. People knew what they wanted in those days, and took seriously the admonition to be found in an old French book on etiquette: "*Ca sent la province d'arriver avant le commencement d'un concert*." Nowadays nearly everyone is in his seat when the lights go down, and even most of the boxes, those black holes of calculation, are filled at curtain time. But make it your business to uphold tradition, never appear promptly, and when you do arrive, unwrap yourself in leisure. Just because most people are on time, a belated entrance is especially effective these days.

TIME OF DEPARTURE. For the best effect, this should be either at the beginning or in the middle of the last scene. The final portions of opera are usually great musical climaxes. They are the moments into which the composer has poured his most meaningful music. Therefore scenes like "*O terra addio*" from *Aïda*, "*Is' ein Traum kann nicht wirklich sein*" from *Der Rosenkavalier*, and of course the *Liebestod* are strictly to be avoided.

APPLAUSE. This should begin immediately after the tenor has run out of breath with the high C, or precisely at the moment when the love duet stops. This is particularly important in Wagnerian and the later Verdi operas because the orchestral postludes are usually beautiful.

IDENTIFYING OF CASTS. As you well know, the important thing is not what opera is being given tonight but who is singing tonight. If the tenor is not famous, the opera can't be good. (This is axiomatic!) Of course, you are not likely to know beforehand who is singing. So, if in the course of the first act you are puzzled as to who is what, don't wait. Light a little pocket flashlight and look at your program. This procedure has the additional advantage of distracting the attention of virtually everyone in your row. If you do not possess a pocket flashlight, don't hesitate to light a match. The firefighting equipment in most opera houses is good.

TALKING. This is a crude though classic device; it is too elementary to need discussion and should be used only on provocation. However, talking should be kept up during orchestral interludes. This registers one's protests against the composer for providing music when the curtain is down. A young man was invited by a dowager to accompany her to a performance of *Tristan and Isolde*. "I should love to accept your invitation to sit in your box for *Tristan*," he replied. "I have never heard you in *Tristan*." This story is variously attributed to Mark Twain, George Bernard Shaw and Bill Nye. But whoever may have originated it, there still exist members of the Old Guard who haven't heard it and who don't act accordingly.

FLUFFS. When the soprano, who has up to this moment given an intelligent and sensitive performance, makes a glaring error, be sure to show that you caught it. The best method is to jump as if stung by a bee. However, a vigorous shaking of the head will suffice. Effective, also, is an understanding veiled look at your neighbor to let him know that you know that the old gray *mère* ain't what she used to be. (See also "Old Subscriber" Attitude.)

CLICHES. There are two operatic clichés which should be standard equipment for all of the Old Guard. One of these is, "All opera singers are terrible actors." There have been and there exist today a number of exceptions to this rule. There are artists whose acting equipment consists of more than extending hand and arm to see whether it is raining; there are artists who sing the text and portray the character. These exceptions should not disturb your belief. You should continue firm in the faith that operatic artists should be heard but not seen, and that therefore you "like to listen with your eyes closed." I need not be so gauche as to point out that the closed-eye technique can be of immense help if you have had a difficult day.

The second cliché concerns chiefly the Wagnerian music drama. It goes something like this: "I just love Wagner's music, but the singing spoils it." This cliché is still today one of the more popular ones, though it is a belief difficult to support on mere grounds of sense. Sense (musical and otherwise) would prove that Wagner knew that the voice is the most expressive and widest-ranged of musical instruments, that he wrote superbly for the voice, that if he wanted the "Good Friday" music sung, he knew what he was doing, and that if this "Good Friday" music is played in orchestral transcription, it loses something of the character the composer intended for it.

THE PROFOUND ATTITUDE. This is an entirely different approach toward the problem, but there are, of course, more ways than one to skin a category. The Profound Attitude must be handled with discretion. It is an attitude which will not work with *I Pagliacci* but does wonders for *Pelléas et Mélisande*. You imply you are here not to enjoy the music but to undergo a short-wave treatment in cultural therapy. You must wrinkle your brow, be sad and sighing, and in general display the symptoms of malaise. You must make it quite clear that this is not a piece of music written by a man for the enjoyment of everybody but a manifestation of a mystic and anomalous rite to which only presbyters hold the secret.

IT USED-TO-BE-BETTER or OLD SUBSCRIBER'S ATTITUDE. This is perhaps most important and should be liberally studded with references to the Golden Age of Opera. Assume this attitude and a bitter-sweet smile when you tell people who are just beginning to discover the delights of opera. Name names of the past—both the famous names and the little known names. Aldous Huxley's advice on how to become an art connoisseur is useful here. He counsels that you should look up an unknown painter, deservedly forgotten. Then when people speak of Rembrandt or El Greco you say, "Ah, but have you ever heard of ——?" Nobody has—so you are a connoisseur.

When talking about the old days in disparagement of present performances, select intermission gatherings where your voice will carry well.

About opera parodies in general and one
guide in particular. . . .

3. The ABC of Music

IT WAS A self-critical and self-ridiculing poet who first said,
"It is but one step from the sublime to the ridiculous, Madame."
Heine took that step often; more than one of his lyric poems
carries a ridiculing about-face epigram as a wagging last-line
tail.

Because the sublime is an essential ingredient of opera,
opera can easily be pushed into the ridiculous. It is a short
step and an obvious one. It's no trick to make fun of opera;
it is not difficult to parody it. And many have done so.
W. S. Gilbert did it best. *Pirates of Penzance* is not too dis-
tantly related to the plot of *Il Trovatore*, as Sullivan's music
is recognizably a satire on Verdi's style in particular and the
Italian recitative in general.

Gilbert and Sullivan were unique. But operatic parodies
of various kinds have appeared after almost every new important and successful opera. In the days when it was Music
of the Future, Wagner's music drama was the most popular
target for the parodists. *Tannhäuser* was the one most often
lampooned. A satire written by the Viennese farceur, Johann
Nepomuk Nestroy, was almost more popular than the opera
itself. It was called "A farce of the future, with music of the
past." In it the Landgraf Purzel condemns Tannhäuser to
join a singing society which has been banished because of
too great a fondness for modern music. Tannhäuser may not
return to Purzel's domain until he has lost his voice. So Tannhäuser sings his way through Mozart's *Magic Flute*, through
Weber's *Der Freischütz*, and many another opera. But no
matter how hard he screams, his voice still holds out. Finally,
he comes across the Music of the Future, and though he does
not lose his voice, he loses his hearing. Wagner, by the way.

heard this little piece when it was playing in the Karltheater in Vienna. He liked it, and sent a stick pin to the man who wrote the incidental music for the farce.

Soon after *Tannhäuser* had its scandalous première in Paris, there appeared in the Paris *Journal Amusant* a parody called *Le tanne-aux-airs*. This was full of those inbred puns in which the French delight. The leading lady was called Elisa-bête. There were a Vol-franc, a Ritter-grog and a Lent-grave. Twenty years later, or about the time that the Metropolitan Opera opened in New York, another French journal, *La Vie Parisienne*, did better. It published a guide to all music, with particular attention to opera—"a guide for experts who do not understand anything about it." Here it is, in part:—

MUSICAL A B C
or What One Should Feel and Say in Listening
to the Great Masters

AUBER: Praiseworthy personality. Enthusiasm unnecessary. It is sufficient if you speak with respect of this composer.

How To Act During the Performance: It is permitted to converse or to be distracted, to use one's lorgnette, to cough or to blow one's nose. It is even permitted to hum the melodies which the singers up there are singing.

BEETHOVEN: Mighty genius. Bow down in deepest homage. No contradiction!!! That's the way it is.

How To Act During the Performance: Deepest concentration. Everyone has to see that you are paying the closest attention. Solemn silence. Your deep emotion is betrayed only by a hardly noticeable shaking of your head.

BERLIOZ: Misunderstood during his lifetime. Since his death our ears have got used to worse things. Declare that he is extremely strong and awfully interesting. Strange. Strange. Strange.

How To Act During the Performance: Your glance should be wild and half-demented. Your hands clenched, your throat dry. And put as much cotton in your ears as you can stuff into them.

CHOPIN: It is imperative to love Chopin as one loves Musset.

How To Act During the Performance: Try to roll your eyes up to your hairline the way Sarah Bernhardt does when she speaks love poetry. Also let a bitter smile play about your lips.

GOUNOD: Not one dissenter. The whole world is enraptured. Sway with the world in your enthusiasm. He wrote three things: *Faust, Faust,* and *Faust.* All the exclamations you can think of. Begin with "ideal" and go on to "divine."

How To Act During the Performance: Crouch and clutch yourself. Tremble, shiver and give forth all signs of sensuous delight. Then murmur in an ecstatic voice inarticulate sounds like "mmmm-oooh."

MOZART: One either loves him to the point of insanity or one finds him insipid. It is a question of taste and temperament. Also of education. Therefore you will do well to feel your way around and get the other man's opinion before you voice your own.

How To Act During the Performance: Listen without any sign of excitement. From time to time make a noise with your closed mouth which may remind one of the bleating of a peacefully grazing sheep. This shows that these peaceful melodies are related to the pleasures of a shepherd.

MEYERBEER: Practically the whole world is agreed on admiring him. Few adversaries. Therefore you may praise safely.

How To Act During the Performance: Make a sad face as if you were making your will and repeatedly say "terrific" in a decided, solemn tone. Nothing more, but roll the r's properly. Don't say too much. "Terrific" covers the subject.

MASSENET: His position is not as yet clarified. A few adore him, others do not acknowledge him.

How To Act During the Performance: Cup first your right ear, then your left, not to lose anything. Your body should be in a relaxed attitude. Lean your head on your hand and give your eyes a longing expression. The safe procedure is to find everything charming. You don't have to believe it, of course.

OFFENBACH: There are some who want to burn his scores. That is exaggerated. You simply say that he has talent.

How To Act During the Performance: Do not be dignified. Rock to and fro. Put on an embarrassed air, then put your left thumb in your vest and hook your right thumb in your trouser pocket. Then say, "Crazy," and smile with a tolerant smile.

ROSSINI: Don't spare the praise. The Swan of Pesaro. The creator of *William Tell.*

How To Act During the Performance: Applaud every bar and scream "Bravo! Bravi! Brava!"

VERDI: You can say that you prefer to hear all the works he wrote before *Aïda* performed on the barrel-organ. But that is enough criticism. Beginning with *Aïda,* declaim, "I am filled with admiration." If you follow this suggestion, you will be taken for an accomplished connoisseur.

How To Act During the Performance: Throw your arms in the air and scream at *Aïda* performances. As to the rest, pfui! bah! pooh!!!

WAGNER: As a Frenchman you detest him in direct proportion to the degree of your patriotism. As a listener, it depends on how much you can stand. Say: "I confess that it remains incomprehensible to me. Certainly that is my fault. My ears hurt me. My God! I think I am becoming deaf!"

How To Act During the Performance: Leave.

4. *Private Performances*

THE ADMIRABLE CUSTOM of having the public step up to the box office and put down its money is comparatively recent. During the seventeenth and well into the eighteenth century most performances of operas—or at least the best performances—were private.

Those royal and aristocratic personages of Europe who could afford it ordered operatic evenings strictly for their own enjoyment or to impress important visitors and friends. The première of Cimarosa's *The Secret Marriage*—to cite one example—was a private performance given for the Emperor of Austria and a few of his court. The story goes that the Emperor was so delighted with the opera that he invited all the singers to supper afterward. While wining and dining, they discussed the merits of the work, and the Emperor suddenly expressed a desire to hear the opera again. Everyone returned to the theater, and the whole opera was given again the same evening. This undoubtedly constitutes the longest encore in operatic history.

The most famous private performances, however, are not those which were commanded by eighteenth-century Hapsburgs or Bourbons, but those more recent ones which Ludwig II of Bavaria ordered for himself. Wagner's royal patron, misanthropic and abnormal, could not bear to hear plays and music in mundane company. So time and again he sat alone in the opera house and listened enraptured to the unfolding of the musical sagas in which he had taken so passionate an interest.

Later, when Wagner was building his Bayreuth theater, he offered to perform the whole *Ring* for Ludwig without any other spectators. Ludwig not only accepted this offer, but asked for three complete performances. However, these were never given. (What actually happened was that Ludwig, arriving in Bayruth in the middle of the night in a train which stopped at a private siding, attended the final rehearsal of the complete *Ring*. He left immediately after the *Götterdämmerung* rehearsal, but returned for the third series of public performances, three weeks later.)

I have come across a little study by Henry Channon of "The Ludwigs of Bavaria" which tells some extraordinary facts about the private performances given at Ludwig's command.

It seems that Ludwig's love for such performances started when he first wandered into the Hof-Theater in Munich while Wagner was holding a rehearsal. The King was so moved by the stillness of the empty auditorium and the out-of-the-world atmosphere that he returned again and again. As he became more and more shy of all humanity, as he fled more and more from the real world, and, like Pirandello's Henry IV, surrounded himself with make-believe, as the theater and play-acting grew to be his chief absorptions, he demanded these unique performances not only of Wagner's works but of other operas and plays also.

In the beginning the performances were actually only working dress rehearsals, and the King indulged himself in what most of us would like to do but few of us can, that is, amateur stage directing. Later he commanded special performances for the sole purpose of attending them alone. The first of these took place in 1871 and the last in 1885, shortly before his death. All in all, according to Channon, 210 private performances were given, comprising forty-five operas and some plays.

All worldly noises had to be shut out of the theater. The scene shifters wore felt slippers; the auditorium was in total darkness, and the performances usually began at midnight. Ludwig would recline alone in the royal box, which was hung with heavy red velvet. Sometimes the ghostly atmosphere of the theater would affect the actors and they would be nervous and fearful of the King.

In later years the performances became more and more elaborate and therefore more expensive. The King even employed a special playwright, Karl von Heigel, who was commissioned to write spectacles containing pomp and flamboyancy in the style of the Bourbons, whose spiritual heir Ludwig now felt himself to be. One of these performances was said to have cost more than fifty thousand dollars.

These performances were not confined to the Hof- and the Residenztheater in Munich. When Ludwig returned to the fantastic place in the mountains which he had built for himself, private performances were given on his estate. Linderhof, which was the name of the King's residence, was a Bavarian imitation of Versailles done with Bavarian bad taste. One house of the estate contained an ornate series of sitting rooms and galleries but only one single bedroom, and a small dining room where a table fully laid rose from a trapdoor (just as it does in the fairy tale by Grimm) so that the King could dine quite alone without contact even with servants, in company only of the marble busts of Marie Antoinette and Louis XIV. He contemplated building an entire opera house on his estate, but this plan was never carried out. He did have, at some distance from the main house, a replica of Hunding's hut. Here under a tree Ludwig and a few of his retinue, dressed in hides and bearskins, would drink mead from drinking horns. At other times and in a changed mood, he would retire to a Moorish kiosk which he had acquired at the Paris exhibit of 1867, and dressed in an Arab costume, he would smoke long pipes and sip Turkish coffee. He also built a grotto with artificial stalactites; an illuminated waterfall rushed to a subterranean lake past a statue of the Lorelei. The background was a huge painting of Tannhäuser in the Venusberg. He mixed up all styles and symbols. Capri and Versailles were represented as well as the Wagnerian backgrounds. The decorative motives were both the swan and the fleur-de-lis.

To this retreat, which he called Meicost Ettal (an anagram of *L'état c'est moi*), Ludwig would invite actors and give spectacles. One of Ludwig's last intimates was the famous actor, Joseph Kainz.

Ludwig's doings in general and his private performances in particular were so absorbing a topic of general European gossip that even so un-Bavarian a writer as Mark Twain took notice of them. You may remember that in *A Tramp Abroad* Mark Twain describes a private performance. Whether this performance actually took place or whether it is a product of Twain's imagination I don't know.

At any rate, Mark Twain writes that in an opera which was performed privately for Ludwig, a storm was supposed to occur. "The mimic thunder began to mutter, the mimic wind began to wail and sough, and the mimic rain to patter. The King's interest rose higher and higher; it developed into enthusiasm. He cried out:

" 'It is good, very good, indeed! But I will have real rain! Turn on the water!'

"The manager pleaded for a reversal of the command; said it would ruin the costly scenery and the splendid costumes, but the King cried:

" 'No matter, no matter, I will have real rain! Turn on the water!'

"So the real rain was turned on and began to descend in gossamer lances to the mimic flower beds and gravel walks of the stage. The richly dressed actresses and actors tripped about singing bravely and pretending not to mind it. The

King was delighted,—his enthusiasm grew higher. He cried out:

" 'Bravo, bravo! More thunder! more lightning! turn on more rain!'

"The thunder boomed, the lightning glared, the storm winds raged, the deluge poured down. The mimic royalty on the stage, with their soaked satins clinging to their bodies, slopped around ankle deep in water, warbling their sweetest and best, the fiddlers under the eaves of the stage sawed away for dear life, with the cold overflow spouting down the backs of their necks, and the dry and happy King sat in his lofty box and wore his gloves to ribbons applauding."

5. *Perils of the Opera House*

IT IS NOT the Phantom of the Opera House I wish to talk about, but less ghostly nuisances.

Chariots which upset, curtains which descend before they are supposed to, revolvers which fail to fire, shawls the fringes of which become entangled in unlikely places, ladders which fall down, wigs which are knocked off in the excitement of a stage duel, swords which are not supposed to wound but do—all these are perils common to the stages of both opera and the theater. But the opera stage has one peril of its own, one almost exclusively reserved for its expansive precincts, one which makes the opera stage-director old before his time: that is the presence of animals.

An animal on the stage inevitably spells trouble. Unfortunately the appearance of animals is called for in many operas. Operatic literature contains a small but well-stocked zoo. The chief trouble-makers are the Wagnerian works with their range from the dermochelys coriacea (turtle) to the callisaurus dracontoides (dragon).

Did Wagner believe that these animals could ever be convincingly set on the stage, whether played by real animals, by contraptions or by an unlucky super? Did he think that the bear at the beginning of Siegfried could ever be anything but a childish and an uncomfortable illusion? Wagner was a supremely practical man of the theater. He must have known—he did know—that even if animals behave themselves and cause no accident, they are sure scene stealers. They have but to enter and the eyes and the worries of the entire audience are concentrated on them.

Perhaps his own love for animals led Wagner to a mistake in practical stage judgment. There was hardly ever a time in Wagner's life when a dog was not part of the household. Animals were part of saga and lore, that world which he loved. They had to become part of his work. But even before the first *Die Walküre* reached the stage in Bayreuth, two of the animals he had written into the score, namely the pair of rams which draw Fricka's chariot to the colloquy with Wotan, were eliminated. Though Wagner had ordered the chariot from the same English firm which constructed the first Fafner dragon, it was not used. Fricka walked on, and the rams remained merely a stage direction.*

At the first Bayreuth festival Grane was cast carefully: he was a beautiful, gentle horse. But though his behavior was exemplary, he had to suffer the indignity that many an actor has come to know: his part was cut. He still made his appearance in the first and the last acts of *Götterdämmerung*. But he was eliminated from the scene in *Die Walküre* in which Brünnhilde presages death to Siegmund because Wagner realized that the presence of the horse during the long scene might distract the audience from the Wälsung and the Walküre.

Nor has Grane, as far as I know, appeared in *Die Walküre* since. He still appears in the *Götterdämmerung*. Why? The argument is that Brünnhilde speaks to him directly in her final speech, and it would be awkward to have her address her words to an invisible animal backstage. Still, it is, I think, more awkward to have him on the stage. Half the audience worries more about Grane than about Brünnhilde. And Brünnhilde worries about him. I remember when he ruined Frieda Leider's closing speech merely by normal friskiness. Poor horse, he has only to twist his head to make everyone nervous. I suggest that he be retired altogether.

---

*I am told that the rams were used in early productions of *Die Walküre* at the Metropolitan. I have also been told the contrary. Does anyone remember seeing the rams?

An animal doesn't have to be alive and kicking to be troublesome. Even mechanical animals can cause mishaps. Everyone around the opera house knows the story of Leo Slezak, who was about to make his entrance as Lohengrin when the swan-drawn conveyance went off too soon and left without him. He turned to the stagehand next to him and asked, "When does the next swan leave?" We can only be thankful in this connection that Wagner did not carry out his original intention of having the swan sing; it is a fact that in the sketch of *Lohengrin* Wagner had given the swan a few lines to sing. He went so far as to set these lines to music, but with better judgment he subsequently eliminated them.

There is another animal around the opera house which appears with annoying frequency, though it takes no part in any well-known opera. This is the cat. Its most famous appearance was on the occasion of the première of *The Barber of Seville*. A cat marched across the stage during the first finale and helped to turn the evening into a fiasco. A cat also appeared most unexpectedly during one Metropolitan performance of *Tristan and Isolde* (it sat on the prompter's box licking its face), but the results were less severe.

In one opera, Humperdinck's *Königskinder*, geese are an essential part of the action. When *Königskinder* was given at the Metropolitan, Farrar played the Goosegirl and caused a commotion at the première by appearing before the curtain carrying a live goose under her arm. The *Königskinder* was also given in Chicago when the Metropolitan was on tour. There the opera was so well liked that the management decided to schedule an extra performance. Then it was discovered that the geese were missing. Upon inquiry, the management was informed that the stagehands, who believed that the geese had played their parts and were no longer needed, had eaten them. . . .

The disappearance of the geese leads me, by direct progression, to the disappearance of the prima donna: it was perhaps the strangest mishap in operatic history. When Verdi's *I Vespri Siciliani* was to be given its première at the Paris Opéra, the lady who was to sing the principal part, a Mlle. Sophia Cruvelli, suddenly vanished a few days before the performance. The Paris police went to work, but two weeks after her disappearance they had unearthed no trace of her whereabouts. Verdi declared officially that he was ready to withdraw the opera. A judgment was taken out against the singer. Since, like all opera singers, she was an employee of the state, it was possible for the state to set the fine, and this was fixed at the large sum of a hundred thousand francs, the equivalent of twenty thousand dollars. The furniture of her apartment and her personal property were seized. More days went by and nothing was heard of her. The newspapers became furious. *La France Musicale* published an article which said: "Here is a theater which reckoned on her, which paid her more handsomely than any artist had ever been paid; here is a musician, Verdi, honor and probity itself, who leaves the country of his triumphs, Italy, for the express purpose of coming to consecrate to the singer more than six months of his time and the finest inspirations he is capable of; here is a poet, M. Scribe, who sketches out a splendid part for this lady, whose name had become a talisman for our French theater. What ingratitude!" Then as mysteriously as she had disappeared, she returned. It seems that she had simply decided to go off on a holiday, though not alone. She had taken a trial honeymoon journey with a baron whom shortly afterward she married. Her only excuse was that the person who was to inform the management of the opera house of her departure had forgotten to do so. But here she was back and quite willing to brave the wrath of the Parisian public by singing again. The rehearsals of *I Vespri Siciliani* were re-

sumed and Mlle. Cruvelli, refreshed by her holiday, threw
herself into the work with passion. She made her reappear-
ance before the Parisian public not in this opera but in Meyerbeer's *Les Huguenots*, as Valentine. When Valentine enters,
the Queen questions her; the first words she says to her are:
"Tell me the result of your daring journey." When the
Parisians heard the line, they burst into laughter and Cruvelli
was forgiven.

6. *De Superstitione*

How superstitiously we mind our evils:
The throwing down of salt, or crossing of a hare,
Or singing of a cricket, are of power
To daunt whole man in us."
JOHN WEBSTER: *The Duchess of Malfi*

A SUPERSTITION, as someone has said, is that which others believe and we do not. Superstitions were a favorite subject of the erudite Sir James George Frazer, he who wrote *The Golden Bough;* but even the less learned among us find it titillating to toy with them. With their origins comfortably lost in the forest of history, they seem to be thin yet noticeable threads which link us to our own past; they are threads which give us a slight feeling of kinship to that valiant Roman who used to be afraid of black cats; they are threads which may lead right back to the cave of the big, bad witch. Superstitious people are members of an ancient club.

Most creative artists are superstitious. Wagner believed that the number thirteen had a special mystic significance for him. Wagner was born in 1813, his *Tannhäuser* was first performed on the thirteenth of March, his name contained thirteen letters (he conveniently forgot the Wilhelm), and he died on February 13. While Wagner considered thirteen lucky, Chopin had a horror of that number, nor would Rossini ever invite more than twelve guests to dinner. Chopin also believed that Mondays and Fridays were evil days and would not begin a composition on those days.

In no department of the arts have superstitions reigned more tyranically than in the theater. Someone described the theater as a madhouse with the opera as the branch for the incurables; it can be well imagined, therefore, that singers carry with them an excess quota of superstitions.

In the theater one must never say the last line of the play during rehearsals. In the opera house one must never, never whistle backstage. In the theater a black cat is good luck; the old Haymarket Theater in London used to have a trained black cat around to put the actors in good humor. In the opera house a black cat is a poisonous animal.

Caruso, confident and sensible though he was, none the less had his superstitions. On his dressing table there were all kinds of lucky charms, old playbills, dilapidated stuffed animals, broken *objets d'art*. He treasured any gift that happened to arrive on a night when he felt that he had sung especially well. All this rubbish had to go with him wherever he sang, and the less respectable the collection looked, the better he liked it.

Neither Jean or Edouard De Reszke would walk under a ladder, and both of them disliked being photographed, for they believed it brought them bad luck. Edouard would never ride a white horse. Lilli Lehmann used to come to the opera house two or three hours before the beginning of the performance, put on her costume and make-up, and then sit for an hour in stony and regal silence on a chair—all for luck. Scotti could not sing unless a certain rag doll was on his dressing table, a doll his mother had given him when he was a boy. Pinza now has the same foible; his doll has a gray knitted dress and a very broken face. Tettrazini had a special superstition concerning a dagger. It was one which she first used in *Lucia di Lammermoor* and which one night, when she happened to be singing unusually well, fell from her hand and stuck upright in the floor. Thereafter she used the dagger as a barometer: she would drop it each time before going onstage; if it again stood upright that meant she would have a success—or, if it fell flat, a failure!

Selma Kurz, the Viennese coloratura, believed that she would sing well if she saw a chimney-sweep before the performance. Her manager used to hire one to saunter accidentally past the stage door. On one occasion, seeing the sooted man, she called him over, reached into her purse, and gave him a tip; whereupon the honest fellow said, "Not necessary, Madame. I have already been paid."

The *Credo in superstitionem* has by no means diminished in our own times. It is of course elementary that one must never wish a singer good luck before a performance. If you visit Lauritz Melchoir backstage, you must wish him "*Hals und Beinbruch.*" This, though German, is now an international wish, all rights reserved for all singers, including the Scandinavian. It means, "Here's wishing you a broken neck and leg." Another traditional wish is "*Imbocca lupo;*" it means, "Your head in the wolf's mouth," and it is used with gusto by Metropolitan Manager Edward Johnson. Spitting three times—or saying "toi, toi, toi," the more refined form of the same thing—is another potent charm. Gertrude Wettergren always asked to be kicked three times before she went on stage. In the French opera the good luck word is one which cannot be printed in a family book like this. It means what you think it means.

Rosa Ponselle used to walk to the opera house from her hotel. Risë Stevens believes that it is bad luck to put a pair of shoes on the table. Kerstin Thorborg's good luck charm is a little elephant, and she is convinced that snow also augurs well for her singing. Zinka Milanov hates the number seven. Gerhard Pechner believes that stepping on the stub of a burning cigarette will bring him good luck—a belief shared by the New York Fire Department. Licia Albanese is a serious student of dreams, and Wilfred Pelletier a collector of good luck penguins.

Helen Jepson refuses under any circumstances to go back

to her dressing room once she has left it. Rose Bampton will never have a manicure on the day she sings. Herbert Janssen carries three chestnuts with him in his costume, and always puts his right foot on the stage first. Nadine Conner carries a red garter with her and pauses to take ten breaths before going on the stage. Baccaloni owns a lucky piece which was forged for him by steel workers when he was singing in South America. Just before Leinsdorf made his debut at the Metropolitan, a friend of his urged him to eat something, and handed him an apple. He ate one apple and then another and still another, but claims to have absolutely no recollection of having done so. Now, before every performance, he eats an apple for good luck.

Lotte Lehmann (like Martinelli) had pictures of all her family in her dressing room and meticulously kissed each picture before going on the stage. Helen Traubel, inspired possibly by the Lone Ranger, cuts a notch in her spear every time she sings Brünnhilde. Every time she sings Isolde she cuts a notch in the handle of the torch.

Of course, writers of books on opera are quite free of these foibles—knock on wood!

A final hymn to
opera and operagoing. . . .

7. *Excitement in the Opera House*

MOST OPERAGOERS today know "The Golden Age of Opera"
only by hearsay. What was it like, this benign age? What
was it like, they wonder, to go to the Metropolitan and to
have in one season the choice of hearing Bonci, Caruso,
Chaliapin, Dippel, Plançon, Scotti, Cavalieri, Eames, Farrar,
Fremstad, Gadski, Homer and Sembrich?

The recollection of that seignoral period is put forth with
varying force by the surviving ear-witnesses, the extremists
claiming that present-day singers really know nothing—very
little, at any rate—about singing, that the art of singing died
with Caruso, and that it is no longer worth while going to
the opera because we have no really great singers to sing
for us.

Though I yield to none in admiring a beautiful voice, I still
think it is worth while to go to the opera. I think so even
though I could be brought to admit that there are very few
singers today who can compare in virtuosity with the great
stars of the golden age, and none who can compare to
Caruso. I make this admission with some hesitancy because I
suspect that the recollection of the golden age is daubed over
with the same roseate varnish which makes all pictures of the
past and of youth seem more glamorous than was actually
the case, and that all was not always quite so perfect as it is
now mirrored in remembrance. Let us grant, however, that
we are suffering a decline of the larynx. Let us admit that
no sounds poured forth by singers today are as velvety as
those of a past generation. Have we something today which
makes up for this loss? Do our performances possess a quality
which past performances did not possess? Can we define a
virtue characteristic of present-day performances?

It is always dangerous to generalize. It is doubly dangerous to generalize in art. It is trebly dangerous to generalize when one speaks of something so variable and so inconstant as an opera performance. Nonetheless, after having read many accounts of by-gone performances and after talking to old-timers and listening to old records, I have come to the conclusion that present-day good performances have an over-all quality which comes nearer to realizing the composer's intention and to giving us a true representation of the opera as a whole than many of the star-studded performances of the golden age. The virtue of our performances—when they are good ones—is fidelity to the composer's wishes. This brings about an integrated performance, which in turn brings about a particular satisfaction. If that satisfaction differs from the enjoyment that an overwhelming personality and voice can produce, it is nonetheless strong cheer and deep pleasure.

In our better performances today the conductor is captain. He not only has achieved the importance which by the logic of music should be his, but he has also become a box-office draw. He has become popular with the audience, he has made an effective appeal to the public's imagination. He is, in the good sense of the word, the star of the performance. The result of his ascendancy is an improvement in the all-over quality of the performance. He cannot spirit forth a good performance without good singers. But he can give us the beauty of the music without having in his troupe one singer who brings the house down.

Give me singers who are musical and who are devoted to their task, give me a great conductor, give me a stage manager with brains, and then give me plenty of rehearsal time, and I'll bring you a performance which you needn't trade for one of the golden age; I'll bring you a performance of which the critics will say that it has "style."

A performance that has style has excitement. Style communicates itself immediately to the musically untrained as well as to the critic. It is directly and strongly felt by the plain opera lover: it is by no means a matter to be understood or appreciated only by professionals. It is the essential ingredient for the coming-alive of music, as essential as James Barrie considered charm to be to a woman: "If you have it, you do not need to have anything else; and if you do not have it, nothing else will help."

Do you believe that this ingredient was always present in the performances of a past age for which so many nostalgic sighs are breathed? I wonder. I wonder what we would think today of Adela Maria Patti, known as "divina," one of the earlier divinities of the golden age. She who commanded an honorarium of between five and six thousand dollars per performance (somebody figured out that this came to about forty cents for each note she sang in *Lucia*), she who introduced *Home Sweet Home* into the Lesson Scene of *The Barber of Seville*, she who in the big ensemble numbers used to open her mouth, go through the motions of singing, but actually saved her voice for the solos—must often have been, with all the delights that she aroused, an equivocal pleasure. As long ago as 1890, a music critic writing for the London *Star* under the name of Corno de Bassetto, but now better known as George Bernard Shaw, wrote about Patti: "It is still possible for a prima donna to bounce on the stage and throw her voice at the heads of the audience with an insolent insistence on her position as a public favorite, and hardly the ghost of a reference to the character she is supposed to impersonate. An ambitious young artist may easily be misled by illustrious examples of stage misconduct. To tell an average young opera singer that she is a Patti or a Nilsson is to pay her the highest compliment she desires. Yet Madame Patti's offenses against artistic propriety are mighty ones and millions. She seldom even pretends to play any other part than that of Adelina, the spoiled child with the adorable voice; and I believe she would be rather hurt than otherwise if you for a moment lost sight of Patti in your preoccupation with Zerlina, or Aïda, or Caterina."

Even Caruso, at least in his young days, must have sometimes been a trial. We have already seen that when Caruso played Pinkerton, one critic was moved to write: "No one would expect (from him) an impersonation with even a tittle of dramatic illusion." If that was even partially true, then we may assert with confidence that there are many singers today who give us more than a tittle of dramatic illusion though none of them can come near to matching Caruso's voice.

In any event, different ages produce different results. The theater changes, and we change with it. Why look to the past? Would we like the past if, by the magic of some time machine, it were brought before us intact?

In that unforgettable film, *King Henry the Fifth*, we were taken to the Globe Theater and were shown how a play was staged and acted in Shakespeare's time. That was the idea, and a fascinating idea it was. But actually what we saw was not a performance by Elizabethan actors; what we saw was a performance given by today's actors working in a replica of the Globe Theater. Had we seen genuine Elizabethan acting, it would have been so strange to us as to be well nigh incomprehensible. Burbage, the original Hamlet, was undoubtedly a good Hamlet for Elizabethan audiences, though he may have been "fat and scant of breath." But we would not sympathize with nor tolerate his performance today. Nor would we accept—to shift centuries quickly—an eighteenth-century performance of *Hamlet*, of which we have pictorial evidence, when Hamlet was garbed in lace and curly wig, with one of his stockings carefully ungartered to make sure that all the audience understand that he was mad. Nor need we go so far back in time. The filmed record of Sarah

Bernhardt's acting of the duel scene in *Hamlet* shows us that the goings-on were little short of grotesque, according to our style of acting.

There is no doubt, of course, that Bernhardt was a great actress. I simply want to make the point that styles in acting change as surely, if not as quickly, as styles in women's hats. And this is quite as true of acting styles in opera. It is true even of singing styles. And I question whether the singers of the late nineteenth or early twentieth century would satisfy us now if we were to hear them today exactly as they sang and acted then.

You may perhaps wonder why I say that singing, which is sound emitted according to precise directions laid down by the composer, should change with the passing time. But it does change. There can never be precise directions laid down. Even if there were, we would read the directions differently. To convince ourselves of this, we have only to make the experiment of listening to some old operatic records, allowing, of course, for the fact that these records were made before modern recording methods, and listening not for beauty but simply for the style of singing, for such things as phrasing, duration of notes and rubato. It is a disillusioning experience. The singers on these old records take what seem to me unforgivable liberties with the music that the composer wrote down. (I must interrupt myself to say that I am speaking generally and not of individual performances, certain of which are still wonderful.) They bear down heavily. They change tempi arbitrarily. That was their style. It is not the style we understand. For we have been tutored by modern musical performances and by modern acting.

Yes, performances of operas and plays must constantly be renewed and refreshed. They must change, if they are not to become museum pieces rather than an interpretation in a living thater. Let's take a favorite opera, *Die Meistersinger*, as one example. Even though the early performances of this opera had the benefit of Wagner's personal direction and the enthusiasm and devotion of the singers who worked for him, I believe today we should not like those performances were we able to witness them. Max Graf has pointed out that the first *Meistersinger* performances were what is called in German *wuchtig*. It was a style of wide and significant gestures, of big women and men—and bigger beards. Hans Richter, who conducted the performance, was himself a man with a massive beard. His baton was more of a bat than a baton, not the little stick that we are used to today but a heavy stick with a heavy handle. His down beat was emphasized with a great display of power. And this very beat determined the style of conducting, which was broad and ponderous. The first Stolzing was Hermann Winkelmann, a heroic figure, trained by Wagner himself and one of his favorite artists. His picture shows that as the young Walther he too was made up with a full and manly beard, that his bearing was that of an older man rather than a youthful, romantic knight. The same is true of Gustav Walter, another early interpreter of the part. And in a contemporary painting by Ferdinand Leeke we see Walther—idealized, to be sure, in the fashion of the sentimental German painter—again as a man almost old enough to be Hans Sachs, bearded and somber. The beards (which Tannhäuser and Lohengrin wore also) are perhaps merely a question of fashion. But the musical and declamatory style—new and stimulating for those days—would strike us false today.

When Gustav Mahler staged *Die Meistersinger* in the Vienna Opera, the style had already changed. The heavy and massive had given way to the pointed and humorous. Mahler accentuated the comedy in *Die Meistersinger*. He lightened the declamation of the singers. He accelerated the rhythms of the orchestra.

Mahler was a great conductor, and his staging of *Die Meistersinger* must have been delightful. Yet the work is done still differently today. When given under Toscanini in Salzburg, *Die Meistersinger* was something new again. The opera became a continuous parade of exquisite, almost unbearably beautiful tunes. It was music overwhelming by the sweetness, the tenderness and the opulence of its sound. It was singing music from the first note to the last. Here was an interpretation—to be sure, an exceptionally great one, indeed, an incomparable one—which again differed from previous performances.

It all amounts to this: that we see a work differently from time to time. But it is, of course, the peculiar property of a work of art that it can be viewed in different ways and still be seen in its own light. The light is true if it emanates from the work itself and is not an artificial beam flooded on it by some forced or fancy interpretation.

If I have convinced you that opera can be exciting even when no altogether stellar singers are present, and that the very change in performances which we sometimes decry adds to the excitement of theatergoing over the years, then I'd like to point out in addition that many very fine singers can be seen and heard today. I purposely say "seen and heard:" it is the total effect which is important. My criterion for judging singers is a simple though a vocally unscientific one. I have in my mind an idea of how a character in the opera should sound and act. Sometimes I hear a performance which is not too far away from my imagined sound and sight. Such a performance gets a passing mark. But every once that I say: this is it, this is what I have imagined, this is the in a while I come across a performance which is so persuasive character. Stefan Zweig once said that men like Dickens and Balzac and Dostoievsky created worlds so real and so convincing that when you met a person in real life, you said, "He

is a Dickens character. . . . He is a figure out of Dostoievsky."
Here a similar transference takes place: we identify the character of the opera with a particular interpreter. Performance
and previous imagination meet. And later, when we think
of the character in the opera, we automatically think of the
singer who has thrilled us. Albanese as Violetta in *Traviata*,
Rose Bampton as Kundry in *Parsifal*, Sayao as Susanna in
The Marriage of Figaro, Paolis as Cassio in *Otello*, Garris as
David in *Die Meistersinger*, Leonard Warren as the Count in
Il Trovatore, Baccaloni as Don Pasquale, Pinza as Don Giovanni—these are a few such performances which make attendance at the opera an exciting experience. . . .

Nothing I have said in the foregoing will, I hope, be interpreted as an excuse for the bad performances that we frequently get. Opera in our country is staged too often with
an almost incredible old-fashionedness and sometimes with
astonishing lack of taste. Singers are allowed to take leading
roles before they are ready to do so. Many do not even know
the meaning of the words which they are singing. Others,
even good singers, have to appear with inadequate rehearsals,
and the resultant performance is a loose shambles in which
routine covers embarrassment. On too many nights is the
odor of the opera house a musty odor smelling of dead or
misunderstood tradition. On too many nights do we get
shoddy instead of silk.

But it is equally absurd to conclude that there is not sufficient excitement still to be obtained in the opera house, or that
singing and operatic acting are lost arts.

In some ways the opera lover is a fortunate fellow! His
is a love which need never be dulled by sameness. One of
the things that make opera-going stimulating is the unpre-
dictability of the performance. No two performances, even
if given with the same cast, are ever alike. A good cast sometimes gives a performance that is out of sorts. On the other

hand—and I'm sure you have had this experience—a performance from which not too much is expected sometimes comes
alive with such force and power that you sit up in your
chair, that your attention and your emotions are engulfed
by the music, that perhaps you shed tears; the whole evening
remains memorable to you. One speaks of an electric performance, though it is more a matter of spontaneous com-
bustion than of electricity.

One thing is certain: Because every performance is different and because music is so imaginative an art, we can enjoy
hearing the same opera over and over again. We can hear
certain operas all our life and derive something new from
each performance. There is no suspense left in an opera performance—how many people in the audience do not know
that Siegfried will waken Brünnhilde and that Almaviva will
get his Rosina?—but there is something better than suspense.
It is the spell of the indefinable, the free, the never-to-be-ex-
hausted beauty of music.

The hearing of music is, at its best, the pleasure of a re-
transversal of familiar ground, a re-experience of something
already experienced. This twice-told tale has its own suspense.
We wait with wonder and held breath for the moment that
is to come. We know what is to come—but how will it sound
this time? Will it strike us again with the same force? Will
its beauty be as noticeable? Will the wave lift us as high?
Will the world burst once more into sunshine when Hans
Sachs in his monologue of the third act arrives at the moment
when he sings "now came St. John's day" and the orchestra
opens up to proclaim the light of that day? Will we be once
more called upon to summon all our power of pity when
Otello turns to the dead Desdemona and tells us that she is
"pale, tired, mute—and beautiful"? And is it possible to respond again to the charm, the zephyr-like and yet so precisely
designed charm, of Zerlina's *"Batti, batti"?* It appears that it is.

As we hear these operas again we hear new things in them. Or we hear the old things in a new way. However it may happen, there is a new element present. Great music is a self-renewing pleasure. I believe that the characteristic of newness is a quality that music possesses to a greater degree than do the other arts. Thus, there is no end to the enjoyment of the great operas, because music can hardly ever be heard to the end—its entire content can hardly ever be brought to the surface—and because each performance is a new performance.